Current Trends in Information: Research and Theory

Forthcoming topics in *The Reference Librarian* series:

•Finance, Budget and Management for Reference Services, Number 19
•Reference Services and Public Policy, Number 20
•Information and Referral in Reference Services, Number 21
•Information Brokers and Reference Services, Number 22
•Expert Systems in Reference Services, Number 23
•Library Use Skills and Research Strategies, Number 24
•Samuel Rothstein, Reference Services and Education, Number 25
•Serials and Reference Services, Number 26

Published:

Reference Services in the 1980s, Numbers 1/2
Reference Services Administration and Management, Number 3
Ethics and Reference Services, Number 4
Video to Online: Reference Services and the New Technology, Numbers 5/6
Reference Services for Children and Young Adults, Numbers 7/8
Reference Services and Technical Services: Interactions in Library Practice, Number 9
Library Instruction and Reference Services, Number 10
Evaluation of Reference Services, Number 11
Conflicts in Reference Services, Number 12
Reference Services in Archives, Number 13
Personnel Issues in Reference Services, Number 14
The Publishing and Review of Reference Sources, Number 15
Reference Services Today: From Interview to Burnout, Number 16
International Aspects of Reference and Information Services, Number 17
Current Trends in Information: Research and Theory, Number 18

Current Trends in Information: Research and Theory

Edited by
Bill Katz and Robin Kinder

School of Library & Information Science
State University of New York at Albany

The Haworth Press
New York • London

Current Trends in Information: Research and Theory has also been published as *The Reference Librarian,* Number 18, Summer 1987.

The Haworth Press, Inc., 12 West 32 Street, New York, NY 10001
EUROSPAN/Haworth, 3 Henrietta Street, London WC2E 8LU England

Library of Congress Cataloging-in-Publication Data

Current trends in information.

Published also as the Reference librarian, no. 18.
Includes bibliographies.
1. Reference services (Libraries) 2. Information services. 3. Library science—Research. 4. Library science—Technological innovations. I. Katz, William A., 1924- II. Kinder, Robin.
Z711.C87   1987   025.5'2   87-17724
ISBN 0-86656-574-4

Current Trends in Information: Research and Theory

The Reference Librarian
Number 18

CONTENTS

I. THEORY AND RESEARCH

**The Influence of Theory and Research in the Practice of
Reference Services**   **1**
    Bill Katz

Can There Be a Theory of Reference?   **7**
    S. D. Neill

    The Reference Process   7
    Theory   8
    The Bibliographic Bridge   10
    Theories of Communication   11
    A Series of Problems   15
    Conclusion   17

Research and Practice in Librarianship: A Cognitive View   **21**
    Nigel Ford

    Research Approaches   22
    Librarianship and the "Human Factor"   25
    "Humanistic" Paradigms   26
    Research Approaches in Contrast   29
    A Cognitive View of Research   30
    Integration   32
    Research in Librarianship and Information Science   35
    Balance in Research Approaches   38
    Research and Practice   40
    "Truth" and Pragmatism as Research Goals   42

The Wider Scope of Information Research 49
 Una Mansfield

The Information Sciences 50
Sciences with a Cognitive Perspective 52
Artificial Intelligence 54
Cognitive Neuroscience 56
Semiotics/Linguistics 56
Philosophy 59
Sciences with a Socio-Technological Perspective 60
Computer Science 62
Information Science 64
Library Science 65
Sciences with a Systems Perspective 66

Unobtrusive Testing and the Role of Library Management 71
 Charles R. McClure
 Peter Hernon

Managerial Responsibilities 73
Suggestions for Implementing Unobtrusive Evaluation 77
Research Opportunities for Unobtrusive Evaluation 79
Reporting Unobtrusive Results to Staff 82
The Context of Unobtrusive Evaluation 82

**The Information Specialist and the Reference Librarian:
Is the Complete Librarian Obsolete?** 87
 John E. Leide

The Reference Librarian 88
Information Access in Developing Countries 89
The Information Specialist in North America 89
Librarian Technicians 90
Technology in Information Transfer 91
The Specialist/Librarian Librarian/Specialist 92
Conclusion 93

Toward Expert Inquiry Systems 95
 Glynn Harmon

An Inquiry and Information Need Model 96
Expert Inquiry: An Example 98

Intelligent Inquiry: Rule Bases   100
Alternative Approaches   103
Conclusion   104

Public Libraries and Society in the Information Age   107
            Arthur W. Hafner

The Public Library as a Public Agency   108
The Role of the Library in Democracy   109
The Public Library in the Information Economy   111
Library Optimization in the Information Age   114
Conclusion   117

II. INFLUENCE OF THEORY AND RESEARCH PRACTICE

**In Pursuit of Windmills: Librarians and the
Determination to Instruct   119**
            Connie Miller
            Patricia Tegler

Historical Interpretation   121
Research and Library Skills   124
Insecurity   125
New Goals   127
Connection   129
Mutual Dependence   131

**To See Ourselves as Others See Us: A Cooperative,
Do-It-Yourself Reference Accuracy Study   135**
            Eleanor Jo Rodger
            Jane Goodwin

Methodology   136
The Process   138
Implementation   140
Findings   141
Management Response to Findings   144
Conclusions   146

Bibliographic Control of Conservative Periodicals   149
            H. Rorlich

Objectives 150
Setting 150
Purpose 151
Methodology 152
Findings 153
Conclusions 155

**The Use of Bibliographic Tools by Humanities Faculty
at the State University of New York at Albany** 157
Susan S. Guest

Introduction 157
Method of Investigation 159
Description of the Questionnaire 160
Analysis of Data 162
Conclusions 170

III. THEORY

**Application of the Finite Difference Calculus to the
Observation of Symbol Processes** 173
Charls Pearson

Introduction 174
The Finite Difference Calculus 181
Symbol Production Processes 186
Mathematical Developments 188
The Echelon Counter and the Finite Difference Model 192
Caveats 196
Summary 197

**Contemporary Trends in Applied Metatheoretic Research:
A Case Study About Information Metatheory:
A Fragment** 199
Nicolay Stanoulov

Communication—What About? 200
Some Special Problems in a Metatheory 203
Inferences About Information Theory Provoked by Its
Metatheory 208
Conclusion 209

"On Fire or on Ice": Prefatory Remarks on the Library in Literature   **211**
Daniel Peter Walsh

Introduction   211
The Texts—Narratives and Basic Semiotic Analysis   213
Ice   214
Fire   220
Conclusions   233

IV. PRACTICE: ONLINE

Online Searching and Its Place in the Library School Curriculum   **239**
Tillie Krieger

Need for Online Searching Ability   240
Early Training   242
Online in the Curriculum   243
Three Approaches   246
Current State   247
Introducing Online Searching   248
Online Searching in the Curriculum   250
The "End User"   251

Development of a Bibliographic Database on a Videotex Type System   **255**
Emil H. Levine

Menu versus Key Term Retrieval   258
Card Catalog-Subject Indexing Model   260
Key Term Model   260
KWIC/KWOC Model   260
Menu Model   261
Determining Indexing Requirements   261
Initial Menus   264

Computer Aided Indexing at NASA   **269**
Ronald L. Buchan

Part I: NASA Thesaurus Activity   269
Part 2: NASA Lexical Dictionary Activity   274

Managing Database Information: An Index to Online Databases   279
    Steven D. Atkinson
    Michael Knee

Introduction   280
Background   281
Hardware/Software/Printer   281
Personal Pearl   282
Conclusion   289

WESTLAW: Online Legal Reference Searching in a Social Science Library   291
    Richard Irving
    Henry Mendelsohn

Acquiring WESTLAW   292
Policy and Procedure   293
Advantages of WESTLAW   294
Case Law Databases   295
Enhanced Access Flexibility   296
Timeliness   300
Time Efficiency   302
Collection Enhancement   304
Added Features   305
Conclusion   305

Current Trends in Information: Research and Theory

I. THEORY AND RESEARCH

The Influence of Theory and Research in the Practice of Reference Services

Bill Katz

In the good old days, i.e., a decade or so ago, one might show less than passionate concern with the theory of reference and information services. There were the users, the reference works and the librarians. The combination seemed predictable and hardly required a philosophical or theoretical framework to explain the interactions involved. Or so it seemed. Even then, though, the enchantment of the new technology threatened the engaging combinations; and confusingly one discovered that accepted levels of service no longer seemed acceptable. The ostensibly secure reference librarian acknowledged, if only in slighted research studies, that some 50 percent of the time the answers given from the reference works to the users were either downright wrong, or inadequate. The heretical notion that theory might at long last do something to at least explain the change and the stentorian errors gradually made itself acceptable.

Theory today has to do with reality in most, if not all areas of reference services. The so called practical aspects of the art is no longer cut loose from the universe of ideas and conjecture. The reality of reference services today is that it depends on research and theory to survive. To see things from this perspective simply consider the articles in this issue. Furthermore, work at, or observe the activities in a typical reference situation and try to forget, if you will, the pressure exerted from such research activities as CD-Rom disks, end-user online systems, videotex and significant quest for improved services. One may think that in a small library all of this may be put behind one, but living together through interlibrary loan and interactive cataloging plans even makes this retreat impossible.

There are obvious differences between daily answering questions and theory and research. Still, few of these differences involve total and direct opposites. The best reference librarian is necessarily something of a theorist, a researcher, if only in an effort to improve service, to better understand why X or Y has such difficulty presenting a query.

This is not to deny there are barriers between theory and practice, or at least research and practice. This may correspond more to a situation in particular than in general. For example, almost any issue of the *Journal of Documentation* (to name only one of a dozen such periodicals in the field of theory and research) is densely packed with technical data, with approaches which stress theory. The assumption here is twofold. First, the reader is well versed in the jargon and technical language employed and is able to follow the normally mathematical explanations. Second, more often than some of the contributors or editors admit, the journals measure a universe which is so totally divorced from the experience and education of the average reference/information librarian that it is exceedingly out of the reach. Most of the people involved with these journals (and sometimes the monographs of a similar nature), do not make a direct impact by what they have in common with the working reference librarian. The impact comes indirectly from what constitutes technical exploration and ideas which eventually may, or may not be translated for the working librarian.

These journals are the life of philosophy and theory and research. The sometimes seemingly formless results may tomorrow lead to a practical turn which will be of vital concern to the reference librarian at the desk. They are, therefore, necessary and in their way as practical as their functions may seem foreign to some.

Another group tend to be more technicians than theorists, and they often surface in the standard library journals. Here the focus is on basic considerations of not "how we do it," but "how you should do it." Some of the articles do bridge the theory-practical gap, but all too often they invoke the ghosts of those experts from the more theoretical journals. The intended bridge builders between the practical and the theoretical normally end with a less than sturdy plank which often collapses under use.

It becomes clear that the person who applies theory to practice had best understand both. As a whole, however, this rarely is the case. The grades of difference between the theorist, the technician and the working librarian need not be that great, but the wrinkle is the lack of proper communication between the three. Sooner or later some do arise who think about all areas, all audiences, and demonstrate the corollary between theory and practice. And that's what this issue is about.

Today it really is not possible to consider an efficient, intelligence reference/information person who lacks a grasp of both theory and practice. The general thinker, the person capable of making connections between ideas and work at a reference desk has become more the rule than the exception. The great modern faith in technology, in research may be somewhat outworn, but no one can go wrong who matches this faith with an appreciation of theory, research, and ultimately the truth. One must not only consider the mission, the objectives, the purpose of reference services, but one must learn to learn about what matters. It is the very soul of the art of reference services to be able to think constructively not only about what has passed, but what is going on and what is likely to happen tomorrow. The notion is hardly unique, and if these papers are representative of the movement, we can say with confidence that the separation of theory, research and practice can no longer be described as practical. Such separation is a denial of what reference services are about.

Neill asks "Can there be a theory of reference," and without argument answers in the affirmative. He explores the meaning of "theory" and concludes that while some aspects of it is inappropriate much of it helps to explain what the average reference librarian is about. Ford makes many of the same points, but from another angle, and offers a telling argument for the integration of research and practice.

Moving to an example of modern day research and theory, Stanoulov shows the "methodological apparatus revealing the logical transition of an existing theory from one to other of its kinds bearing on a well grounded deductive method." The supposition, as with many articles of this type, is that the reader is familiar with the language of the concepts discussed. This is equally true in the broader look at the library in literature. Here, Walsh offers a scholarly appraisal of how literary methodology may be applicable in a historical/cultural view of the library.

The expert inquiry system suggested by Harmon is the ideal "by information scientists and philosophers for many years." It's a primary example of wedding theory and practice. It offers, as the author suggests, a basic analyses of research strategies as applicable in theory as in daily work. Leide takes the intellectual play to its ultimate conclusion with the question asked by almost everyone: "Is the complete librarian obsolete." In reaching an answer he considers the rapid changes in the profession. Hafner is concerned with exploring the underlying rationale for the public library in a democratic society. He develops the theory of its role and how it is affected by transition from industrial to an information economy.

Miller and Tegler believe that at least one theory—the instruction of laypersons in the use of the library—is wrong and been self-destructive. They illustrate time and time again how a wrong headed theory can interfere with efficient practice and, in a real way, undermined the profession. Rodger and Goodwin examine another massive problem, this time at a local level. The puzzle of measuring reference accuracy is examined, and a carefully worked out methodology is offered. The article is representative of the class in that it not only analyzes a particular situation, and offers conclusions, but demonstrates how the same approach may be used by other libraries.

The classic unobtrusive testing methodology is examined by McClure and Hernon is relationship to library management and the sometimes failure of reference services. They show how a theory is turned into a practical tool—a tool which will help in library decision making and improve service.

As many of the authors in this issue point out or imply, the new technology has brought theory into the practical field of reference services. In a necessary effort to understand the workings of an online search, it is important to have a grasp of what heretofore has been more intellectual puzzle than real problem. If, a few years ago, one might devote scores of user studies to the hows and whys of asking questions, and just as readily leave them to gather dust, today they are considered of major importance in evaluating the efficiency of the online interview and search. This is equally true of ideas which apparently had little or no relationship to the reference desk. Today many of those intellectual puzzles, those carefully considered ideas are applied to not only online work, but daily reference services.

Library schools are aware of the real connection between online training and reference services. Krieger offers a valuable survey of where and how online searching is taught and the problems involved. The need for improving educational aids is the theme of Levine's paper, which stresses the various uses of videotex and user preferences for various systems and approaches. He stresses the importance of appreciating user requirements instead of simply the technology *per se*.

Buchan gives an actual example of how the computer and the index are wed to produce the fascinating NASA Lexical Dictionary and the thesaurus. Turning to the revolutionary microcomputer Atkinson and Knee explain the various functions of the computer in the library and then turn to the ever present problem of determining which database to search. They offer a model, customized index which can be employed in other libraries.

Theory, practice or talk—when it finally comes down to it, the real question is how well the question is answered by the reference librarian. This issue concludes, fittingly enough, with a description of how this goal is achieved via a well known legal system, Westlaw. Irving and Mendelsohn study the features and conclude it is extremely valuable for anyone, not just trained attorneys, seeking legal and related types of information. Most important, they show how on a daily basis the database may be studied and employed to increase the efficiency of the average reference librarian.

Can There Be a Theory of Reference?

S. D. Neill

I shall answer the title's question in the affirmative. Before I do, I intend to take an unscientific sample of theoretical papers and show how they are not theories of reference but are descriptions of what goes on in reference work, or are techniques for doing reference, or are applications of theories from other disciplines. In the end, I will identify a tentative theory of reference and thus answer the question. That is, although the theory of reference I propose might prove inadequate, it is sufficiently close to the mark to enable me to say that there can be a theory of reference. First, however, I must clarify what I mean by "theory" and what I mean by the words "the reference process."

THE REFERENCE PROCESS

The calendar which describes the reference course I teach calls it "information sources and services." While it is about those things, it is even more about the process of referring inquirers to sources of information to meet a specific need. Mainly it is about referring people to "the literature." It is about *reference*.

The reference process has its beginning with the question being asked of the librarian and ends with an answer being accepted. That is the limited definition. The process really begins with the formation of the question in a situation experienced by the person who will become the inquirer. Asking the question of a librarian, usually in an institutional setting, is the second stage in the process. Search-

Professor Neill is at the School of Library and Information Science, University of Western Ontario, London, Canada N6G 1H1.

ing for the answer in the collection and having it accepted is the third stage. There is a fourth stage, and that is the use the inquirer makes of the answer.

For the librarian, the action begins with the asking of the question, but the process of finding the answer is, or should be, based on an understanding of the first and last stages — how and why people ask questions and how they use the information or knowledge they accept as the answer.

THEORY

A theory explains. Some say it is the overall interpretive framework which guides our study of a phenomenon. These are very general definitions. A theory of reference will answer the question "why is the reference process the way it is?". But before we can have a theory of reference we must have a description of what it is and, since it is dynamic, how it moves. Because the process involves at least two human beings interacting, the description will be complex and often tentative. For instance, a detailed description of the part played by memory has only recently been attempted (White, 1983; Neill, 1984).

We need to look at an overall framework built in a cumulating circle: these are the parts, this is the way they work, these are the skills and techniques for making the parts work well, and this is why there are these parts which work this way with these particular skills and techniques.

However, in the complex process that is human interaction and human thinking it is possible to have theories about what is happening and whether or not the parts identified are in fact the right parts for the process being studied. We can have a theory of what as well as why. Columbus sailed west on the theory that the earth was round. That is no longer a theory; it is a fact. Because much of the reference process is subjective, the patterns are hard to find, and much is hidden, as it is mental work which does not always show clearly in verbal or non-verbal behavior. So we get such researchers as Benson and Maloney (1975), Taylor (1968), Rettig (1978), and Dervin (1977), saying "I think this is what is happening and this is the way it is happening and this is the best way to do it (under certain circumstances)." These are theories in the sense that the authors are saying "I haven't got all the facts, but here's a good guess based on the evidence I have." There will come a time when we are so sure we know the what and how of reference that we can concentrate on an overall interpretive theory.

Nevertheless, a general theory can be postulated when only some descriptive material has been accumulated. Indeed, to guide research questions, some general theory is a necessity, as Ellis (1984) so clearly illustrates. Discoveries of new areas and new skills can be tested against the proposed theory in attempts to falsify or amend it.

If there is a theory of reference, then, ideally it must underlie the whole of the reference process. That is, to have a theory of the reference process we cannot have one theory that explains one part and another that explains a different part. From the generation of the question to the application of the answer is a constant flow — a single-purpose action. A theory that will provide us with an interpretive framework must apply as validly at the beginning as at the ending.

Theory Development

Four elements come into play in theory development: (1) a description of the territory, (2) the categorizing and structuring of parts and patterns, (3) the presentation of a theory as an idea, a possibility, and (4) gathering data to test the theory with more and more rigor. A theory cannot be developed without repeated observations of the field of action and a description of *all* the parts. For the reference interview alone we are dealing with an incredible range, from the physical layout of the library to the cognitive aspects of the inquirer and the librarian. When we add in the peculiar institution which is a library, we add all of the complex relationships people have to information technology and to books in particular.

Everything that comes into play must be accounted for if any test of the theory is to be valid, indeed, if any test of any theory of any part is to be valid; for the sub-theory must fit the overall theory if results are to be relied upon. Otherwise the unknown or discounted variables will persist in invalidating results and the practice will not improve. Thus, information retrieval experiments in laboratory situations do not necessarily generate conclusions that accurately transfer to reality.

The reference process begins with the formulation of the question arising from a problem situation and ends with the use of the answer in the life of the inquirer—from Taylor's theory of levels of question formation to Dervin's constructivist theory of information, which includes the inquirer's interpretation and use of the answer. A general theory of reference will cover all stages and will include in its explanatory power any sub-theory developed for the different events and facets of the process.

Some Examples of Theories

When I teach the basic reference course, I base it on a theory of problem solving which says that every facet of the reference process is a problem soluble by a general problem solving strategy: (1) define the problem, (2) gather information to clarify the problem and suggest solutions, (3) devise a plan, (4) test the solutions, and (5) if not satisfied, go back and re-think from the beginning if necessary. This is the theory I posit as evidence for an affirmative answer to the title's question.

However, in order to discuss the various aspects of the process, I use a number of articles that are theoretical about what and how, that is, they are basically descriptive. I will analyze these briefly to help clarify what I think should count as a theory of reference.

THE BIBLIOGRAPHIC BRIDGE

Benson and Maloney's (1975) "Principles of searching" is a good description of the reference process inasmuch as it identifies the steps that are taken and draws a model or map of the process. It is a different way of drawing a flow chart. Benson and Maloney categorize questions and resources (systems). The sequence of actions to be taken in the process of searching are "principles." These principles are, of course, in the nature of guidelines or rules of thumb. The purpose of the search process is to build a "bridge" between the question and the resources in such a way that there is a match between them. Congruence equals success.

The theory is that success comes when there is a match and that the search process is the bridge that can make that match. There are some who question the best match theory (Belkin, Oddy and Brooks, 1982). Nor would I agree that the bridge between the question and the resource system is one-way, as they picture it. Frequently, the knowledge in a resource, or the words, can help clarify the question or even alter the direction of the inquirer's investigation.

Benson and Maloney's theory is set against one of the "tenets of faith" for reference librarianship that good reference service is a result of the librarian's knowledge of the collection — a concept that has not, they say, been investigated to any degree. (This tenet of faith is another pseudo theory, and one which guided the teaching of reference for many years. It postulates what is important in reference work, but it is not a framework which explains what happens in the reference process.)

Does Benson and Maloney's model constitute a theory? In the sense of being a theory of "what," it is. Columbus risked all on a theory of what. We need to test such theories against experience so that we are secure in our facts. We need to know the facts before we can address the question why, e.g., why the earth is round.

When we ask why Benson and Maloney's theory of action might be successful, we could answer that the search process as they describe it is similar to the general process of problem solving and since any question is a "problem," the cognitive processes involved in problem solving will apply. Thus the explanation behind whatever validity is inherent in Benson and Maloney's model would be that this is the way people think when trying to solve a problem.

While Benson and Maloney have given us a framework, it is descriptive rather than explanatory, and it is a description that barely penetrates the surface. It does not, for instance, explore the thinking process at the level of Bates' (1979) search tactics. Bates' tactics are a heuristic for how to do it — alternative ways of thinking in the process of solving the problem of finding sources and answers. Indeed, she notes the relevance of the literature on the psychology of problem solving.

THEORIES OF COMMUNICATION

James Rettig's (1978) "A theoretical model and definition of the reference process" develops the theory that the reference process is really one of interpersonal communication. At the time Rettig wrote, the tenet of faith that good reference work results from the librarian's knowledge of the collection had been clearly displaced.

Rettig's model, contrasted with Brenda Dervin's (1977, 1983) constructivist model illustrates how a theory can affect our view of what is actually happening in the reference situation.

Rettig presents a simple communication model involving a source (the inquirer), a message transmitted through a channel (the voice), to a destination (the librarian), who receives it (by ear) and decodes it (in the brain). Noise is added to this base — in the reference process, noise is semantic noise. A resource, as a medium, is linked to the librarian and to the inquirer. The significant factor in this model is that its theoretical base is Shannon's theory of communication, which Rettig cites (on page 21). Actually, he cites Warren Weaver's introduction to Shannon's theory (Shannon and Weaver, 1949).

Weaver attempts to extend Shannon's engineering theory to include meaning and the effect of meaning on the conduct of the receiver. This is the theory which was, for many years, the generally accepted paradigm (interpretive framework) in the study of mass communication. It is a theory that understands the receiver to be an object to be "hit" by a message and "get" it. Such an understanding is an inaccurate view of the receiver when the receiver is a human being. Weaver "imagines" another box in Shannon's diagram which would be labeled "semantic noise," re-labeling Shannon's "noise" as "engineering noise." The problem of understanding the message must then take semantic noise into account. To make sure the desired total message meaning arrives at the destination, Weaver says an adjustment can be made in the original message so that "the sum of message meaning plus semantic noise is equal to the desired total message meaning at the destination" (p. 26). There is no consideration of the interpretive acts on the part of the receiver as a result of personal background (Ellis, 1984, has good examples of this in the information retrieval milieu), or of the feelings of the receiver vis à vis the message itself.

Rettig's model includes feedback from the inquirer to the librarian and back again. In fact, although Rettig does not say so, we are dealing with *two* sources and *two* receivers. The model is far more complex than either Shannon and Weaver or Rettig depict it.

That Rettig accepts the source-to-receiver model, that is, that it is source-oriented, is clear from his view of the librarian selecting, cataloging, and classifying the resources in anticipation of the needs they will eventually satisfy. The purpose of this preliminary organization of the collection is to "allow information to flow efficiently from information sources to those who need information" (pp. 27-28). This is a third "source" in the model, and this source is a collection of messages written by experts. In this set-up one wonders what the word "efficiently" in the above quotation means. The inquirer is faced with the formidable task of finding an answer in a system organized by someone else on principles as yet unknown, except that the letters and language are familiar.

It is the model that Dervin (1983) describes as the bullet or hypodermic theory of communication. The meaning of the message, as decided by the source, is expected to get into the head of receivers exactly as intended and ought to produce a certain specified effect on behavior. If it does not, the fault is in the receiver. Librarians have similar expectations of subject terms and classification codes. Librarians who, consciously or unconsciously, live by this (Rettig's) model, see users as bad guys who cannot formulate a question or readily understand catalogues or indexes to reference tools.

For Dervin (1977), each inquirer comes from a unique problem situation which no preconceived classification or list of descriptors will match perfectly. No answer will have the same effect on all inquirers or even on the same inquirer at different times. For one person, a given piece of information may be calming, for another it may provide motivation.

For Rettig, the interpersonal communication aspect controls the search process and all "ancillary" activities depend on it. Dervin (1977) finds the more interesting focus to be the use made of information: "How did the individual find the information useful?" She claims that, for librarians, functional utilities are to circulate books or transfer information; for the individual user, the functional utility is more likely to be "instructions, clarifications, reinforcements, answers, ideas, companionships, confirmations, assistances, escapes" (p. 25). The question for the librarian, therefore, is "how can the 'something' which will be functional for the individual, be delivered?" To answer this question, the librarian needs to know how information helps or why it does not.

With Dervin's theory, the whole focus has changed because the theory of communication is different from Rettig's. The fundamental difference is that the creative nature of the receiver of information, grounded in a unique situation in time and space, is taken into account.

Theories of interpersonal communication slight search strategies and knowledge of resources. A comprehensive theory of reference cannot slight any facet. It must underlie and explain all sub-theories that might be applied at different stages. The importance of Rettig and Dervin is that they have gone below the surface of the reference process and beyond a description of steps to identify cognitive and, in Dervin's case, affective elements in the interpersonal communication stage.

But are these theories of reference or theories of communication applied to an aspect of reference? The constructivist theory of communication tells us why neutral questions are appropriate in the reference interview and why we need to know about question formation (in a way that Taylor did not) and why we need to know about the use of information because of the unique and subjective nature of personal problem situations. But it does not tell us why the whole process operates the way it does, except as it sees that process as a process of solving problems.

Memory Theories

Marilyn Domas White goes deeper into the cognitive area than has been done before when she applies Minsky's theory of (memory) frames to reference work. Memory lies below the communication process of the reference interview, and, as Neill (1984) has shown, below the search process as well. But are these theories of reference, or descriptions of one part of the cognitive territory of reference as highlighted by theories from other disciplines? Neither Neill nor White develop a theory of reference. They apply theories of memory to reference activities in order to describe them.

It should be noted that White recognizes the problem solving base: "Reality begins at the second level with constraints posed by problem-solving abilities and the problem itself" and "(Levels) Q2 and Q3 are influenced greatly by the user's problem-solving skill . . ." (p. 44).

The Filters

Finally, I think we should ask if Robert Taylor's (1968) five filters in the question negotiation process are theoretical in any sense other than being a concept of "what." Taylor's is one of the most cited articles in librarianship. Why? Certainly because the five filters identified for the first time the basic parts of the reference interview—the parts of the inquiry the librarian needs to know: (1) the subject, (2) the objective and motivation of the inquirer, (3) the personal characteristics and background of the inquirer, (4) the relationship of the question's terminology to the library keys, and (5) the anticipated or acceptable answer. Filters two, three and five are information needed to help clarify the subject. With a little effort we can see these factors stretching back into Dervin's problem situation and ahead to the possible use to be made of the information. Taylor was aware of the play of the personal. But nowhere does Taylor specifically mention the problem solving process that underlies the filters. He has identified how the librarian finds out about the subject and hints at the beginnings of the search process (filter four). But why are these filters necessary in the question negotiation process? One answer is that the negotiation process is a process of problem solving and the filters are specific instances of general problem solving strategy.

A SERIES OF PROBLEMS

Indeed, it is possible to treat each filter as a problem to which general problem solving strategy can be applied. More than that, each step in the reference process, from the inquirer's recognition of an anomolous state of knowledge, to deciding to ask a librarian, to putting the information to work, is a problem. The reference process from start to finish is a sequence of problems. This is one explanation of the reference process (for an elaboration see Neill, 1975, 1985). There may be others, but one, even tentative, theory which encompasses every facet of the action is enough to say there can be a theory of reference.

The question we have been addressing is not why there is a reference process or what is the reference process or how it is done, but why the reference process is the way it is. To say that the process is "mainly" a communication process, or "most importantly" a process of interpersonal communication, or "most importantly" a knowledge of tools, does not answer the question why it is what it is. It is a communication process of a peculiar kind where problems are presented explicitly and arise implicitly out of the very nature of the communication between two human beings in an institution that has a knowledge resource which is actively present to a greater or lesser degree in the minds of each participant. To solve the problems, techniques based on communication theories are useful, use of memory is essential, understanding human nature is required, and knowledge of the ways of analyzing the search process as well as knowledge of the tools are all necessary for good results. But these are the what and how — the parts and how they work and how they can be worked — not the why.

Librarians are and always have been more interested in what and how. After all, these are very difficult to know and do, perhaps can never be known completely and certainly rarely done perfectly. Perhaps that is why articles on reference service policies were mistakenly called theories (Bishop, 1915). In librarianship, the levels of service "theory" does not explain what is happening in any of the stages of reference. Some part of the interview and search can be influenced by a levels of service policy, but policy is a force external to the process and we are looking for a theory that explains the process both at its worst and at its best. A theory must be able to explain all cases. It must hold in the most abbreviated and the most extensive of reference instances.

On the Use of Theory

Theoretical articles seem too far removed from practice to warrant more than a "so what" comment from readers and journal referees. A good example of this is Richard Derr's (1984) categorization of questions. Derr attempts to base all questions asked in libraries, if not all questions period, on eight categories organized as "conceptual presuppositions." Derr concludes: "This paper has identified two fundamental properties of questions; namely, they have a structure that consists of a subject and a query, and they presuppose a limited number of basic categories of human thought" (p. 189). Since librarianship deals with questions, a speculative discussion of question types seems to me to be relevant. But Derr's paper drew a negative response from a reader ("Question on 'Questions'," 1985) who designated himself (or herself) as a "pragmatic reference librarian." This person declared Derr's contribution to be "useless" and "twaddle." Derr replied that plans for systematic testing of the concepts were underway. Neither critic nor author seemed able to accept a purely speculative article as part of the world of library literature. Everything in that world has to be useful immediately or tested empirically. The study of librarianship seems limited in its range to the practical.

Theory is useful. Witness the results of adopting a communication theory such as Dervin's *vs.* Rettig's adaption of Shannon and Weaver. However, even Rettig's theory is useful, for it starts us looking at the reference interview as a communication process, focusing our thinking on that area and away from others. Even a weak theory, such as the problem solving theory proposed here as a theory of reference, is useful. Weak theories are usually based on few observations and often the nature of the phenomena studied is not clear cut (Eysenck, 1985). Still, such theories direct attention to areas which might yield useful discoveries if examined systematically.

If the theory holds, that is, if it is strong enough to predict what happens consistently, it becomes a theory widely, if not universally, accepted. At that point researchers build on it with confidence and produce useful results for the profession. These results themselves help prove the strength of the theory.

CONCLUSION

Can a theory of reference be seen as, or contribute to, a theory of librarianship? This question could be asked substituting "cataloging," "classification," and "administration" for the word reference. My first guess would be that any theory of cataloging or classification would not be reducible to problem solving. Rather, these activities are involved with organizing and managing bodies of knowledge and bits of information *in records*. These are not interactive as are persons in the reference process. Knowledge must be manipulated as an interlinked structure of larger and smaller disciplines; information must be organized in the context of such a structure.

Administration could be seen as a study of problem solving situations. The difference is that administrators must arrive at solutions to their problems, for better or worse, while people in referencing situations need not *solve* anything (Neill, 1985). As Belkin, Seeger, and Wersig (1983) so clearly explained, most everyday human problems are "treated," not solved. Dervin and Fraser's (1985) discovery of the multitude of uses of libraries supports this idea.

Ultimately, the profession of librarianship is a service and it may be that theory is here inappropriate. A service is tied up with a view of the nature of persons as learners and therefore is tied into cultural values and political beliefs. When Alvin Schrader (1984) attempted to give us a theory of library and information science, he presented a theory of "what." Indeed, in the abstract to his thesis, he admits, with more humility than necessary, that his conceptualization constitutes a "rudimentary descriptive theory of library and information science," but yet a "more adequate and more powerful description of the domain than those definitions so far posited." His description of library and information science as "the domain of the symbolic culture access system" (374) may nevertheless be an adequate paradigm within which empirical studies of problems generated by any general theory of reference can be undertaken.

REFERENCES

Bates, Marcia J. (1979). Information search tactics. *Journal of the American Society for Information Science, 30*(4, July), 205-214.

Belkin, N. J., Oddy, R. N. & Brooks, H. M. (1982). ASK for information retrieval: Part 1: Background and theory. *Journal of Documentation, 38*(2, June), 61-71.

Belkin, N. J., Seeger T. & Wersig, G. (1983). Distributed expert problem treatment as a model for information system analysis and design. *J. Info. Science, 5*(5, Feb.), 153-167.

Benson, James & Maloney, Ruth Kay (1975). Principles of searching," *RQ, 14*(4, Summer), 316-320.

Bishop, W. W. (1915). The theory of reference. *Bulletin of the American Library Association, 9*(4, July), 134-139. (See also Rettig's [1978] discussion of the literature.)

Derr, Richard (1984). Questions: definitions, structure, and classification. *RQ, 42*(2, Winter), 186-190.

Dervin, Brenda (1983). An overview of sense-making research: Concepts, methods, and results to date. Presented at the International Communications Association Annual Meeting, Dallas, May 1983. Seattle, Washington, School of Communications, University of Washington, 1983.

Dervin, Brenda (1977). Useful theory for librarianship: Communication, not information. *Drexel Library Quarterly, 13*(3, July), 16-32.

Dervin, Brenda & Fraser, Benson (1985). *How libraries help.* Sacramento, CA: California State Library.

Ellis, D. (1984). The effectiveness of information retrieval systems: The need for improved explanatory frameworks. *Social Science Information Studies, 4*(4, Oct.), 261-272.

Eysenck, H. J. (1985). The place of theory in a world of facts. In K. B. Madsen & Leendert Moss (eds.), *Annals of Theoretical Psychology, Vol. 3.* New York: Plenum Press, 17-72.

Neill, S. D. (1975). Problem solving and the reference process. *RQ, 14*(4, Summer), 310-315.

Neill, S. (1984). The reference process and certain types of memory. *RQ, 23*(4, Summer), 417-23.

Neill, S. D. (1985). The reference process and the philosophy of Karl Popper. *RQ, 24*(3, Spring), 309-319.

"Question on 'Questions'," *RQ, 24*(4, Summer), 519-520.

Schrader, Alvin Martin (1984). *Toward a theory of library and information science.* Ann Arbor, MI: University Microfilms International.

Rettig, James (1978). A theoretical model and definition of the reference process. *RQ, 18*(1, Fall), 19-29.

Shannon, Claude E. & Weaver, Warren (1949). *The mathematical theory of communication.* Urbana: University of Illinois Press.

Taylor, Robert S. (1968). Question-negotiation and information seeking in libraries. *College and Research Libraries, 29*(3, May), 178-194.

White, Marilyn Domas (1983). Conference encounter model. *Drexel Library Quarterly, 19*(2, Spring), 38-55.

Research and Practice in Librarianship: A Cognitive View

Nigel Ford

The over-riding impression of the results of the not inconsiderable research efforts of the last decade is one of unfulfilled promise. The mass of "so-what" research findings have barely ruffled the surface of practice or usefully deepened intuitive or experimental understanding. (N. Roberts)[1]

Arguably, all is not well with research in librarianship. It has been criticized as generally being more talked about than practiced. When it is practiced, it may often be narrow and compartmentalized, of disturbingly varied quality, and of transitory value.[2] What Harris has termed "ostrich librarianship" has lost the profession its pride of place in the pecking-order for research and development funds and facilities:

Librarians, who have nurtured the information business over this century, have manifestly failed to maintain their proprietary rights. . . . Non-librarians and even anti-librarians are now forcing the pace. The information trade is largely in the hands of systems analysts, educational technologists, marketing executives, and post office engineers. They are doing the research and they are producing the goods with resources which might once have gone into libraries.[3]

What good quality research is done must find its way through "the barriers of resistance (and ignorance) that exist in librarianship

Mr. Ford is a Lecturer, Department of Information Studies, University of Sheffield, Sheffield S10 2TN, South Yorkshire, England.

towards research."[4] Nor is it easy to find universally acclaimed research and development successes even in areas which would seem to be relatively straightforward and uncontroversial (compared, that is, with psychological and sociological research) such as the development of information retrieval systems. For example, as Peter Vickers, of Aslib's research department, pointed out:

> A nasty corollary is that if I cannot easily find what I know to be present, there is zero chance of my finding anything I am unaware of. Our beautiful on-line retrieval systems suffer from similar limitations.[5]

Nor are similar criticisms emanating from a number of different countries hard to find.[6]

But if research is merely "systematic inquiry made public"[13] can it really be that librarians are uninterested and researchers incompetent? Or could it be because of intractable problems in the very nature of knowledge, the problems faced by librarianship, and the problems of human perception and cognition — as Roberts has said:

> the knowing, perceiving processes of individual researchers . . . How and why research problems are seen as such; how "solutions" are arrived at; why individual responses vary despite identical information "inputs"; etc?[14]

I would argue that it is necessary for us to examine the processes of research in some detail in order to try to shed light on such questions.

RESEARCH APPROACHES

> It is the aim of any scientific theory eventually to provide laws which unify substantial areas of knowledge and make predictions possible. (L. R. B. Elton and D. Laurillard)[15]

A central function of research activity is *prediction*, which allows us the possibility of *control*. If we can predict that action C will result from circumstances A and B, we can bring about C by engineering A and B to be present, or avoid C by preventing A or B. We are essentially looking for economic ways of representing otherwise unmanageable volumes of discrete information, to reduce data to underlying principles in the form of explanations, models, theories, principles and laws. These, it is hoped, can be applied to other contexts, allowing us to predict and possibly control.

"Scientific" Paradigms

> I believe that (informatics) will become the *fundamental* social science, assuming much the same role in the social disciplines that physics has in the physical disciplines. (B. C. Brookes)

Traditionally, research in the physical sciences has concentrated on analyzing complex situations into component parts, studying each part, then re-assembling the parts into the original whole with increased understanding. In subjects like chemistry, the purity of substances can be controlled, and the behavior of pure samples can be generalized to all other pure samples subjected to the same conditions.[13]

As adopted by many researchers in a number of social scientific disciplines, including librarianship and information science, the scientific method retains many of the features mentioned above. The main difference is that the purity of phenomena being studied cannot be controlled in the same way as substances in chemistry, and there is difficulty in predicting the behavior of individual variables from one sample to another. Consequently, representative samples are sought in the hope that the experimental sample will accurately represent other samples to which the research results are to be generalized. The use of random samples, as opposed to samples chosen according to the researcher's judgments, allows us to subject the process to testing in accordance with the mathematics of probability.[17] This allows an estimation of the extent to which research results are likely to have occurred by chance. Based on this, levels of "statistical significance" are generally interpreted as indicating predictive power from the experimental sample to other similar samples.

A number of assumptions underlie the adoption of this paradigm, namely that:

— we can increase our understanding of complex wholes by analyzing them into component parts, better understanding the parts, then re-assembling them to form the whole

—we can discover universal laws of behavior: that is, we can identify variables which when subjected to the same conditions behave in exactly the same way in all similar samples.

These basic assumptions themselves involve other assumptions, namely that:

—we can measure individual variables in isolation from one another: as opposed to the philosophical argument that phenomena can only be defined and known through their relations with other phenomena[13]
—having done so, we can profitably re-link them using statistical relationships.

These assumptions require a strong emphasis on

—quantitative data, in the sense of large volumes of data, economically reduced to statistical form
—"statistical significance" testing in order to predict to other samples in the search for universal laws
—reducing subjectivity in order to promote the most widespread consensus (as opposed to individual idiosyncrasy) possible, which will increase levels of statistical significance. Attempts to reduce subjectivity may be aimed at the generation of hypotheses; the constructs and categories used in the research design, and the analysis of the data
—searching for (and often unjustifiably inferring from correlations) discrete relationships, particularly cause and effect relationships, involving "diachronistic" time scales (discrete event A, for example, being antecedent of discrete event B) as opposed to a "synchronistic" time scale (in which events are interlinked more closely)[15,20,21]

and may often result in a prescriptive application of the research results—that is, since "universals" are being sought, and universals apply in all other similar contests, then interpretations of data obtained within such a framework may themselves be framed in terms of universality and take the form of prescriptive instructions (e.g., tape/slides are or are not the most effective way of presenting certain aspects of library instruction)[22] rather than more tentative suggestions of possible interactions between variables which the reader may test out for himself in different contexts.

If research is a question of performing a logical analysis of the research problem, and if data must be obtained in relatively large quantities and in a form that allows common analysis, then it may also be assumed that it is both possible and desirable to stick to research designs which are predetermined by the researchers—in terms of the categories used for analysis and data collection, and the focus and sequence of the inquiry.

LIBRARIANSHIP AND THE "HUMAN FACTOR"

our main unit of measurement, and our only source of justification—(is) the individual. (N. Roberts)[22]

However, when applied to the study of social and psychological man, this scientific paradigm may be criticized on two main counts. Research results are

—generally less consistent than those produced in the physical sciences
—often not particularly valid in "real life" contexts.

The physical sciences abound with relatively well established relationships in the form of models, principles and laws with high reliability. In this way, formulae can be combined in complex ways and applied to a variety of situations, so that, say, the stresses at play in a massive bridge can be calculated with sufficient accuracy to allow an acceptable balance between costs and safety standards.

When we bring in psychological and sociological factors, however, levels of consistency—and therefore predictability—drop relatively. Explanatory models and formulae in these areas provide much less consistent results. Our problem is that these human factors are central to our concerns.

Despite an apparent preoccupation with inanimate phenomena such as mathematical theories of communication and the development of computerized systems, librarianship and information science are essentially social. They do contain overtly social scientific aspects such as the cultural role of the library, the psychology of library management, and the increasingly cognitive viewpoint in information retrieval studies. [14,24-28] However, even apparently less "human" technological aspects — such as recall and relevance formulae, biblio models and library service statistics — are essentially records of cognitive operations and transactions in the communication process between two (or more) individuals, including the producer of an information source and the information seeker.

Within this context, if we are to persevere with the "traditional" scientific paradigm, then we must attempt to maintain levels of statistical significance by obtaining more data per variable — either by obtaining larger total samples, or by reducing the complexity of variables being studied.

For example, larger samples should be required to establish at a given level of statistical significance that, say, stable introverts tend to spend longer hours working in the library, than to establish at the same level of significance that running increases heart rate. Yet to maintain viability in terms of research time and effort, rather than simply increase total sample sizes, it may often be necessary to reduce the complexity of the constructs and relationships being studied. Yet since the sociological and psychological sciences must deal with complex situations, often only a small and arguably superficial facet of any situation may tend to be analyzed — therefore results may not be particularly valid in the complex contexts in which research is most urgently needed. Paradoxically, such concentration on relatively isolated constructs and simple relationships may also often mean low levels of reliability insofar as simplistic models may have less predictive force over time and across different samples. This may induce a vicious circle keeping both ecological validity — or relevance to "real life" situations — and reliability low.

"HUMANISTIC" PARADIGMS

It is not realistic to expect the reduction of (human) behavior to laws, because it is not possible to isolate individual components of behavior in order to establish the relations between them. (L. J. Cronbach)[29]

Another solution is to adopt alternative paradigms. Finding origins in philosophy in Germany in the nineteenth century,[30] alternative "interpretative" paradigms have been developed in fields such as social anthropology and humanistic psychology which are now influencing research in fields such as the study of teaching and learning, which previously had made predominant use of "traditional" scientific assumptions and methodology, [15,31,32] and information science and librarianship. [33]

As applied to the study of sociological and psychological man, "interpretative" paradigms rest on certain basic assumptions, which may be described in both positive and negative terms — negative terms — negative in order to show their difference from the "traditional" scientific paradigm described above.

- the "whole" is more than simply the sum of the parts, and cannot be fully understood by means of isolating, analyzing, testing, then reassembling the parts. Complex situations must also be studied in their entirety.
- human behavior is too complex necessarily to allow us to reduce it to universal laws. It is also necessary to study complex interacting phenomena which may interact differently in different contexts. [34,35]
- instead of separating and defining variables in isolation from one another, phenomena must also be studied within the context of their interactions. When we do this, attention must shift from discrete things and events themselves, to the relationships — and systems of relationships — between them. The researcher's task is to "interpret the system of relationships in terms of simpler underlying structures on which the observed situations are built." [36]
- "relationships" cannot solely be conceived of as discrete causes and effects within a "diachronic" time scale (discrete event A preceding and causing discrete event B). Rather, relationships must also be seen as complex patterns of mutual interaction.
- findings that relate to restricted contexts, as opposed to those having universal applications, are valid. Rather than search exclusively for basic laws on which to base predictions, it is valuable to try to understand underlying structures operating in a specific contexts. This means that models are developed which are *not* "simplified descriptions of *all* of relevant reality," but rather are used to "unify limited aspects of a particular reality." [37] Several different models may be applicable and valid to the same reality. Models may be useful within the

context of "frames,"[38] and different situations may be viewed from a variety of such frames, or vantage points. Ironically, such a conception of "models" accepted in the physical sciences, has been largely ignored in the application of traditional scientific paradigms to the study of social and psychological phenomena.[15]

Research paradigms are a case in point. Those discussed are not mutually exclusive — each can be relevant to the same reality — but take different standpoints and select different aspects of that reality for study, like lights shining onto an object from different angles. The object may appear very different vantage points, but through their interaction overall understanding may be increased.

This approach often involves an emphasis on detailed case studies involving much contextual data from a relatively small number of situations, and qualitative data and analysis.

Because of the relevance of partial models, and because of the complexity and interrelatedness of variables

— it is both possible and desirable to place more emphasis on qualitative data and analysis, even if (as is usually the case) this means reduced quantity, as statistical significance is relatively less central a concept.

— "experiential" data[39] is permissable and desirable, i.e., data gleaned from the participants' experience of the situation being investigated. In scientific paradigms, this type of data is not desirable, insofar as it risks a reduction in the quantity of strictly comparable data on account of subjective idiosyncrasies.

— the researcher need not be constrained by the need to keep rigidly to a pre-determined research framework. He can seek to explore individuals' perceptions of their experience, and can focus on what the individual considers salient even though this is likely to differ from individual to individual.[40]

This paradigm assumes

— "a recognition of man's unique capabilities of self-conscious reflection and appraisal of his experiences. The researcher is required to take on a role akin to that of a sympathetic listener, seeking to understand through empathy in intuition the perspective or world view of the person or group of people in whom he is interested."[41]

Yet the limitations of more interpretative paradigms must not be overlooked. As Entwistle and Hounsell note

. . . the very sensitivity and flexibility which are the essence of illuminative research are also its Achilles' heel . . . research reports can appear too much the product of the researcher's personal perspective and of the idiosyncrasies of the specific situations examined.[41]

RESEARCH APPROACHES IN CONTRAST

As each paradigm marks out boundaries and establishes its own rules of discourse, there is a danger that territorial advantage will be sought through confrontation rather than mutual understanding—and the outcome of a pitched battle is more likely to be schism than synthesis. (N. J. Entwistle & D. Hounsell)[42]

Is there any way out of the dichotomy between what Ford[43] has called on the one hand the supply of "highly reliable answers to highly meaningless questions" risked by "traditional" scientific paradigms; and on the other hand, the supply of highly "meaningful questions with highly unreliable answers" risked by interpretative social scientific paradigms?

Unfortunately these research paradigms may often be seen to be in competition—as Entwistle[44] notes, "It is almost as if the one perception . . . necessarily destroys the other." Yet these two views are perfectly compatible—so long as neither is interpreted or assumed to represent either *all* reality, or the *most important* aspects of reality. In the former case, they would be mutually exclusive: in the latter, likely to be highly disputed. But why should an awareness of the complementary nature of, and the ability to integrate different research perspectives be so hard to achieve? I would argue that research into cognition may help us to understand.

A COGNITIVE VIEW OF RESEARCH

What we can see from one point of view we cannot see from another. . . . With one kind of observation certain aspects become visible: with another kind of observation we see something else. We cannot arrive at a procedure of observation which makes all the various aspects visible simultaneously. (F. Morton and L. Svensson)[45]

If we view research paradigms as the products of human cognition, it is hardly surprising if the distinctions discussed seem to reflect distinctions identified in research into cognition itself. The two research paradigms discussed may be thought of as essentially different in the extent to which an *analytic* or a *holistic* view is taken. Towards one end of such a dimension, research approaches are characterized by logical, sequential analysis. The research problem is typically broken up into manageable component hypotheses, each of which is tested. More complex hypotheses are built on the basis of those already tested. Other paradigms, however, are characterized by a more holistic approach, in which complex hypotheses may be handled without waiting to be built up from tested sub-hypotheses. To some extent different levels of uncertainty would seem to be inherent in these different approaches. The researcher pursuing a relatively holistic approach must sustain greater uncertainty in the sense that he is dealing with complex and relatively untested hypotheses at the same time, in comparison with the relatively "secure" logical steps of more analytic approaches. These differences seem to reflect fundamental differences in the way we process information from the level of concept learning through strategies for learning complex academic topics to broad specialization in arts and science.

Echoing Bruner's findings in the field of concept formation,[46,47] more recently Pask has investigated students' learning of complex academic subjects.[48-51] He has identified learning styles susceptible to this distinction. Based on laboratory experiments using sophisticated techniques of computer-monitoring of students' learning processes, and on research in more "ecologically valid" normal learning contexts, he has identified two distinct but complementary components of understanding. *Comprehension learning* relates to building up a description of what may be known in a subject — usually involving obtaining a broad overview by forming complex and relatively speculative hypotheses about how individual topics are inter-related, making rich use of analogies and relating what is being learned to personal experience. *Operation learning* relates to mastering procedural details – usually involving forming relatively narrow, simple hypotheses and testing them out before moving on to the next topic, logically and sequentially. This analysis has been applied to a wide range of complex subjects in disciplines including science, anthropology and history. Examples are as diverse as biological taxonomies, the menstrual cycle, the operon, spy networks, reaction kinetics and Henry VIII's reign! Certain individuals may be better at one or other type of learning. Comprehension learners would seem to pursue relatively complex hypotheses often obtaining an overview without going on to test its validity more systematically. Operation learners, on the other hand, tend to progress logically and sequentially, testing out narrower and more simple hypotheses before going on to the next, but often not achieving the overview. Versatile learners, however, can combine both elements and achieve full understanding.

The same dimension may also be useful in distinguishing between *divergent* and *convergent* thinking. The "divergent thinker" excels in tasks requiring him or her "to think fluently and tangentially."[52] "The highly divergent thinker tends to be relatively unconcerned about strict observation of rules, somewhat unconventional, impulsive and willing to take risks."[53] The convergent thinker excels at tasks requiring him to converge on the one "right answer" by logical processes. Indeed such differences seem to reflect C. P. Snow's "Two cultures." Generally thought processes in the Arts would seem to emphasize relatively holistic untested (in any objective sense) and intuitive hypotheses, whereas "traditional" science has largely been more analytical – emphasizing the more logical testing of relatively narrower hypotheses and building up understanding in a logical sequential way. It is interesting to note that Hudson found strong correlations between divergent thinkers and choice of arts, and convergent thinkers and choice of science subjects in the sixth form.

Witkin and others[54] review over 25 years of research into differences in cognitive style which pervade a wide range of individuals' activities including perception, body-concept, defenses, social orientation, learning preferences, subject interest and career choices. Relatively *field-independent* individuals tend to be interested in areas requiring cognitive skills – articulation, analysis or structuring — not emphasizing relationships with people. Relatively *field-dependent* individuals, on the other hand, tend to favor areas requiring social, interpersonal relations in which such abilities in analyzing and restructuring are not emphasized. These differences are pervasive and relatively stable. The pervasive strand of differences in this distinction seems to be the extent to which different individuals are able to free what they are perceiving or thinking about from the context in which it is found or presented. The "embedded figures" test of field dependence/independence, for example, seeks to measure how successfully people can perceive particular shapes embedded in more complex patterns. This ability seems to extend to perceptions about the self — the extent to which the individual perceives her/himself as distinct from the context of those around her/him. Whilst not wishing to stretch the similarities to far — and I accept the highly speculative nature of my suggested links between different cognitive styles — once again this distinction between the analytical extraction of parts from their context on the one hand, and on the other hand, the concern with keeping the parts within their contexts seems familiar.

It may well be that such distinctions reflect not just individual differences *between* — but also fundamental biological distinctions *within* each individual. Recent advances in neurological sciences [55-58] have suggested that the left hemisphere of the brain is

a rational-linear mind specializing in sequential processing logical analytical thinking and verbalization. . . . This is the mind that requires structure and order, which processes perception and sensory input in logical and linear modes. [59]

The right hemisphere

houses spatial perception, holistic understanding, perceptual insight . . . visualization and intuitive ability. Its mode is metaphoric, analogic and holistic. . . . This side of the brain thrives on multiple relationships processed simultaneously. [60]

INTEGRATION

it is . . . important to recognize the limitations created by being a human being on the one hand, and trying to be a scientist on the other. Part of the objectivity necessary for a social scientist depends on a recognition of his inevitable subjectivity. (N. J. Entwistle)[61]

There is some evidence that certain individuals tend to adopt one or other consistent type of thinking—which I have argued characterize different research paradigms—across different situations and in different contexts. Bruner found such consistency. Pask noted that the differences he found seemed to reflect fundamental styles of information processing.

Other individuals, however, seemed equally able to adopt different approaches. In Pask's research, "versatile" learners could achieve both "comprehension" and "operation" learning. Certain of Hudson's sample were classified as "all-rounders," performing well on tests of both divergent and convergent thinking.

Indeed, there is evidence that without both types of thinking the quality of learning and knowing is much reduced. Pask claims that the combination of *both* "comprehension" and "operation" learning is necessary for the full understanding of any topic. Comprehension learning without operation learning leads to what Pask has termed *vacuous globetrotting* in which the broad description or overview of the way in which the topics making up a subject are inter-related is not valid—i.e., it will not stand up to detailed testing. Operation learning without comprehension learning leads to *improvidence* in which the individual cannot see the wood for the trees.

Neurological research has also indicated the essentially *integrated* and *complementary* role of the left and right hemispheres of the brain. Indeed

cerebral organization as the basis for processing information and constructing expressive behavior must be understood as more than simple lateralization of cerebral functions. Cerebral organization must also be interpreted in terms of inter-hemispheric integration . . . (both) are crucial to the successful and complete processing of information.[62]

Although the left hemisphere is thought of as controlling, for example, linguistic functions such as reading, there is evidence that right hemisphere functions are also necessary in verbal processing, including letter recognition.[63,64] The essential role of intuition as a complement to rational "scientific" thought even in the progress of scientific knowledge has been described by Popper.[65]

> The way knowledge progresses, and especially our scientific knowledge, is by unjustified (and unjustifiable) anticipations, by guesses, by tentative solutions to our problems, by conjecture.

Traditionally scientific research has sought to minimize subjectivity not only in the testing of, but also in the generation of hypotheses by an emphasis on observation. Popper, however, proposes an alternative view of scientific research succinctly described by Entwistle as

> . . . an iterative model . . . in which tentative theories are refined through error elimination, but never perfected. Within this view science progresses by demanding that . . . there should be a process of conjecture and refutation. . . . These conjectures are . . . controlled by empirical test.[66]

Polanyi[67] goes further in that he

> rejects the normal idea of scientific objectivity and the mechanical procedures often implied by the logic of scientific discovery . . . (and) stresses the importance of creative imagination in physical science . . . (and) personal knowledge of empathetic theorizing, supported, but not dominated by empirical testing.[68]

And arguably, in the Arts, distinction between creativity and banality may be interpreted in similar terms. Although the Arts thrive on complex hypotheses about human nature and experience which are relatively untested in an analytic "scientific" sense, their quality also depends ultimately on the testing of their validity in terms of other people's experience. A lack of such validity, tested in the public arena, is surely the hallmark of the purely eccentric and banal.

RESEARCH IN LIBRARIANSHIP
AND INFORMATION SCIENCE

Research . . . is rarely premised upon an agreed version of "information man." Economic science needed an agreed generalized notion of economic man to progress. Does information science need a similar abstraction? Research activities give no indication. (N. Roberts)[69]

Yet a distinct lack of balance — and some tension — between the two paradigms is apparent in a number of research fields, including that of librarianship and information science. A lack of balance between the two, I would argue, has been a prime cause of:

- the lack of application of research findings in library practice; and
- the poor quality of much research in librarianship and information science.

Most research has in my view not taken sufficient account of the *individual*. By "individual" I mean two things:

- the individual (sense A) and a human being, as opposed to non-human, technological phenomena; and
- the individual (sense B) as unique, as opposed to groups of people.

I believe that research has not "taken sufficient account" of the individual in the sense that

- it has concentrated on technological phenomena to the relative exclusion of the individual in sense A;
- where it has studied the individual in sense A, it has concentrated on groups of individuals to the relative exclusion of the individual in sense B.

A prime cause, I would argue, is an over-emphasis on conceptions of research, and of "evidence," based on paradigms developed in the physical sciences. The reader may or may not agree with my assessment of the main thrust of research conducted to date. Few — and I would not claim to be amongst them — are able to take an impartial overview of all or even most research in these areas. Indeed the usefulness of the concept of "all" or "most" research is limited. Research takes many forms and is conducted at many different levels in terms of quantity, quality, importance, applicability and effectiveness. However, more important than assessing past efforts are questions relating to future decisions facing individual researchers and those guiding groups of such individuals who must decide priorities and balances in selecting what is worth investigating, how the research is to be conducted, and the nature of what will constitute acceptable and useful "evidence."

Despite an increasing research attention to psychological aspects of librarianship and information science,[28,70,71] and an increasing number of studies making use of such "interpretative" features as case studies, experiential, qualitative interview and "thinking aloud" data,[72-77] most research has concentrated on relatively technological aspects — the development of techniques and systems. Although essentially evidence of cognitive transactions, records of satisfaction rates, levels of recall and relevance, issues and requests have generally been used in large scale quantitative analyses geared to developing essentially mathematical type models of library and information activities.

Where it has studied social and psychological "information man" more explicitly, research has tended (with notable and an increasing number of exceptions) to use "traditional" scientific paradigms, in which individuals are subordinated to statistical patterns. (Unfortunately, using this approach, it is possible for example for a change in some system to result in improved statistical performance for up to 40% of users.)[13] Often, models of activities do not have "ecological validity." Where they have been developed from the study of isolated variables often in experimental conditions, they may be highly abstracted and not relevant to the complexities of "real life" human situations in which practicing librarians must work. However, this is the type of research likely to result from the research paradigms predominantly in use until recently in librarianship and information science.

If this is the case, it is not surprising to note Roberts' comments on the current state of research in librarianship and information science, in which

> Research is synonymous with narrow and compartmentalized forms of study . . . separate research projects fail to convey

the impression of contributing to a common pool of ideas shaped by a consensus of professional imperatives. . . . The current assumption appears to be that once a piece of research is completed then it is completed forever. The consequence is that much research is characterized by its static, snapshot, quality and, as such, quickly relegated into irrelevance and history by the flux of circumstance.[69]

These are just the results likely to be produced by an overemphasis on "scientific" paradigms. Such approaches lack the more "holistic" element which would allow the (admittedly relatively speculative) overview of highly complex situations necessary for the integration of isolated studies and the development of an integrated model of complex Man the Information User.

Indeed, it is tempting to view much research in terms of what Pask[49] has termed *improvidence* — the result of operation learning without comprehension learning, in which the mapping out of the wood, and an understanding of its ecology, is obscured by a preoccupation with measuring and observing individual trees. On the other hand, much discussion, current opinion and practice goes ahead without the benefit of being grounded in research. This I would describe in terms of *vacuous globetrotting* — comprehension learning without operation learning in which rich — but untested and invalid — generalizations may be made.

It is interesting to note that librarianship and information science are in many ways analogous to education. All are concerned with a wide range of activities from technological systems through human perception and cognition to attitudes and values. All are concerned with the communication of information and with developing systems of making information accessible to information seekers in response to their needs. All have come across what I would argue are very similar difficulties in the research field.

Research in librarianship and information science must avoid following — yet appears to be following — the vicious circle characterizing much research of recent years in education. Aping the traditional scientific paradigm, research[15,78,79] has largely concentrated until recently on quantity to the relative exclusion of quality. Constructs have been isolated, and measured and correlated with other isolated constructs. Universally valid theories, as opposed to more variable context-dependent models, have been sought. The result has been twofold — research pervaded by "no significant results" on the one hand; on the other the same mass of "so-what?" results identified by Roberts in librarianship and information science.

Addressing the American Psychological Society, Cronbach notes that in research in education the traditional scientific paradigm of

> Model building and hypothesis testing became the ruling ideal, and research problems were increasing chosen to fit that mode. Taking stock today, I think most of us judge theoretical progress to have been disappointing. [80]

Entwistle and Hounsell note that

> Research on student learning was for many years the almost exclusive province of the experimental psychologists. . . . Typically, the experiments undertaken, while being sophisticated in research design, were trivial in content. [81]

Within the scientific paradigm adopted by much educational research, the need for large-scale collection of data susceptible to numerical analysis led to a concentration on *quantity* at the expense of *quality* in education. Not surprisingly, there has recently been increasing interest in the conscious rejection of such quantitative paradigms in favor of interpretative or "illuminative" ones. [31,32]

I would suggest that these dichotomies may be deep-rooted, on two counts.

Firstly, the contexts in which people work create their own rigorous and precise parameters of information need, in terms of the nature of "evidence" which is relevant, acceptable, influential and decisive — and the scope, focus and conceptualization of what constitutes the problem needing research.

Secondly, individuals may develop habitual and pervasive styles of processing information, which may strongly influence their areas of interest and choice of profession. Such cognitive styles may be more, or less appropriate in relation to certain features of "research" and "practice."

BALANCE IN RESEARCH APPROACHES

As teachers, we have all had students and younger colleagues complain that they cannot find the right methods to study problems in which they are interested. All too often we help them reshape their problems so that the available methods can be used. In the process, the original problem is often lost. (E. G. Mishler)[82]

The researcher's problems may be governed by factors other than attempting to find answers to relevant, meaningful questions. Occasionally, research methodology may assume a greater reality than the research problem. To the practitioner faced with a problem, this approach is no better than the proverbial searching for a lost coin not where it was dropped, but rather where the light is better!

There may be also considerable forces of tradition, and forces of incentives and controls which mould the way researchers go about research, in particular institutions, funded by particular bodies and/or supervised by particular individuals. All of this may be coupled with individual researchers' own deep rooted cognitive styles and beliefs about the nature of investigation, reality and truth. Whilst it may be easier for the researcher to change his/her paradigms than for the proverbial leopard to change its spots, nevertheless, the willingness of individuals to integrate different approaches in their own work and in their evaluation of the work of others may be difficult to acquire.

What is needed, I would argue, is a sensitive and informed interaction between different research paradigms building on the strengths and being aware of the limitations of each — in Pask's terms, achieving versatile learning leading to a full understanding — and an acceptance that

> The two paradigms ("scientific" and "illuminative") contain the tension of opposites — a thesis and antithesis out of which a fruitful synthesis might be anticipated, but is still far from being achieved. . . . Yet the methodologies of competing paradigms could be used alongside one another, each providing distinctive yet equally valid types of evidence.[41]

Although there may be a tendency for studies to learn predominantly towards one or other approach in that there is a certain logical consistency between features characterizing different approaches,[83] a number of recent and continuing research projects exemplify such interaction.

For example a study involving collaboration between Sheffield University's Centre for Research in User Studies (now Consultancy and Research Unit) and the Centre for Applied Research in Education at the University of East Anglia, focussing on library access and use at sixth-form level, used "generalisation across descriptive case studies . . . based upon condensed fieldwork involving tape-recorded interviews, observations and collection of documents, including both qualitative and quantitative data."[84]

In the field of learning, the qualitative analysis of introspective interview data from small samples of students have yielded a number of distinctive study approaches,[85,86] characterized by high levels of "ecological validity" — relevant to realistically complex learning in natural learning situations — unlike the majority of constructs previously identified in the field of learning by larger scale more quantitative methods. Techniques for measuring these and other constructs relating to learning in large-scale samples by means of questionnaire data collection and statistical analysis have subsequently been developed,[87] and the original constructs have been refined in this close interaction of relatively qualitative and quantitative methods.[88] This interaction has involved the close cooperation of different research teams in the Universities of Lancaster and Gothenburg.

This is not to argue that complementary approaches are not desirable or possible within smaller scale studies. Indeed, rich intuitive and holistic speculation can be found in discussions of results in cases where a "traditional" analytic scientific approach was used. Many relatively quantitative studies are based on hypotheses generated from more qualitative experiences and observations. Relatively holistic qualitative studies may often be pursuing further lines of interest suggested by the results of more analytic quantitative ones.

RESEARCH AND PRACTICE

. . . is such a practically-minded field, with a fractured intellectual tradition and a deep sense of professional inferiority, sufficiently open to the play of ideas and the highly critical temper that an active group of intellectuals can bring to bear upon librarians' work and thinking? (P. Dain)[89]

I would argue that generally (a) much *research* in librarianship and information science has been characterized by a "scientific" (rational/linear; partist; "operation learning") type of thinking, whereas (b) much *practice* in librarianship and information work is characterized by a "humanistic" (intuitive/simultaneous; wholist; "comprehension learning") type of thinking.

The trouble is that *both* types of thinking are necessary for high levels of understanding. This type of *research* tends to lead to evidence which may be relatively more *reliable* but relatively less *relevant*. This type of *practice* is based on evidence which is more *relevant*, but which may be relatively less *reliable*. The result is that when attempts are made to make interpretations relevant to practice from research data, they are often unjustifiably far removed from those data. This leads to poor, incomplete understanding in both research and practice, and a gap between the two. Practicing librarians work in complex, holistic contexts dealing with individuals as well as groups. It is hardly surprising if research results from studies reflecting narrow, partist and quantitative assumptions and foci are often not seen to be relevant.

Within a context already biased towards "scientific" type studies, what is needed, I would argue, is an increased emphasis on the gathering of interpretative type evidence relating to the individual — his information needs, habits, skills and processes. However, without some form of control of standards, a proliferation of interpretative research could lead to vast quantities of eccentric and idiosyncratic data, analyses and interpretations. (One aid to control suggested by Stenhouse would involve the setting up of a central archive of case study data possibly in microform. Stenhouse[90] argued for a national center. This approach would allow not only relatively objective scrutiny of research studies, but also the re-use of data in other studies — subject to a solution of copyright and privacy questions.)

We must also promote increased interaction between practitioners and researchers. However, this presupposes rather more widespread practice and acceptance of research in librarianship and information science throughout the library profession.

Researcher-Practitioner Interaction

Yet in both cases we may be talking about a fundamental difficulty stemming from deeply differing types of information needs and styles of thinking, inherent in the different contexts of (a) different types of *research*, and (b) *practice*.

If one accepts that such differences may be deep-rooted, then the problem of closing the gaps between researcher and practitioner cannot be considered to be one of simply "educating the practitioner" in the sense of putting on courses in which he is introduced to, and required to go through the motions of analyzing, interpreting and conducting, "Research." Any assumption that information which individuals may be perfectly able to comprehend, manipulate and apply within the context of a *course* will necessarily be accepted, found useful, or applied in a *work* context, are open to question. Many students may "go through the motions of" using information which they find of little value other than that of enabling them to pass a course and obtain a qualification.[91,92]

Within the context of "teaching" research, we must approach learning not only at "cognitive," but also at "affective" levels. Cognitive and affective aspects of learning have been analysed separately.[93,94] However, to think of them as separate may be unhelpful — in teaching, unproductive. Recent taxonomies have attempted to integrate these areas.[95] Recent research in learning has identified links between "cognitive" learning processes and styles, and more "affective" characteristics such as motivational orientations, study attitudes and features of personality.[87,96,97] Recent teaching approaches have concentrated on reaching the individual at this deeper level. Recent work reported by Shaw, Thomas and Augstein,[98,99] for example, represents an attempt to enable students to become aware of, evaluate and change the basic constructs through which, if one accepts Kelly's[100] personal constructs theory, they interpret experience and, more specifically, formulate their approaches to study.

"TRUTH" AND PRAGMATISM AS RESEARCH GOALS

It is conceivable that, to future generations, our conceptions of what constitutes "evidence" in relation to the study of human thought and behavior may be just as interesting — perhaps more so — as the results based upon such evidence. (N. Ford)[101]

However, at a more fundamental level, those concerned with research in librarianship and information science must pay urgent attention to the balance between searching for "universal truths" and pragmatism.

One function of research, besides that of adding new knowledge on which future researchers may build, is surely to affect the practice of librarianship and information sciences. If this is so, then crucial variables must be the nature of evidence, its presentation and support, most likely to have a particular effect in a given context. Yet with exceptions there is remarkably little evidence of systematic study of the variables on which librarians base their practice and, more particularly, changes in their practice. For example, what might be the balance of emphasis that a particular librarian, or group of librarians might place, in relation to changing their practice, on (a) the fact that a particular set of research data related to 1,000 library users, and findings were significant at a level of $p <$ 0.025; or (b) the extent to which the researcher's conclusions and interpretations are intuitively acceptable to him, irrespective of sample size and level of statistical significance? If the balance is towards (b), then the production of less "scientific" but more intuitively "meaningful" evidence becomes more useful at least for certain purposes.

Within the context of applied research accepted standards of statistical significance, their precise empirical basis, and their theoretical assumptions about the predictability of man and his susceptibility to scientific study, must themselves be evaluated in terms of their relative usefulness within particular contexts, rather than remaining largely unquestioned yardsticks of some universal truth. [43]

If researchers fail to make their contribution to closing the research/practice gap, by overemphasizing the search for secure universals at the expense of relevant pragmatism, then it may not be so outlandish to modify the quotation from Dain, which introduced this section, to read:

> . . . is such a theoretically-minded field, with a fractured intellectual tradition and a deep sense of academic inferiority, sufficiently open to the play of ideas and the highly critical temper than an active group of *practitioners* can bring to bear upon *researchers'* work and thinking?

Not only has practice something to learn from research. Research has much to learn — and cannot be conceived as separate from —

practice. We must strive to achieve a more active and sustained dialogue and interaction between the two.

NOTES

1. Roberts, N. (1980). Review of Heriksen, T. IRFIS 3. *CRUS News,* *9,* 17-18, p. 17.

2. Ibid.

3. Harris, K. G. E. (1980). Ostrich librarianship? *Library Association Record, 82,* 569.

4. Redfern, M. (1981). Review of "Research methods in librarianship techniques and interpretations" by C. H. Busha & S. P. Harter. *Library Association Record, 83,* 39.

5. Vickers, P. (1981). (Reported in) Needles in haystacks. *Library Association Record, 83,* 14.

6. Bibliotek (1977). Biblioteksforskning — en grim aelling. *Bibliotek, 70,* 446-448.

7. Bogens Verden (1978). Vived for Lidt om bibliotekerne. *Bogens Verden, 60,* 150-15.

8. Carlsen, S. (1976). Forskningen pa forskningsbibliotekerne. *Bibliotek, 70,* 218-219.

9. Dain, P. (1980). The profession and the professors. *Library Journal, 105,* 1701.

10. Maguire, C. (1977). Research and librarians: Is there a connection? In *Proceedings of the 19th conference, Library Association of Australia* (A. Batt, ed.). Library Association of Australia Conference Committee, Hobart, Tasmania, pp. 295-301.

11. Renborg, G. (1978). Biblioteksforskning? Vad menas? *Biblioteksbladet 63,* 163-164.

12. Wilson, P. (1976). Barriers to research in library schools: A framework for analysis. *Journal of Education for Librarianship, 17,* 3-19.

13. Stenhouse, L. (1980). The study of samples and the study of cases, *British Educational Research Journal, 6,* 1-6.

14. Roberts, N. (1978). Forum: Comments on the developing cognitive viewpoint in information science — Brookes. *Journal of Informatics, 2,* 84-86, p. 86.

15. Elton, L. R. B. & Laurillard, D. M. (1979). Trends in research on student learning. *Studies in Higher Education, 4,* 87-102, p. 99.

16. Brookes, B. C. (1978). Forum: Comments on "The developing cognitive viewpoint in information science" — Brookes' response (to N. Roberts' comments). *Journal of Informatics, 2,* 86-89.

17. Fisher, R. A. (1935). *The design of experiments.* Edinburgh, Oliver & Boyd.

18. Bradley, F. H. (1908). *Appearance and reality.* New York, Macmillan.

19. Moore, G. E. (1922). *Philosophical Studies.* London, Kegan Paul, Trench, Trubers & Co. Ltd.

20. Elton, L. R. B. (1977). Methodological themata in educational research. *Research Intelligence, 3,* 36-39.

21. Entwistle, N. J. (1973). Complementary paradigms for research and development work in higher education. Conference of the European Association for Research and Development in Higher Education, Rotterdam.

22. Baldwin, J. F. & Rudolph, R. S. (1979). The comparative effectiveness of a slide/tape show and a library tour. *College and Research Libraries, 40,* 31-33.

23. Roberts, N. op. cit. Reference 14, p. 86.

24. Brookes, B. C. (1978). Forum: Comments on "The developing cognitive viewpoint in information science" — Brookes' response (to N. Roberts' comments). *Journal of Informatics, 2,* 86-89.

25. Ford, N. (1979). Cognitive psychology and "library learning." *Journal of Librarianship,* 25-38.

26. Ford, N. (1980). Relating "information needs" to learner characteristics in higher education. *Journal of Documentation, 36,* 99-114.

27. Glossop, M. (1978). Sociological ideas and librarianship. *New Library World, 79*, 25-28.

28. Keen, E. M. & Armstrong, C. J. (1980). *Visual processing in information retrieval searching: A collection of research papers*. Department of Information System Studies, College of Librarianship Wales, Aberystwyth.

29. Cronbach, L. J. (1975). Beyond the two disciplines of scientific psychology. *American Psychologist, 30*, 116-127.

30. Outhwaite, W. (1975). *Understanding social life*. London, Allen & Unwin.

31. Entwistle, N. J. & Hounsell, D. (1979). Editorial. Student learning in its natural setting. *Higher Education, 8*, 359-363.

32. Nisbet, J. (1980). Educational research: The state of the art. In *Rethinking educational research* (W. B. Dockrell & D. Hamilton, eds.). London, Hodder & Stoughton, pp. 1-10.

33. *Social Science Information Studies, 2*(4).

34. Biggs, J. B. (1979). Individual differences in study processes and the quality of learning outcomes. *Higher Education, 8*, 381-394.

35. McKeachie, W. J. (1974). The decline and fall of the laws of learning. *Educational Researcher, 3*, 7-11.

36. Elton, L. R. B. & Laurillard, D. M. op. cit. Reference 15, p. 89.

37. Ibid. p. 90.

38. Entwistle, N. J. (1977). *Changing approaches to research into personality and learning*. Institute of Education, University of Goteborg, Sweden (Report No. 59.).

39. Marton, F. (1978). *Describing conceptions of the world around us*. Reports from the Institute of Education, University of Goteborg, No. 66.

40. Parlett, M. & Hamilton, D. Evaluation as illumination. In *Curriculum evaluation today: Trends and implications* (D. Tawney, ed.). London: Schools Council.

41. Entwistle, N. J. & Hounsell, D. op.cit., Reference 31, p. 361.

42. Ibid. p. 363.

43. Ford, N. (1980). Levels of understanding and the personal acceptance of information in higher education. *Studies in Higher Education, 5*, 63-70, p. 67.

44. Entwistle, N. J. (1979). Stages, levels, styles or strategies: Dilemmas in the description of thinking. *Educational Review, 31*, 123-132.

45. Marton, F. & Svensson, L. (1979). Conceptions of research in student learning. *Higher Education, 8*, 471-486, p. 484.

46. Bruner, J. S. et al. (1956). *A study of thinking*. London, Wiley.

47. Floyd, A. (1976). *Cognitive styles*. Milton Keynes, Open University.

48. Pask, G. (1976). Conversational techniques in the study and practice of education. *British Journal of Educational Psychology, 46*, 12-25.

49. Pask, G. (1976). Styles and strategies of learning. *British Journal of Educational Psychology, 46*, 123-143.

50. Pask, G. *Learning styles, educational strategies and representations of knowledge: Methods and applications*. Progress Report 3 to the Social Science Research Council on Research Programme HR2708/1. Richmond, Surrey. Systems Research Ltd.

51. Entwistle, N. J. (1978). Knowledge structures and styles of learning: A summary of Park's recent research. *British Journal of Educational Psychology, 48*, 255-265.

52. Hudson, L. (1968). *Contrary imaginations*. Harmondsworth, Penguin.

53. Kennet, K. F. & Cropley, A. J. (1975). Uric acid and divergent thinking: A possible relationship. *British Journal of Psychology, 66*, 175-180, p. 176.

54. Witkin, H. A. et al. (1977). Field-dependent and field-independent cognitive styles and their educational implications. *Review of Educational Research, 47*, 1-64.

55. Bogan, J. (1975). Some educational aspects of hemispheric specialization. *U.C.L.A Educator, 2*, 24-32.

56. Raina, M. (1979). Education of the left and right. *International Review of Education, 25*, 7-20.

57. Samples, B. (1975). Education for both sides of the human mind. *The Science Teacher, 42.*

58. Samples, B. (1977). Mind cycles and learning. *Phi Delta Kappan*, May.

59. Raina, M. op. cit. Reference 56, p.10.

60. Samples, B. op. cit. Reference 58, p.688.

61. Entwistle, N. J. op. cit. Reference 38, p.33.

62. Raina, M. op cit. Reference 56, p.11.

63. Levy, J. (1976). Evolution of language lateralization and cognitive function. In R. Harnad, H. Sreklis & J. Lancaster (eds), *Origins and evolution of language and speech.* New York: New York Academy of Science.

64. Zalma, R., Reynolds, C. R. & Kaufmann, A. S. (unpublished). Handedness, cerebral dominance, and lateralization of cortical functions: An integrated review of research. Athens, GA, University of Georgia.

65. Popper, K. R. (1963). *Conjectures and refutation: the growth of scientific knowledge*. London, Routledge and Kegan Paul.

66. Entwistle, N. J. (1977). *Changing approaches to research into personality and learning.* Institute of Education, University of Goteborg, Sweden (Report No. 59).

67. Polanyi, M. (1958). *Personal knowledge.* London, Routledge and Kegan Paul.

68. Entwistle, N. J. op. cit. Reference 38, pp. 25-26.

69. Roberts, N. op. cit. Reference 21.

70. Belkin, N. J. (1977). *Linguistic and cognitive models of information and state of knowledge.* British Library Research and Development Report 5381. London, The British Library Research and Development Department.

71. Belkin, N. J. et al. (1979). *The representation and classification of anomalous states of knowledge and information use in interactive information retrieval.* In IRFIS 3. Proceedings of the 3rd International Research Forum in Information Science, Oslo, August 1st-3rd, 1979 (T. Heriksen, ed.), Oslo, Statens Bibliotekshoke, 2 vols.

72. Beswick, N. (1975). *Organizing resources: Six case studies. The final report of the Schools Council Resources Center Project.* London, Heinemann Educational Books.

73. Fjallbrant, N. (1977). Evaluation in a user instruction programme. *Journal of Librarianship, 9*, 83-95.

74. Harris, C. (1977). Illuminative evaluation of user education programmes. *Aslib Proceedings, 29*, 348-362.

75. Ingwersen, P. & Kaae, S. (1979). User-librarian negotiations and information search procedures in public libraries: Analysis of verbal protocols. Copenhagen, Royal School of Librarianship, (presented at the 3rd International Research Forum in Information Science, Oslo, August 1st-3rd, 1979).

76. Lancaster, F. W. (1977). *The measurement and evaluation of library services.* Washington: Information Resources Press.

77. Stenhouse, L., Harris, C. & Etherington, W. (1979). *Project proposal – Library access, library use and user education in academic sixth forms.* Center for Applied Research in Education, University of East Anglia.

78. Evans, K. M. (1968). Planning small scale research. National Foundation for Educational Research.

79. Cronbach, L. J. op. cit. Reference 29.

80. Ibid. p. 169

81. Entwistle, N. J. & Hounsell, D. op. cit. Reference 31, p. 359.

82. Mishler, E. G. (1979). Meaning in context: Is there any other kind? *Harvard Educational Review, 49*, 1-19, pp. 17-18.

83. Marton, F. & Svensson, L. op. cit. Reference 45.

84. RADIALS (1980). *Library access and sixth-form studies.* B.L.R. & D. funded project 1980-1982. Details in RADIALS 30/2/270, p. 37.

85. Marton, F. & Saljo, R. (1976). On qualitative differences in learning. 1. Outcome and process. *British Journal of Educational Psychology, 46*, 4-11.

86. Miller, C. & Parlett, M. R. (1974). *Up to the mark: A study of the examination game*. London, Society for Research into Higher Education, London.

87. Entwistle, N. J. & Wilson, J. D. (1977). *Degrees of excellence: The academic achievement game*. London, Hodder & Stoughton.

88. Entwistle, N. J., Hanley, M. & Ratcliffe, G. (1979). Approaches to learning and levels of understanding. *British Educational Research Journal, 5*, 99-114.

89. Dain, P. op. cit. Reference 9, p. 1701.

90. Stenhouse, L. (1979). The problem of standards in illuminative research. *Scottish Educational Review, 11*, 5-10.

91. Ford, N. (1979). Study strategies, orientations and "personal meaningfulness" in higher education. *British Journal of Educational Technology, 10*, 143-160.

92. Ford, N. op. cit. Reference 43.

93. Bloom, S. (ed.) (1956). *Taxonomy of educational objectives. Handbook I: Cognitive domain*. London, Longman.

94. Krathwohl, D. R. et al. (1964). *Taxonomy of educational objectives. Handbook II: Affective domain*. London, Longman.

95. Steinaker, N. & Bell, R. (1978). The experiential taxonomy: A fresh approach to teaching and learning. In *International Yearbook of Educational and Instructional Technology 1978/79* (A. Howe & A. J. Romiszowski, eds.), pp. 71-77, London, Kegan Page.

96. Biggs, J. B. (1979). Dimensions of study behavior: Another look at ATI. *British Journal of Educational Psychology, 46*, 68-80.

97. Entwistle, N. J., Hanley, M. & Hounsell, D. (1979). Identifying distinctive approaches to studying. *Higher Education, 8*, 365-380.

98. Shaw, M. L. G. & Thomas, L. F. (1979). Extracting an education from a course of instruction. *British Journal of Educational Technology, 10*, 5-17.

99. Augstein, S. H. & Thomas, L. F. (1979). Conversational investigations of student learning — Methods and psychological tools for learning-to-learn. *Core, 2*(1), Fiche 7, Frames G3-G13.

100. Kelly, G. A. (1955). *The psychology of personal constructs*. New York: Norton.

101. Ford, N. op. cit. Reference 43, p. 101.

The Wider Scope
of Information Research

Una Mansfield

Spectacular advances in science pose their own peculiar problems. A major breakthrough in understanding, accompanied by radically new methods and highly technical tools, can sorely upset the established order. Scholars may feel inadequate, because of their inability to maintain any reasonably comprehensive view of the new order or to acquire the skills needed to use the novel tools and methods. This can lead to the proliferation of ever narrower specialties, as scientists try to carve out manageable niches in the new domain, and to a loss of disciplinary coherence in the professions based on these sciences.

At the mid-point of this century, such a revolution occurred in the scientific study of information. The year 1948 saw the publication of two epochal works. First, Wiener's book, *Cybernetics; or Control and Communication in the Animal and the Machine,* provided the related insights that there is an essential unity in the set of problems in communication and control, whether they are to be studied in the machine or in living tissue, and that the computing machine represents an ideal model of information processing in the nervous system. Then, Shannon's paper, "A Mathematical Theory of Communication," clarified the concepts of *uncertainty* and *information* and provided a quantitative measure of each. This quantum leap in understanding was followed, in 1949, by the development (by von Neumann) of the world's first stored-program electronic digital computer, one of the most powerful tools ever available to science.

An experienced researcher, Una Mansfield may be found at 144 Gaybrook Lawns, Malahide, County Dublin, Ireland. The author wishes to acknowledge that this article "draws heavily on contributions to a collective volume I edited with the late Fritz Machlup (Machlup and Mansfield, 1983). My thanks to all of the contributors involved, in particular to Allen Newell and Patrick Wilson, whose influence has been especially strong.

Together, these events marked a turning-point in scientific research; von Neumann himself predicted that whereas, in the past, science had dealt mainly with the concepts of energy, power, force, and motion, "in the future, science would be more concerned with problems of control, programming, information processing, communication, organization, and systems" (Burks, 1970, p.3). The emergence, in the immediate post-war period, of several powerful one-theorem fields, such as information theory, control theory, decision theory, game theory, operations research, system theory, linear programming, and (later) dynamic programming, gave added fillip to this new direction of science. The awesome challenge of mechanizing intelligence, together with the need to manage the post-war explosion in the volume of recorded information, provided fertile ground for experimenting with the new tools and methods. Academic disciplines were subdivided and supplemented to cope with the surge of research activity. New professions were spawned, while established professions, such as librarianship, were forced to reassess their roles.

It has been difficult to get a clear picture of the new order in information research, partly because of the incredible speed with which developments have piled up, one upon the other, and partly because of the sprawling nature of the intellectual terrain. But now, nearly four decades after the initial breakthrough, perhaps we can posit the emergence of a new group of sciences, *the information sciences*, which includes a number of autonomous areas of study and several subfields of larger areas, some quite new and many arising out of the reorganization of traditional disciplines, all having a focus on a particular aspect of the phenomenon of information or its processing (Machlup and Mansfield, 1983, pp. 19-20).

THE INFORMATION SCIENCES

The information sciences are highly diverse. To underscore this diversity, Machlup has provided us with a scholarly analysis of the many meanings of the word "information" — from the literal to the metaphoric — in use across the disciplines (Machlup, 1983, pp. 641-661). Like the natural sciences or the social sciences, the information sciences neither have nor need a unified conceptual framework or many common fundamental postulates or axioms. Nevertheless, it is possible to group these sciences according to their general perspectives on information research: (1) empirical sciences that study information-processing by intelligent entities (human, animal, and machine) — *the cognitive perspective*; (2) empirical sciences that study information in industry and in society, with emphasis on the role of technology in its processing and communication — *the socio-technological perspective*; and (3) formal sciences that provide a theoretical base for many of the activities under (1) and (2), as well as for other parts of science — *the systems perspective*.

1. The Cognitive Perspective

Disciplines holding this perspective are known collectively as *cognitive science* (to be described later); they are

> artificial intelligence (i.e., the cognitive part of computer science)
> semiotics/linguistics (esp. psycholinguistics, neurolinguistics, and computational linguistics)

together with the *cognitive elements* of the following disciplines:

> psychology (e.g., cognitive psychology, neuropsychology, and computational psychology)
> neuroscience (e.g., cognitive neuroscience; brain theory)
> philosophy (e.g., philosophy-of-mind; epistemology)
> anthropology (e.g., cognitive anthropology; anthropological linguistics)

2. The Socio-Technological Perspective

> computer science (incl. parts of artificial intelligence)
> information science (i.e., the field that grew out of the documentation movement)
> library science

together with the *information elements* of the following disciplines:

> communication science (e.g., telecommunications)
> management science (e.g., management information systems; database management)

economics (e.g., economics of information and knowledge)
sociology (e.g., sociology of knowledge)

3. The Systems Perspective

information theory
cybernetics
system theory

Although the above disciplines and subdisciplines may appear to be a wildly heterogeneous lot, many have been influenced by the same Zeitgeist and share common approaches and methods. Perhaps the single most important influence on the information sciences, given their objectives of mechanizing intelligence and managing recorded information, has been the abstract conception of computation as *symbol-processing*.

Another strong influence has been the mechanization of logic, which led to the notions of *control, mechanism*, and *intelligent automata*. Work in logic (Turing, 1986), in psychology (Craik, 1943), and in neurology (McCulloch and Pitts, 1943), that developed parallels between computing and nervous activity in the brain, has had far-reaching effects. And the cybernetic thesis that *purpose* could be formed in machines by feedback (Rosenblueth, Wiener, and Bigelow, 1943) set the stage for Wiener's cybernetic revolution of 1948 and for the integrated study of mind, brain, and machine that followed.

Finally, Shannon's *mathematical theory of communication* (1948) had instant and universal appeal, and has been applied (indeed, sometimes misapplied) in all of the information sciences, as well as in other (mainly engineering) disciplines.

Let us look, then, at the scope and content of the three distinct sets of information disciplines. Space permits only a cursory glance at each, but the overall picture may help the reader to assess the broader context in which his or her own specialty operates.

SCIENCES WITH A COGNITIVE PERSPECTIVE

The disciplines listed under (1) above as having a cognitive perspective on information research are known collectively as "cognitive science." In the late 1970s, researchers in artificial intelligence and cognitive psychology came together with those linguists and philosophers-of-mind who emphasize *symbol-processing*, thus consolidating more than twenty years of cooperation among them. The resulting field is still a loose federation and no integration of the cognitive elements of the separate disciplines has occurred. But the ideals of cognitive science are firmly based and have been formalized in several ways.

For instance, in 1977, volume one of the journal *Cognitive Science* appeared. In 1978, an advisory committee submitted a report on the state-of-the-art in cognitive science to the advisers of the Alfred P. Sloan Foundation (Sloan Report, 1978). In 1979, the first meeting of the Cognitive Science Society was held in San Diego. Both the editorial board of *Cognitive Science* and the governing body of the Cognitive Science Society contain a broad distribution of members from the contributing fields, notably psychology, artificial intelligence, and linguistics. By the late 1970s, several dozen centers dedicated to the study of cognitive science had been created at major American universities and commercial research laboratories.

Cognitive science is described as an empirical natural science that studies "the principles by which intelligent entities interact with their environments" (ibid., p. 1). The "natural kind" to which its theories apply are those systems that are governed by *representations* or by knowledge and goals — the human information-processor is merely a special case of the more general theory of information-processing that it seeks.

Some of the related questions on the cognitive-science agenda are: "How is information about environments gathered, classified, and remembered? How is such information represented mentally and how are the resulting mental representations used as a basis for action? How is action coordinated by communication? How are action and communication guided by reason?" (ibid., p. v). So, the most immediate problem areas to be tackled are "representations of knowledge, language understanding, image understanding, question answering, inference, learning, problem-solving, and planning" (Collins, 1977, p. 1). In fact, the field is motivated by a search for a systematic theory of representation. Within cognitive science, "the theoretical and methodological apparatus of one subfield is being increasingly applied, and sometimes improved, to answer questions in another" (Sloan Report, 1978, p. 2.).

There is an overriding theme that, more than any other, appears to characterize the field of cognitive science:

> Computation, information processing, and rule-governed behavior all depend on the existence of physically-instantiated *codes* or symbols that refer to or represent things and properties outside the behaving system. In all these instances, the behavior of the systems in question (be they minds, computers, or social systems) is explained not in terms of intrinsic properties of the system itself, but in terms of rules and processes that operate on *representations of extrinsic things*. (Pylyshyn, 1983, p. 78)

This leads to the hypothesis that cognition consists in manipulating physically-instantiated symbols (whether in a brain or a machine); Pylyshyn expresses it as "the quite literal proposal that cognition *is* computation" and points out that cognitive science and computer science converge precisely at this point (Pylyshyn, 1983, p. 117). Critics object, however, to the over-emphasis on computation by cognitive scientists. They point out that the human mind is much more complicated than any known computational system, and that while symbol-manipulation may be one kind of intelligence, it is almost certainly not the only kind.

ARTIFICIAL INTELLIGENCE

The predominance of the computational view of intelligence in cognitive science may be attributed to the influence of one very dynamic member-discipline, artificial intelligence (AI, for short). AI is the part of computer science concerned with the creation of computer programs that exhibit behavioral characteristics identified as "intelligent" in humans: knowing, learning, reasoning, problem-solving, understanding language, and so on. And, in conjunction with the rest of cognitive science, AI has adopted the larger scientific goal of constructing an information-processing theory of intelligence.

Artificial intelligence came into being in the mid-1950s, just as soon as computer memories became powerful enough to accommodate the large, complex programs that it requires. AI has remained a part of computer science and has contributed to mainstream computer-science activities, such as studies of user/computer interaction (e.g., designing timesharing systems, inventing interactive languages, and developing personal computers). But its main focus is on building intelligent systems, as can be gleaned from some of its terms and slogans: *symbol-processing, physical-symbol system, symbol manipulation, information-processing model of cognition, cognition as computation, expert system, knowledge engineering.* Initially, work in AI was dominated by a search for general problem-solving methods; the key terms were *learning, classification,* and *search.* But, since the early 1970s, the emphasis has shifted toward designing forms of knowledge representation and the development of expert systems, with the key terms changing to *planning, knowledge representation,* and *semantics.* (The reader may be interested to note the distinction between expert systems and knowledge engineering: the former seeks to substitute computer intelligence for human intelligence, while the latter aims to amplify human intelligence by building new knowledge structures to aid understanding.)

Because of the ubiquitous nature of the computer, AI has links with all of the information sciences. Minsky has commented on its links with its nearest neighbors:

> With computer science [AI researchers] try to understand ways in which information-using processes act and interact. With philosophy we share problems about mind, thought, reason, and feeling. With linguistics we are concerned with relations among objects, symbols, words, and meanings. And with psychology we have to deal not only with perception, memory, and such matters, but also with theories of ego structure and personality coherence. (Minsky, 1979, p. 400)

With its engineering-orientation, AI opted initially for work on *performance* tasks, such as problem-solving (games, puzzles, theorem-proving, etc.). It is in this area of problem-solving, as well as that of concept formation, that it has had its strongest influence on psychology. Since the mid-1970s, however, AI and psychology have worked on different levels: AI at the symbol level and cognitive psychology at the level of overall memory structures.

Although the influence of the computational view can be seen in much of the current research in cognitive, developmental, and educational psychology, the view widely held in AI that physiological implementation is theoretically independent of questions about computational mechanisms has alienated some psychologists. However, all agree that AI has introduced a new rigor into research in psychology and philosophy-of-mind; the exercise of implementing a theory in a computer program forces clear thinking and the avoidance of mentalistic terms.

COGNITIVE NEUROSCIENCE

Mention of "physiological implementation" brings us to the role of cognitive neuroscience within cognitive science. When scientists started out to study intelligence, one group concentrated on programming (using discrete systems) while another studied pattern-recognition (using continuous systems). The first group, the AI researchers, looked to psychology for inspiration and guidance; the second group, the cyberneticists and brain theorists, turned to neurophysiology. Thus, the physical forms in which representational systems reside became a separate field of study, leaving a gap, which still persists, between AI and cognitive psychology, on the one hand, and brain theory, on the other.

Basic neuroscience, of course, is a part of biology. Cognitive neuroscientists are those members of the discipline who have undertaken the task of designing cognitive systems that show how the human mind/brain system works, thus providing a framework within which to test the theories of the cognitive scientists. For example, recent findings by cognitive neuroscientists point to the possibility of a modular organization of information-processing in the brain, rather than to a single cognitive system in charge of all information-processing, as had been assumed. This puts constraints on the theories of cognitive science.

SEMIOTICS/LINGUISTICS

Semiotics, the science of signs, includes linguistics, the science of language. But there is a clear division of labor between the semioticians and the linguists, and each group has developed its own terminology and research style. Although the term "semiotics" was used as far back as the time of the Greek Stoic philosophers, modern semiotics began with the work of the American philosopher, Charles Sanders Peirce. Laferrière defines semiotics as "the study of signs, i.e., of those entities which affect communication between interpreters of signs. Quite a variety of things can function as signs. A word, a sentence, a gesture, a facial expression, a photograph, a diagram, etc., are all signs because we their interpreters are more concerned with what they *stand for* or represent than with what they are merely *in themselves*" (Laferrière, 1979, p.434).

This brings out an important distinction between the kinds of signs or symbols studied in semiotics and those of concern, say, to computer scientists. Semiotics focuses on the symbols that humans use in order to convey meanings, not on symbols that function directly as intrinsic causes of behavior, the way symbols do in computers. The symbols of the semiotician require an intelligent agent to interpret them, and derive their meaning from their social and conventional context.

Signs are of interest to information scientists generally as the most elementary carriers of meaning and information, and some scientists maintain that the basic science of information concerns the structure of signs and how they are processed. Semiotics certainly has provided an elaborate framework for the study of signs, including their ranking along a presyntactic, syntactic, semantic, and pragmatic dimension.

Linguistics is a well established, culturally distinct discipline with strong roots in the humanities, and only a handful of linguists participated in the information revolution of the early 1950s. However, one such linguist/philosopher, Noam Chomsky, proved to be extremely influential and spearheaded what is now known as "the Chomskian revolution" in linguistics, in course of which he developed the theory that an understanding for grammar is an innate characteristic of humans. The algebraic character of the new linguistics, together with the idea of generative rules characterizing behavior systems, is in tune with the new scientific Zeitgeist. Nalimov, the Russian mathematician, has commented that "Chomsky's theory of context-free languages is clearly a mathematical subject generated by linguistic problems," and noted that "linguistics has also acquired some purely engineering aspects. The problems of machine-translation, working out languages for computers, and especially the problem of 'man-computer dialogue', have added engineering features even to such a purely humanistic field as semantics, though the principal problems of semantics have retained their humanistic core" (Nalimov, 1981, pp. 204-205).

A principal issue in determining the relations between linguistics and some of the newer information sciences was the distinction between *competence* and *performance* (Chomsky, 1963). Linguistic competence is the general knowledge a speaker has of the language, in particular, of the generative grammar of the language. Performance is the actual production of utterances, which can be affected by other factors, such as stress, cognitive limits, etc. The competence/performance distinction makes useful operational sense for linguistics, because there are two sources of evidence about human language capabilities: the actual utterance and the judgment of grammaticality.

But this distinction between competence and performance served to separate the sciences concerned primarily with performance, namely, artificial intelligence, computational linguistics, cognitive psychology, and psycholinguistics, from mainstream linguistics. This separation has persisted, with the study of linguistic theory being carried out independently of the study of computational mechanisms that enable the sentences of a language to be produced and recognized. But, while the performance fields have been able to draw on the findings of mainstream linguistics, there has been no reciprocal flow in the opposite direction, and linguistics proper still fits its traditional mould.

All of this left the field of artificial intelligence in a rather difficult position. Natural language is a unique mental capability, and AI needed to produce programs that could understand natural language. So, in the absence of direct help from mainstream linguistics, it mounted its own effort in the early 1970s, in conjunction with the subfield of computational linguistics. (See, for example, Winograd, 1972.) However, a decade later, the study of human cognition had become widely equated with the study of information-processing models, and pleas were being entered for greater cooperation between linguists and computer scientists, so that studies of competence and performance could be linked.

A partnership that fared somewhat better was that between linguistics and cognitive psychology. Through the new subfield of psycholinguistics, formal linguistic analysis was integrated with psychological investigations of memory to solve problems relating to such matters as span of consciousness, form of mental representations, and learning as a form of problem-solving.

Linguistics ought to be of help to fields such as library science that must grapple with the problem of content representation of published materials. However, the fixation of linguists on the single sentence (as opposed to longer discourse) and their general lack of success in dealing with semantics, has meant that little of value to library scientists has yet emerged from linguistic research.

PHILOSOPHY

Linguistics has always had important contacts with logic and philosophy. As language is the vehicle for human knowledge and judgment, it is considered central to issues involving philosophy-of-mind. In linguistics, traditional philosophic questions can be posed in sufficient detail to permit their subjection to experimental analysis.

Since the time of Descartes, philosophy has also been concerned with the mechanization of mind. This would seem to indicate strong links with the new field of artificial intelligence, yet, in its initial stages at least, AI had little involvement with philosophy. The two fields hold divergent views on a common domain of interest. Newell points to one example of this divergence, the problem of induction, where philosophy is interested in the certainty of induction, whereas AI is concerned with performing the induction (Newell, 1973). Until recent years, those philosophers who did take note of work in artificial intelligence tended to be critical of its limitations. (See, for example, Dreyfus, 1972; Searle, 1980.) But, under the umbrella of cognitive science, there are indications that philosophy is now becoming actively involved in the implications of information-processing systems.

One area of philosophy that may have special help to offer AI research is epistemology (the theory of knowledge) and there has been a notable increase in epistemological work within AI in the last few years. (See, for example, Bobrow, 1980.) Work in AI deals with the nature and functioning of knowledge, and progress in the subfield of knowledge engineering, in particular, stands to gain from the findings of philosophical epistemologists. A statement by a benign philosopher-critic of AI, Margaret Boden, is appropriate not only to this theme, but also to round off our brief discussion of the disciplines with a cognitive perspective:

> Thus, we need an interdisciplinary epistemology in which computational insights are integrated with philosophical un-

derstanding and psychological and biological knowledge. Indeed, the need for a genuine interdisciplinarity is a prime lesson of the computational approach. Workers in AI have much to learn from the insights of psychologists, linguists, physiologists, biologists, and philosophers, who, in turn, can benefit from their computationally informed colleagues. (Boden, 1983, p. 235)

SCIENCES WITH A SOCIO-TECHNOLOGICAL PERSPECTIVE

Whereas cognitive science deals with the subset of information problems inherent in *information within intelligent systems*, this group of disciplines focuses on problems related to *recorded information* (or knowledge): its generation, classification, processing, storage, retrieval, display, use, transfer, and accessibility. The domain of study embraces both the *activity* of processing and the *substance* that is processed, irrespective of the type of media involved. Indeed, it can be argued that it was the need to accommodate the powerful electronic media, with their revolutionary potential for information handling, that caused the major upheaval in this part of the information sciences and brought forth new fields of study and new scientific methods.

Unlike cognitive science, the disciplines holding a socio-technological perspective have not formalized their cooperative research effort. It is tempting to claim that the American Society for Information Science (ASIS), with its journal, performs this function, but that would not be quite accurate, as ASIS has members from across the entire spectrum of the information sciences, including many who hold a cognitive perspective (King, Krauser, and Sague, 1980). Cooperation within this second group is evidenced more in the blurred lines of demarcation between the three main disciplines: computer science, information science, and library science. Information science is allied to both of its neighboring disciplines, as "computer and information science," on the one hand, and "library and information science," on the other. It is possible to isolate studies of the computer (as a complex technical device), at one end of the spectrum, and studies of the library (as an institution that provides generalized access to recorded information and knowledge), at the other; but the large area of information studies is common to all three fields, though each, of course, has its own particular slant on the subject.

As we have seen, the domain of study includes two distinct elements: the *activity* of processing and the *substance* being processed. The processing activity is carried out primarily in computer science. Investigations of the substance of information are carried out on two different levels: on the syntactic/semantic level in computer and information science, and on the semantic/pragmatic level in library and information science. Wilson has called the latter activity "bibliographical R & D" and has provided a novel and useful categorization of its constituents.

Wilson's first category, which he claims to be the most successful, consists of developmental work leading to new products, services, and systems, based on applications of computer technology. This has resulted in an increased stock of know-how, much of it embodied in devices and systems. The second category he describes as attempts at originating bibliographical information, including bibliographical description and content representation. These he judges to have been "strenuous, but much less successful." Wilson's third category covers studies of the characteristics and use of the literature that forms the input to the bibliographical sector. Although these have resulted in the observance of some empirical regularities (e.g., Bradford's Law of Scattering), he says, no genuine scientific laws have yet been discovered (Wilson, 1983, pp. 390-392).

The situation is complicated by the fact that, in addition to bibliographical information, there is a need to organize and manage proprietary or operational information of the sort found in business and industry. It is not clear to what extent the principles of library science apply here, and studies of this type of information have called for cooperation between computer science, information science, and management science, resulting in the creation of such subfields as management information systems, database management, office automation, and so on.

The enormous dependence of information technologies on advances in the field of telecommunications has brought what would normally be thought of as an engineering discipline into the family of information sciences. Evidence of this integration can be seen in the fact that at least one school of library and information science (that at the University of Pittsburgh) is introducing a master's degree program in telecommunications.

It is difficult to think of a social science that does not have to study information and knowledge as part of its general investigations. But two such sciences devote specific efforts to understanding aspects of the information phenomenon. Economics has a specialty known as "the economics of information" that, according to Machlup's estimate, has an accumulation of over 20,000 published titles (Machlup, 1984, Ch. IX). The reader should be aware, however, that this subfield studies the role of information within economic activity, and not the economic considerations that pertain to information as a commodity, as has sometimes been assumed. The implications of information activities in the broader society are examined in a subset of sociology called "the sociology of knowledge."

Rather than comment on the progress of research in the socio-technological sector, on which many of my fellow-contributors will be reporting, I will confine myself to some brief remarks about the three main disciplines involved.

COMPUTER SCIENCE

Computing machines originated in electrical engineering, but the enormously complex task of designing, programming, operating, and maintaining the all-purpose digital computer soon gave rise to the development of a separate discipline, computer science. The mid-1960s saw the creation of the first departments of computer science, and the Association of Computing Machinery published its first undergraduate curriculum in 1968 (ACM, 1968).

Computer science has been defined as "the study of phenomena related to computers" (Newell, Perlis, and Simon, 1967); "the study of algorithms" (Knuth, 1968); "the study of information structures" (ACM Curriculum Committee, 1968; Wegner, 1970); and "the study of the management of complexity" (Dijkstra, 1972). These definitions reflect not only the wide spectrum of interests within the field, but also the increase in the complexity of the domain of computer science as it developed. The field is classified as an empirical science, despite the inclusion of several essentially mathematical specialties.

Computer scientists themselves are divided on the issue of whether the *activity* of information-processing or the *substance* being processed is the central concern of their discipline, with the latter group advocating a semiotic approach to computer studies. But all are agreed that one of the strengths of computer science lies in the fact that the knowledge-component (theory) and action-component (applications) have been kept together. Practical results suggest relevant theory, and theoretical results can increase the effectiveness of action.

Newell and Simon claim that "computer science is a scientific enterprise in the usual meaning of that term: that it develops scientific hypotheses which it then seeks to verify by empirical inquiry," and go on to cite their physical-symbol-system hypothesis as a case in point (Newell and Simon, 1976, p. 125). But theoretical work in computer science has grown only slowly, and most of its theories are borrowed from physics, mathematics, electronics, and modern logic. It is as an engineering discipline that computer science has displayed the incredible dynamism that has affected all of science. There is scarcely a discipline where it has not found fruitful application as a provider of tools and models. But our interest is in the fields with which it shares its research interests:

> Computer scientists . . . conduct research and publish papers in engineering, mathematics, economics, sociology, psychology, linguistics, philosophy, library science, the biological sciences, business, law, and the humanities, as well as in other cross-discipline areas such as communications and information theory, control theory, and general system theory. (Pylyshyn, 1970, p. 61)

It is interesting to note the inclusion of most of our information sciences, although the list was drawn up more than fifteen years ago. Computer science is involved (through its subfield, artificial intelligence) in the cognitive group of disciplines, and is a heavy user of the theories emanating from the systems group of disciplines. This makes it one of the most penetrating and influential members of the new breed of information sciences.

INFORMATION SCIENCE

The choice of the name "information science" for the field that grew out of the documentation movement of the 1950s and early 1960s has proved unfortunate. The terms "information" and "science" are both ambiguous, and their combination in the title of the new field has been criticized from various standpoints. Some critics want to know which of the multifarious meanings of "information" is intended, and some challenge the status implied by the word "science." For our purpose, the difficulty arises when the singular "information science" is used in a broad sense to describe a heterogeneous set of activities—what we call "the information sciences"—thus forcing the search for a unifying conceptual framework where none exists. Wilson says that if these "information scientists are correctly named, they have a generic claim to the title but not a specific claim. They may be information scientists, but they are not the only ones—they constitute only a particular species of the genus information science . . . library scientists might also claim to be information scientists; library science would be the name of the species, information science the name of the genus" (Wilson, 1983, p. 394).

Information science, in the narrow sense, may well evolve into an autonomous discipline. It is the youngest of the information sciences and any attempt to assess its true nature or potential may still be premature. I understand that several of the pioneers in this area are preparing their own histories of its evolution, and these publications may help clarify its objectives and activities. In the meantime, we can note its origins in the documentation movement, its initial concern with mechanized information retrieval, and its current activities within "the bibliographical R & D group" (described above). We can also note the fact that information technology has created new activities (e.g., networking, teleconferencing) and called for new ways of performing old tasks (e.g., cataloging, indexing), and that scholars from the narrow "information science" field are meeting these challenges. It is hoped that a better name will be found to describe what they do. English-speaking Europeans use the term "information technology" (IT, for short) to describe similar activities. It seems to fit.

LIBRARY SCIENCE

We have already seen that library science cooperates with information science to undertake research and developmental work in the bibliographical R & D sector. It also undertakes research studies on its own library sector: historical studies of libraries and library services; studies aimed at improving current management of libraries as institutions; and studies related to the formation of service policies, including economic considerations. In the present fiscal climate, studies aimed at cost containment, particularly through the introduction of new information technology in libraries, are receiving priority funding.

But, however important these studies may be to libraries as institutions, the unique feature of librarianship remains unchanged. Shera describes this as "the mystery of the substantive content of recorded knowledge, with a view to making this content accessible to others." He reminds librarians that their central concern is with *sociological* and *psychological* phenomena, and not with physical objects and processes. And he recommends research at the level of *symbolic interaction* (a process by which people relate to their own minds and the minds of others), which would provide "for the contributions of philosophy, linguistics, and psychology in the formulation of its (the library's) unique purpose" (Shera, 1983, p. 386).

As the concern of librarians is primarily to serve the human user of information, one assumes that their links with and interest in the cognitive disciplines should be at least as great as those with their technological neighbors. For instance, knowledge-engineering activities within artificial intelligence may be of particular relevance to library science, in view of their potential to radically alter the forms in which knowledge will be presented to the user in future. Knowledge engineering involves restructuring existing knowledge so that it can be flexibly presented in different formats for different contexts of use, and computer-aided learning is an important subfield of knowledge engineering. Indeed, computers provide a new dimension for communication among a community of scholars that could fundamentally change the sociology of creating and using knowledge in all academic disciplines, and libraries as institutions may have to reassess their roles to accommodate these changes.

It has been said that the major figures in the history of American librarianship were "doers rather than thinkers"; that they were concerned with *process* rather than *purpose*. Current developments in other areas of the information sciences may force a re-examination of the purpose of libraries as institutions, and a consequent new direction for research activities in library science, in which the librarian's unique role as guide to the intellectual content of recorded information may become a more central theme.

SCIENCES WITH A SYSTEMS PERSPECTIVE

We now come to a disciplinary grouping of a different sort. Formal — indeed, essentially mathematical — in character, these fields provide a theoretical base for the information sciences, as well as for many other disciplines. They are *general system theory* — the science of relations; *cybernetics* — the science of controls; and *information theory* — the science of transmissions of information (Machlup and Mansfield, 1983, p. 41). Explication of the technical aspects of these complex fields is beyond the scope of this article. Let us, rather, try to discover what the labels stand for, and how these disciplines relate to each other and to the other fields in our survey. Each of the fields has been given a narrow and a broader definition; and each has suffered from inappropriate application in areas where the mathematical expertise available was inadequate for a full understanding of the underlying theory.

When used in the narrow sense, the term "information theory" spans two levels. At the basic level, it denotes a class of problems concerning the generation, storage, transmission, and processing of signs and signals over channels of communication, in which a *particular measure* of information it used. (This is Shannon's theory.) On a higher level, but still in a narrow sense, "information theory has been taken to include any analysis of communications problems, including statistical problems of the detection of signals in the presence of noise, that make *no* use of an *information measure*" (Elias, 1959 and 1968; emphasis added). In the broader sense, "information theory has been used as a synonym for the term 'cybernetics' and thus includes the theories of servomechanisms, automata, communication, control, and 'other kinds of behavior in organisms and mechanisms' " (ibid.). This latter use was prevalent in the U.K., while, in the U.S., Shannon's theory and its later developments retained the label "information theory," which is still used in the same narrow sense.

The restricted definition of "cybernetics" limits it to the area of *control information*. Wiener's essential insights were that a control state as dependent on the pertinent information flow; and that the scientific laws governing control are universally applicable, and therefore independent of the usual dichotomy between living and nonliving entities. Cybernetics, in this sense, covers *control, homeostasis*, and *feedback information*, and provides an array of coopted mathematical specialties for use in researching these problems. In the broader sense, the term "cybernetics" has been used to cover any study of complex systems that is aided by a computer — a usage so broad as to cover even mathematical economics. This broader usage was most prevalent in the U.S.S.R, where cybernetics, as "the science of controls" enjoyed great popularity in the post-Stalinist period.

Several philosophers-of-science have placed cybernetics within the orbit of general system theory.

> Cybernetics is a method of examining interactive parts of any system of communication and control, with particular emphasis on feedback and homeostasis. It is part and parcel of general system theory, which is concerned with these and also other relations among parts of a whole and between the whole and its environment. General system theory, which thus comprises cybernetics, is a method of organizing one's thinking in terms of interrelated elements in closed or open sets. (Machlup and Mansfield, 1983, p. 17).

This broad field of *general system theory* has attracted philosophers, economists, and behavioral scientists, among others, while the narrow field of *mathematical system theory* remains the preserve of the mathematicians. The latter provide mathematical models and simulations of complex systems in all fields of academic endeavor; but there is a strong belief among scientists that the key problems in system theory are those for which no easy mathematical solutions will be found.

As already mentioned, these three formal sciences, information theory, cybernetics, and general system theory, provide a theoretical base for all of the information (and some other) sciences. However, great care must be taken in applying theories across disciplinary boundaries; Elias's warning about the application of information theory might well apply to the other two fields as well:

... the fact that entropy has been proved in a meaningful sense to be the unique correct information measure for the purpose of communications does not prove that it is either the unique or a correct measure to use in some other field in which no issue of encoding or other changes in representation arises. The measure may, indeed, be useful or even unique for another application, but that fact *must be demonstrated in the target field*. (Elias, 1983, p. 500; emphasis added)

NOTE

1. The burgeoning information sciences call for new links among scholars already at work and for a novel approach to the education of new generations of researchers. Margaret Boden has stated the case as it applies in cognitive science; I believe her words apply equally to the wider group of information sciences:

> Mere intellectual communication across the boundaries of these several disciplines is not enough. We also need mutually cooperative research by people who (albeit specializing in one area) have a familiarity with other fields and a commitment to their intellectual integration. This . . . will require modifying current educational practices, so that students are no longer socially separated — and even intellectually opposed — by traditional academic labels. (Boden, 1983, p. 235)

BIBLIOGRAPHY

ACM Curriculum Committee on Computer Science, "Curriculum '68: Recommendations for Academic Programs in Computer Science," in *Communications of the ACM*, vol. 11 (Mar. 1968), pp. 151-197.

Bobrow, Daniel G., ed., Special Issue on Non-Monotonic Logic, *Artificial Intelligence*, vol. 13 (Apr. 1980), pp. 1-172.

Boden, Margaret A., "Methodological Links Between Artificial Intelligence and Other Disciplines," in Machlup, Fritz and Mansfield, Una, eds., *The Study of Information: Interdisciplinary Messages* (New York: Wiley, 1983), pp. 229-236.

Burks, Arthur W., ed., *Essays on Cellular Automata* (Urbana: University of Illinois Press, 1970).

Chomsky, Noam, "Formal Properties of Grammar," in Luce, Robert Duncan; Bush, Robert R.; and Galanter, Eugene, eds., *Handbook of Mathematical Psychology*, vol. 2 (New York: Wiley, 1963), pp. 323-418.

Collins, Allan, "Why Cognitive Science?" in *Cognitive Science*, vol. 1 (Jan. 1977), pp. 1-2.

Craik, Kenneth J. W., *The Nature of Explanation* (Cambridge: Cambridge University Press, 1943).

Dijkstra, Edsger W., "Notes on Structured Programming," in Dahl, Ole-Johan; Dijkstra, Edsger W.; and Hoare, C. A. R., *Structured Programming* (London and New York: Academic Press, 1972).

Dreyfus, Hubert L., *What Computers Can't Do: A Critique of Artificial Reason* (New York: Harper and Row, 1972; rev. paperback ed., 1979).

Elias, Peter, "Coding and Information Theory," a paper written in 1959, reprinted in Evans, C. R. and Robertson, A. D. J., eds., *Cybernetics* (Baltimore: University Park Press, 1968), pp. 253-266.

Elias, Peter, "Cybernetics: Past and Present, East and West," in Machlup, Fritz and Mansfield, Una, eds., *The Study of Information: Interdisciplinary Messages* (New York: Wiley, 1983), pp. 441-446.

King, Donald W.; Krauser, Cheri; and Sague, Virginia M., "Profile of ASIS Membership," in *Bulletin of the American Society for Information Science*, vol. 6 (Aug. 1980), pp. 9-17.

Knuth, Donald E., *The Art of Computer Programming, Vol. 1: Fundamental Algorithms* (Reading, Mass.: Addison-Wesley, 1968).

Laferriere, Daniel, "Making Room for Semiotics," in *Academe*, vol. 65 (Nov. 1979), pp. 434-440.

Machlup, Fritz, "Semantic Quirks in Studies of Information," in Machlup, Fritz and Mansfield, Una, eds., *The Study of Information: Interdisciplinary Messages* (New York: Wiley, 1983), pp. 641-672.

Machlup, Fritz, *Knowledge: Its Creation, Distribution and Economic Significance, Volume III: The Economics of Information and Human Capital* (Princeton, N.J.: Princeton University Press, 1984).

Machlup, Fritz and Mansfield, Una, "Cultural Diversity in Studies of Information," in Machlup, Fritz and Mansfield, Una, eds., *The Study of Information: Interdisciplinary Messages* (New York: Wiley, 1983), pp. 3-56.

McCulloch, Warren S. and Pitts, Walter H., "A Logical Calculus of the Ideas Immanent in Nervous Activity," in *Bulletin of Mathematical Biophysics*, vol. 5 (1943), pp. 115-133.

Minsky, Marvin L., "Computer Science and the Representation of Knowledge," in Dertouzos, Michael L. and Moses, Joel, eds., *The Computer Age: A Twenty-Year View* (Cambridge, MA: MIT Press, 1979), pp. 392-421.

Nalimov, Vasilii V., "The Penetration of the Humanities into Other Fields of Knowledge," in Colodny, Robert O., ed., *Faces of Science* (Philadelphia: ISI press, 1981).

Newell, Allen, "Artificial Intelligence and the Concept of Mind," in Schank, Roger C. and Colby, Kenneth M., eds., *Computer Models of Thought and Language* (San Francisco: W. H. Freeman, 1978), pp. 1-60.

Newell, Allen; Perlis, Alan J.; and Simon, Herbert A., "Computer Science" letter to the editor, *Science,* vol. 157 (22 Sept. 1967), pp. 1373-1374.

Newell, Allen and Simon, Herbert A., "Computer Science as Empirical Inquiry: Symbols and Search," in *Communications of the ACM*, vol. 19 (Mar. 1978), pp. 113-126.

Pylyshyn, Zenon W., ed., *Perspectives on the Computer Revolution* (Englewood Cliffs, NJ: Prentice-Hall, 1970).

Pylyshyn, Zenon W., "Information Science: Its Roots and Relations as Viewed from the Perspective of Cognitive Science," in Machlup, Fritz and Mansfield, Una, eds., *The Study of Information: Interdisciplinary Messages* (New York: Wiley, 1983), pp. 63-82.

Pylyshyn, Zenon W., "Representation, Computation, and Cognition," in Machlup, Fritz and Mansfield, Una, eds., *The Study of Information: Interdisciplinary Messages* (New York: Wiley, 1983), pp. 115-120.

Rosenblueth, Arturo; Wiener, Norbert; and Bigelow, Julian, "Behavior, Purpose and Teleology," in *Philosophy of Science*, vol. 10 (Jan. 1943), pp. 18-24.

Searle, John R., "Minds, Brains, and Programs" (with peer commentaries), in *The Behavioral and Brain Sciences,* vol. 3 (Sept. 1980), pp. 417-467.

Shannon, Claude E., "A Mathematical Theory of Communication," in *Bell System Technical Journal*, vol. 27 (July and Oct. 1948), pp. 379-423; 623-656.

Shera, Jesse H., "Librarianship and Information Science," in Machlup, Fritz and Mansfield, Una, eds., *The Study of Information: Interdisciplinary Messages* (New York: Wiley, 1983), pp. 379-388.

Sloan Foundation, Advisers of the Alfred P., "Cognitive Science '78." Report of the State of the Art Committee (New York: Alfred P. Sloan Foundation, 1978).

Turing, Alan M., "On Computable Numbers, with an Application to the Entscheidsungs problem," in *Proceedings of the London Mathematical Society*, vol. 42, no. 2 (1936), pp. 230-265.

Wegner, Peter, "Three Computer Cultures: Computer Technology, Computer Mathematics, and Computer Science," in Alt, Franz L. and Rubinoff, Morris, eds., and Freiberger, Walter, guest ed., *Advances in Computers* (New York: Academic Press, 1970), vol. 10, pp. 8-78.

Wiener, Norbert, *Cybernetics, or Control and Communication in the Animal and the Machine* (Cambridge, MA: MIT Press, 1948; 2nd ed., MIT Press and Wiley, 1961).

Wilson, Patrick, "Bibliographical R & D," in Machlup, Fritz and Mansfield, Una, eds., *The Study of Information: Interdisciplinary Messages* (New York, Wiley, 1983), pp. 889-898.

Winograd, Terry, *Understanding Natural Language* (New York: Academic Press, 1972).

Unobtrusive Testing and the Role of Library Management

Charles R. McClure
Peter Hernon

Unobtrusive testing views reference services from a user's perspective and assesses the accuracy with which library staff answer factual and bibliographic questions. Such testing should not be an end unto itself but a means toward improving the *quality* of library services. Libraries should ascertain the quality of services that they currently provide and develop managerial strategies to act upon the results of that assessment. In short, the information that results from the unobtrusive testing must be incorporated into library decision making and planning processes.

Librarians are frequently "shocked" when they read a study based on unobtrusive testing that documents a low accuracy rate for those library personnel tested. After overcoming their initial shock, they typically display skepticism about the studies and rationalize the score, e.g., testing occurred on a non-typical day at the library, the researchers used invalid research methodologies, or other information providers would have performed less successfully on a similar set of questions. They also assume that their library would have tested significantly better than those typically reported in the literature.

Most libraries have not studied the accuracy rate of their public service staff. The body of unobtrusive research studies conducted in academic and public libraries challenge librarians' blind faith that their services are fine and of high quality.[1] Various studies con-

Professor McClure is at the School of Information Studies, Syracuse University, Syracuse, NY. Professor Hernon is at the Graduate School of Library and Information Science, Simmons College, 300 the Fenway, Boston, MA 02115.

ducted over a 20 year period have reached similar conclusions, ones that can no longer be ignored:

- staff members answer correctly a low percentage of test questions
- they infrequently engage in referral, either internal or external to the library
- the length of the search process does not increase the likelihood that a correct answer will be received
- the interpersonal communications skills of some library personnel are limited and these people can be abrasive in their dealings with the public
- staff may fail to negotiate questions.

Taking action on such results from unobtrusive testing is the critical link in improving the quality of library reference services. A reassessment of library management's commitment to reference services and the effectiveness with which those services are offered must be made. Such a reassessment must be conducted in a context that links research related to library management and unobtrusive testing directly to specific strategies for improving the quality of library information services.

This article discusses managerial responsibilities regarding the uses of unobtrusive testing and improving the quality of reference services. It also identifies additional types of unobtrusive testing that may be useful in a public services context. In a 1983 book, we specified strategies by which reference staff might improve the quality of their services.[2] In a more recent work,[3] we report the results from two additional uses of unobtrusive testing and discuss the need to develop ongoing post-MLS educational programs. Ultimately, however, the responsibility for ensuring that patrons' information needs are met, in a timely and accurate manner, belongs to library management.

The underlying theme of this article is that sufficient knowledge exists about library managerial strategies, unobtrusive testing of reference services, and evaluation methodologies to develop strategies whereby the quality of reference services can be reviewed and improved on a regular basis. Indeed, such strategies must be implemented if academic and public libraries are to meet effectively and efficiently the information needs of their clientele. Library management must assume responsibility for the provision of quality information services or future unobtrusive tests will continue to document correct answer fill rates, a performance measure for the number of test questions correctly answered, that hover around 55%.[4]

MANAGERIAL RESPONSIBILITIES

Library managers must possess specific skills if they are to offer leadership regarding the provision of high quality reference services. Katz and Fraley review a number of these skills and identify managerial activities that take advantage of these skills.[5] Some of the most important skills are attitudinal and knowledge-based. To encourage high quality reference services, library managers, both at the organizational and reference department levels, must provide leadership in each of the areas discussed subsequently.

Supportive Organizational Climate

Organizational climate is a psychologically-based method of describing how peoples' value systems coexist with those of the organization. This climate reflects the internal environment of an organization; it is experienced by its members, influences their behavior, and can be described in terms of values held by organizational members.[6] Various factors such as management style, interpersonal skills, and physical facilities may combine to produce an organizational climate. Depending on the outcome of the interaction among such factors, the organizational climate may support and encourage increased staff performance and productivity.

Supportive library organizational climates tend to be those that offer:[7]

—*innovation*: the degree to which a library is ready to pursue innovative practices, policies, and services
—*support*: the degree to which a library maintains mutually supporting relationships between different work groups within that library
—*democratic governance*: the extent to which library staff feel that they have the opportunity to participate in library decision making *(not* the degree to which they actually participate — an important distinction)

—*esprit*: the level of morale and shared purpose among library staff.

There appears to be a link between supportive organizational climates and the quality of reference service.[8] Library managers have a responsibility to:

— understand psychologically-based indicators of organizational behavior
— recognize the importance of management styles, organizational climates, and other managerial considerations as factors that affect the quality of staff performance
— develop management strategies to enhance organizational climates and improve the managerial setting in which staff work on a daily basis.

However, many library managers are unaware of their library's organizational climate; they have neither developed *measurable* criteria nor recognized the impact of such a climate on the provision of high quality reference services.

Emphasizing the Importance of Quality

A primary responsibility for library managers is to increase staff awareness of issues related to the *quality*, as opposed to the quantity, of reference services. Many library reference departments stress quantity of services. For example, recording the number or types of reference questions asked or online searches performed suggests that the quantity of activities may be of greater importance than "how well" the activities are performed. Priorities will have to be decided between provision of *quantity* versus *quality* reference service.

Library management must be committed to excellence and instill that commitment into the reference staff. Attributes which Peters and Waterman identify as contributing to organizational excellence include:[9]

—*a bias for action*: getting on with it, trying alternatives and not being paralyzed into doing nothing about a clearly identified problem

 —*staying close to the customer*: organizations must learn from the people they serve and incorporate that knowledge into daily activities
 —*autonomy and entrepreneurship*: encouragement of risk taking, innovation, and trying new ideas
 —*productivity through people*: the single most important resource in any organization is its staff; they must be treated with respect and concern
 —*hands-on knowledge*: managers must have firsthand information and knowledge about what is happening in their organizations; they must also be visible to employees
 —*stick to the knitting*: stress the provision of services and products which the organization knows best and has the appropriate resources to provide
 —*simple form—lean staff*: organization structures must be uncomplicated, clear lines of authority are needed, and the organization should not be "top heavy" with managers
 —*simultaneous loose-tight properties*: allowing both autonomy for the individual on the "front line" within a firm management framework or policies and clearly defined responsibilities displaying a decentralized style.

This distillation of attributes that foster excellence encompasses both *attitudes* and specific skills. If reference staff observe poor attitudes in library managers and a lack of concern related to quality services, they are also receiving a message about the level of quality managers will accept. In short, library managers need to promote the attitude that excellence and high quality services are primary commitments of the organization.

Encouraging Measurement and Evaluation

Measurement is the process by which numbers are assigned to describe or represent some object or phenomenon in a standardized manner.[10] While measurement may lead to evaluation and evaluation usually requires measurement, the two processes are not the same. Evaluation, as used here, includes measurement and adds components of the research process, planning, and implementation strategies to change or improve the organization or a specific activity.

Developing supportive organizational climates and emphasizing the importance of quality reference services is essential, but not sufficient. Ultimately, a library ought to assess the quality of its reference services and correct answer fill rate. Without empirical evidence — evaluation — describing the level of quality provided, it is difficult to develop effective and meaningful managerial strategies to *improve* reference services.

Academic public service librarians apparently do not believe that formal evaluations of the quality of reference services have much utility. Rather, they maintain that:[11]

- intuitive assessment of performance is as accurate as formal means of evaluation
- there are few rewards and benefits for librarians who do engage in formal assessments of the quality of reference services
- resulting data that assessed the quality of reference services are not likely to be reliable or valid
- even when such data are produced they are rarely incorporated into library decision making and planning.

A key implication of these findings is that library managers do not encourage the use of evaluation methodologies, are unfamiliar with the use of correct answer fill rate and other performance measures, and set an example for their staff that does not encourage the use of such techniques.

A citation analysis of the seminal work on unobtrusive testing, Crowley and Childers (1971),[12] concluded that "unobtrusive procedures have not yet become a component of the standard methods for evaluating library and information service performance."[13] Without greater basic knowledge of qualitative research methodologies, including unobtrusive techniques, library reference services cannot be meaningfully evaluated and strategies implemented for their improvement. Worse, reference service will continue as it is, typically unevaluated and providing "half-right" answers.[14]

The larger issue here is that library managers must develop a positive attitude toward the importance of utilizing empirical data in decision making and planning. They must know how to conduct evaluation research and employ research techniques such as unobtrusive testing in order to describe existing levels of library services empirically. Minimally, library managers should be able to:

- identify reference service areas requiring study
- state research problems and questions
- develop appropriate methodologies to answer the research questions
- collect reliable and valid data
- analyze and report the results
- implement strategies to improve the quality of reference services.

If library managers cannot perform these basic procedures, retooling or gaining basic evaluation competencies is in order.

SUGGESTIONS FOR IMPLEMENTING UNOBTRUSIVE EVALUATION

For purposes of the evaluation of library services, Figure 1 identifies four types of unobtrusive studies that realistically might be conducted in a library setting. Generally, unobtrusive studies test or observe either library staff or library clientele as subjects. There are numerous possible subgroups within these two broad categories of subjects. For example, library staff may be described as either professional or paraprofessional; full-time or part-time; public services, technical services, or management; main or branch library staff; and so forth. Similarly, subgroups of library clientele encompass a wide range of demographic, library use, geographic, or other criteria.

Approach I: Testing Library Staff. This approach is perhaps the best known and has been used in a number of unobtrusive tests of reference services. Hernon and McClure discuss one version of this approach.[15] However, there are many variations to this approach, depending on the specific skills that the evaluators wish to assess. For example, they might examine knowledge of specific reference tools, accuracy with which answers are given, or the use of various interpersonal and question negotiation techniques.

Approach II: Testing Clientele. Although some reference librarians may not realize it, clientele are regularly being "tested" as they attempt to resolve their information needs in the library. This approach simply formalizes the procedures by which staff assess user knowledge of libraries and search techniques. Awareness, use, and assessment of particular library services can be determined by "testing" library users with pre-determined questions that are inter-

FIGURE 1

BASIC TYPES OF LIBRARY UNOBTRUSIVE STUDIES*

UNOBTRUSIVE TECHNIQUE

Subjects	TESTING	OBSERVATION
Library STAFF	I	III
Library CLIENTLELE	II	IV

* Unobtrusive studies of subjects other than library staff or library clientele are possible, but are not the focus of this chapter.

woven into a reference negotiation process or other settings. Or, library staff may work with groups outside the library where students, for example, might be asked questions about the library and its services, or assessed on the extent to which they can resolve predetermined problems.

Approach III: Observing Library Staff. Structured observation of the activities of library staff is a relatively easy and straight-forward approach to study unobtrusively the quality of staff performance. Sophisticated methods that require a proxie to sit in the reference, or another service area, and carefully observe and record the activities of library staff can provide valuable evaluation information about the quality of services provided.

Approach IV: Observing Library Clientele. Structured unobtrusive observations of clientele's use of the card catalog, microform readers, or other equipment (or traffic patterns at the reference desk or in the reference department/collection) are common examples of the application of this approach. In one instance reference librarians were wired with a small microphone and the interview between reference staff and the patrons was recorded for later analysis. [16]

Unobtrusive observation, approaches III and IV, offer a useful means of acquiring qualitative evaluation information. Epstein and Tripodi provide an excellent introductory overview for conducting such observationally based evaluations. [17] The purpose of the observation and the activities to be observed must be clearly articulated. Moreover, the data recording forms that define those activities, and techniques to enhance the reliability and validity of the observation, must be developed. Goodell summarizes how such observational forms are constructed in a library context, how to determine the number of observations that are necessary to achieve particular reliability levels, and which methods are effective for reporting the results. [18]

RESEARCH OPPORTUNITIES FOR UNOBTRUSIVE EVALUATION

A broad expanse of opportunities for unobtrusive evaluation/ research is available for assessing the quality of services provided by library staff. Specific aspects that lend themselves to unobtrusive evaluation include the:

- *accuracy of answering in-person reference questions*: although existing unobtrusive evaluation has concentrated on factual and bibliographic questions, evaluators can design the questions to stress:
  a. specific subject areas, e.g., history, science, or literature
  b. subgroups of library staff, e.g., professional versus paraprofessional, full time versus part-time
  c. types of materials, e.g., knowledge of specific information formats, e.g., microforms, maps, periodicals, government publications, or electronic files.
- *accuracy and appropriateness of referrals*: for which types of reference questions are referrals most likely? Should the referral have been made or could the answer have been obtained from sources available in the library or the department? If a

referral was made, was it to the "best" source? How effective are referral sources in answering questions?

— *ability to negotiate a question successfully*: unobtrusive testing comprises a powerful means to assess the ability of library staff to use specific interview techniques related to open-ended questions, the "why" question, listening skills, and other factors.[19]

— *use of non-verbal communication or other interpersonal skills*: the best means to assess the library staff's knowledge and application of interpersonal skills in the provision of services is to observe unobtrusively those skills; such factors have been shown to be important considerations in the overall effectiveness of information services.[20]

— *use of information resources in the provision of services*: do library staff have specific "favorites" that they rely on to answer reference questions at the expense of sources that might better answer the question but of which they are unaware? Library staff members' use of particular types of information sources for specific types of questions has been inadequately considered as a factor in the provision of reference services.

— *duration of the provision of information services*: staff members may have an "internal clock" that determines the amount of time they will spend with a particular client;[21] a better understanding of how such "internal clocks" impact on the answering of correct versus incorrect answers, referrals, and interpersonal skills is needed.

These topics are suggestive of areas where unobtrusive testing is appropriate and can obtain data that are reliable, valid, and objectively-based rather than perceptual.

The identification of these areas accents the importance of having clearly defined service goals, objectives, and policy statements. The effective evaluation of services in each of these areas depends on having a set of criteria that describe "adequate" or "excellent" performance. Gers and Seward, and Schwartz and Eakin provide useful examples of an evaluation form that can be used for establishing such criteria and as a means for assessing the service provided by library staff.[22] Library management is responsible for describing such criteria in terms of "acceptable" or "model" reference services. Managers must clarify expectations for what constitutes excellence, be able to operationalize those expectations into observable and definable behaviors, and then base unobtrusive evaluations on those criteria.

Although unobtrusive evaluations for library and information services assess staff skills, competencies, and attitudes, the method also examines library clientele as well. For example, observation of the sources that clientele use and patron search patterns also lend themselves to unobtrusive evaluation. Knowledge from such evaluation provides important management information for structuring information services intended primarily to *resolve the information needs of library clientele*.

These unobtrusive methods can be combined with transaction log analysis, which is an assessment of the procedures that one follows when searching for a record in an online catalog, a bibliographic database, or similar interactive computer system. The computer system is programmed to maintain a record of the subject's transactions while he/she uses the computer system. A log of those activities can then be reviewed, based on a set of specific criteria.

Borgman has shown that use of this unobtrusive technique has been most successful in assessing patron's knowledge of online catalogs.[23] Tolle offers a detailed description of the methodology as a means of studying patron's use of the OCLC database.[24] The approach has great potential for assessing a broad range of library services and the skills of library staff and users regarding specific services.

Reference department managers could review the search skills of staff on online bibliographic databases, bibliographic utilities such as OCLC and RLIN, or other interactive computer systems with which they come into contact. An analysis of completed logs constitutes an excellent means for obtaining evaluation information on what *actually* occurs rather than a *perception* of activities conducted during the online session. Further, the assessment of such logs provides a direct link to developing intervention strategies to remedy identifiable problems. Clearly, however, more evaluation needs to employ multiple data collection techniques. Unobtrusive testing, when combined with other techniques, provides management with a more complete assessment of the quality of library services and programs.

REPORTING UNOBTRUSIVE RESULTS TO STAFF

The reporting of unobtrusive tests/observations to the same staff members tested may create difficulties and may be a primary reason why unobtrusive testing of library services is performed infrequently. Where staff believe that they perform at a high level of quality, and if they are confronted with evaluation results suggesting less than high quality performance, they may respond defensively. Library managers may lack both the interpersonal and managerial skills to utilize unobtrusive test results in a positive manner as a catalyst to *improve* the quality of various library services.

Argyris describes a range of individual-organizational defensive routines. He also offers specific strategies by which managers and evaluators can alter those routines and develop strategies that increase overall acceptance of change and while, at the same time, promoting organizational effectiveness.[25]

Equally important, evaluators who present study findings must be conscious of interpersonal and professional issues related to unobtrusive evaluation of library services. They also need special skills in group processes and team building. The focus of the discussions among evaluators, managers, and staff should be on (1) what levels of performance can be reasonably provided for particular services, (2) what steps must be taken to reach acceptable performance levels, and (3) how will library staff know when those levels of performance have been reached.

At issue here is that many library staff have never considered what constitutes an acceptable level of performance for particular services. Nor have library managers been committed to developing and using *measures* by which the performance of a service can, in fact, be described. Given different missions, goals, and priorities of libraries, a correct answer fill rate of 40% may be acceptable *to that library* if the staff are consciously concentrating their resources on other service areas. It is this larger context of using unobtrusive evaluation for planning and setting service priorities that must be better understood.

THE CONTEXT OF UNOBTRUSIVE EVALUATION

Increased attention to formal programs of reference service evaluation is essential in libraries today. As part of that evaluation, greater attention must be given to the use of nontraditional evaluation designs and data collection methodologies. Simply stated, there is little use of formal evaluation techniques, and excessive reliance on survey methods, perceptual data, and data that do not directly provide a *qualitative* assessment of library services. Determining that "X" number of patrons completed a reference transaction is *not* knowing the *quality* of the service that they received. Unobtrusive evaluation techniques that address qualitative performance criteria, such as accuracy of answering reference questions, are powerful means to assess library services.

Accuracy, or other qualitative-based criteria are best assessed in evaluation research conducted within the organization, and, if possible, by organizational members. Generally, case study designs which combine different data collection techniques are excellent beginning points for libraries embarking on this process. Case studies link evaluation directly to making recommendations and developing intervention strategies effective for the particular library. Yin has prepared a practical overview of case study designs and how to implement them in an evaluation study.[26] McClure, Hernon, and Purcell have combined a case study design with a number of data collection techniques, including unobtrusive testing.[27] Hernon and McClure have combined unobtrusive testing with an experimental design. The staff of one library were pretested unobtrusively, administered two interventions (a workshop and a guide accompanied with a slide presentation), and posttested unobtrusively.[28]

Evaluators who use case study designs which include unobtrusive methods and who assess the quality of information services within a particular library should not be that concerned with the external validity of their findings beyond that particular library. External validity, or the degree to which the evaluation results can be generalized, is not an objective for practitioner-based library evaluation. The issue, rather, is to maintain a high degree of reliability and internal validity, that is, the study measures what it is supposed to measure within the organization and findings are correct for *that* particular library at that particular time.[29]

To first improve the quality of any library service, there must be an awareness that evaluation is essential, a willingness to engage in an evaluation process, and adequate competencies and skills on the part of the evaluators. Perceptions and assumptions about what is thought to be occurring in the provision of library services should be validated by programs of ongoing evaluation research. Librarians must accept this challenge of testing their perceptions and assumptions and determine if, in fact, their intuitive assessments match those resulting from formal evaluations.

Apparently, the techniques of evaluation research and unobtrusive methods have been perceived by library practitioners as inappropriate, unnecessary, or perhaps too difficult to conduct. And, of course, there are literally thousands of reasons to justify and rationalize such hesitancy to engage in ongoing evaluation of library services. But the evidence is clear that the *quality* of library services, especially in the area of reference services, requires immediate attention. A formal program of ongoing evaluation is essential if library reference services are to be improved.

Library managers must accept responsibility for the development and implementation of an evaluation program. No longer should they merely read the published results of unobtrusive evaluations and assume that their library performs at a higher rate of accuracy. Clearly, the body of published unobtrusive investigations suggest that library reference service is facing a crisis. Staff experience problems in providing effective and efficient service for questions often regarded as easier than the average. The key issue is whether library managers will assess their local situation and take corrective actions, where necessary, or whether staff will continue to provide "half-right" reference service.[30]

NOTES

1. For a list of the unobtrusive studies conducted in library and information science, see Peter Hernon and Charles R. McClure, *Unobtrusive Testing and Library Reference Services* (Norwood, NJ: ABLEX Pub. Corp., 1986).

2. See Charles R. McClure and Peter Hernon, *Improving the Quality of Reference Service for Government Publications* (Chicago, IL: American Library Association, 1983), pp. 111-160.

3. See Hernon and McClure, *Unobtrusive Testing and Library Reference Services*.

4. Performance measures focus organizational attention on specific areas of services and activities, and seek to determine their overall effectiveness and efficiency. Correct answer fill rate compares the number of correct answers to the total asked.

5. Bill Katz and Ruth A. Fraley, eds. *Reference Services Administration and Management* (New York: Haworth Press, 1982).

6. R. Tagiuri and G. H. Litwin. *Organizational Climate: Explorations of a Concept* (Boston: Division of Research, Graduate School of Business Administration, Harvard University, 1968).

7. Charles R. McClure and Alan R. Samuels. "Factors Affecting the Use of Information for Academic Library Decision Making," *College & Research Libraries*, 46 (November 1985): 483-498.

8. Ibid.; Alan R. Samuels and Charles R. McClure. "Utilization of Information for Decision Making Under Varying Organizational Climate Conditions in Public Libraries," *Journal of Library Administration*, 4 (1983): 1-20.

9. Thomas J. Peters and Robert H. Waterman Jr. *In Search of Excellence* (New York: Warner Books, 1982), pp. 13-16.

10. Abraham Kaplan. *The Conduct of Inquiry* (Scranton, PA: Chandler Publishing, 1964).

11. Charles R. McClure. "Costing and Performance Measures for Academic Library Public Services: A View from the Trenches," *College & Research Libraries*, in press.

12. Terence Crowley and Thomas Childers. *Information Service in Public Libraries: Two Studies* (Metuchen, NJ: Scarecrow Press, 1971).

13. Alvin M. Schrader. "Performance Standards for Accuracy in Reference and Information Services: The Impact of Unobtrusive Measurement Methodology," in Bill Katz and Ruth A. Fraley, *Evaluation of Reference Services* (New York: Haworth Press, 1984), pp. 197-214.

14. Terence Crowley. "Half-Right Reference: Is it True?" *RQ*, 25 (Fall, 1985): 59-68.

15. See Hernon and McClure, *Unobtrusive Testing and Library Reference Services*.

16. Mary Jo Lynch. "Reference Interviews in Public Libraries," *Library Quarterly*, 48 (April 1978): 119-141.

17. Irwin Epstein and Tony Tripodi. *Research Techniques for Program Planning, Monitoring, and Evaluation* (New York: Columbia University Press, 1977).

18. John S. Goodell. *Libraries and Work Sampling* (Littleton, CO: Libraries Unlimited, 1975).

19. Thomas A. Childers. *The Effectiveness of Information Service in Public Libraries: Suffolk Co. Final Report* (Philadelphia: School of Library and Information Science, Drexel University, 1978); William A. Katz. *Introduction to Reference Work*. Vol. II: *Reference Services and Reference Process*. 4th edition (New York: McGraw-Hill, 1982).

20. Helen M. Gothberg. User Satisfaction and Librarian's Immediate and Non-Immediate Verbal-Non Verbal Communications. Ph.D. Dissertation. Denver: University of Denver, 1974.

21. McClure and Hernon, *Improving the Quality of Reference Service for Government Publications*; Hernon and McClure, *Unobtrusive Testing and Library Reference Service*.

22. Ralph Gers and Lillie J. Seward. "Improving Reference Performance, Results of a Statewide Study," *Library Journal*, 110 (November 1, 1985): 32-35; and Diane G. Schwartz and Dottie Eakin. "Reference Service Standards, Performance Criteria, and Evaluation," *Journal of Academic Librarianship*, 12 (March 1986): 4-8.

23. Christine L. Borgman. *End User Behavior on the Ohio State University Libraries' Online Catalog: A Computer Monitoring Study* [Report Number OCLC/OPR/RR-83-7] (Dublin, OH: OCLC Online Computer Library Center, Inc., 1983).

24. John E. Tolle. *Current Utilization of Online Catalogs: Transaction Log Analysis* [Report Number OCLC/OPR?RR-83/2] (Dublin, OH: OCLC Online Computer Library Center, Inc., 1983).

25. Chris Argyris. *Strategy, Change and Defensive Routines* (Boston, MA: Pitman Publishing, Inc., 1985).

26. Robert K. Yin. *Case Study Research: Design and Methods* (Beverly Hills, CA: Sage Publications, 1984).

27. See Charles R. McClure, Peter Hernon, and Gary R. Purcell. *Linking the U.S. National Technical Information Service with Academic and Public Libraries* (Norwood, NJ: ABLEX Pub. Corp., 1986).

28. Hernon and McClure. *Unobtrusive Testing and Library Reference Service*, Chapter 4.

29. David R. Krathwohl. *Social and Behavioral Science Research* (San Francisco, CA: Jossey Bass, 1985).

30. Crowley, "Half-Right Reference: Is It True?"

The Information Specialist and the Reference Librarian: Is the Complete Librarian Obsolete?

John E. Leide

The reference librarian has long been a cornerstone of North American librarianship. Service is an essential feature of the North American concept of library science, and the reference librarian, seen as the mediator between the user of libraries and the information stores which they contain, is an expert, professionally trained in the provision of information services. This is not, however, the only model of information transfer involving libraries.

Another model is based on the concept of the information specialist. This view predicates that, because information needs are becoming so specialized, a subject expert is needed to provide an interface between the user and the information resources. In other words, in order to facilitate the question and answer negotiation or to anticipate information needs, knowledge of the subject domain is more important than knowledge of the system of organization. This model is often seen in developing countries.

The question whether the North American model is obsolete is of particular importance to the future of both North American librarianship and to that of the developing countries. It is the intent of this paper to examine the bases of these two models of information access facilitation in order to understand the underlying philosophical differences.

The author is on the faculty of the Graduate School of Library and Information Studies, McGill University, 3459 McTavish St., Montreal, Quebec H3A 1Y1.

87

THE REFERENCE LIBRARIAN

The concept of the reference librarian is based on a belief that a complete librarian is better prepared to provide the necessary mediating role between the users and information.

The historical precedents of the modern librarian can be found in the scholar librarian (the original information specialist?). A librarian was first a scholar and in addition, perhaps only incidentally, the custodian of books. The early perception of libraries as treasure houses and later warehouses of knowledge supports the view of the library as being fundamentally an organized collection of materials. This image is still prevalent in many European countries as well as those which were exposed to European librarianship under colonial rule.

Two developments led to a change of perception in North American librarianship. First, the increasing amount and availability of printed information (the publication explosion) made it increasingly difficult to maintain the idea that a collection, however well organized, could be a self-service resource; someone was needed to provide an interface between the user's needs and the information store. Second, the development of librarianship as a discipline and the emergence of librarians as a professional group provided an identity for the mediator and prepared the way for the development of formal training programs for the education of practitioners according to predefined standards. Education for librarians developed from on-the-job apprenticeships, through undergraduate programs and the fifth year bachelor's degree, to the master's degree from an accredited library program. It is believed that professional education for information mediators must be firmly based on a broad liberal undergraduate education.

One of the consequences of this model is a common core of basic competencies which underlie any distinctions between librarians serving in the public and technical services. The common knowledges of librarianship are deemed more important than specialized subject expertise which can be learned outside of the basic training, on-the-job if need be.

The information specialist paradigm is founded on the basic premise that access to information can best be facilitated by persons trained in subject disciplines similar to those of the users. This view predicates the absence or unimportance of a common core of librarianship and concludes that increased scholarity in a subject discipline will provide any necessary information mediating knowledges which cannot be learned on the job.

INFORMATION ACCESS IN DEVELOPING COUNTRIES

Information service in developing countries often follows the precepts of the information specialist model. This may be the result of at least three factors: (1) information resources are frequently not plentiful; so that, personal rather than systematic access may suffice, (2) information service is not universally available, but rather, reserved for specialists with a need to know, and (3) programs of formal education in librarianship are few and the barriers of distance and money make access to programs in more developed countries inaccessible. As a consequence, librarians in developing countries are frequently trained in apprenticeship programs similar to those prevalent in the early days of librarianship in North America.

Technological developments, however, do not wait; the types of specialized information desperately needed in developing countries may be too complex for librarians with only a boot-strap education to mediate. The need for expertise to negotiate questions and answers is acute. If professionally trained librarians are not available to perform the necessary information mediation, what other personnel resources can be found?

The gate-keeper of the invisible college may seem to be an expedient anodyne. Since groups of experts working in any field tend to form natural information networks, and these networks informally identify certain individuals as information mediators (gate-keepers for the information transfer), it is natural for this function to be formally recognized. The information specialist is born. It remains to be seen whether the information specialist will self-consciously develop a sense of a new role as an interdisciplinary facilitator balancing the needs of a knowledge of the subject with a knowledge of the system.

THE INFORMATION SPECIALIST IN NORTH AMERICA

The need for subject expertise which may be seen to characterize the information specialist has entered into North American librarianship in two different areas: education and research.

The teacher/librarian is often an information specialist, but his expertise is that of another profession. Before a school librarian can be certified in most states he must also be a certified teacher. In some cases, a teacher may be assigned responsibility for the library—a clear application of the information specialist model. In others, the librarian is a teacher with a library science minor as part of his teaching credential. In most accredited library education programs leading to a master's degree for school librarians, a teaching certification is required as a pre- or co-requisite.

In the research area, special libraries have long been a home for the information specialist. Perhaps because of the technical nature of much of the information, it is natural to appoint one member of the staff to take charge of the information mediating role. In other cases, the receipt of documentation preceeds (and exceeds) its organization. Often a secretary or clerk is given responsibility for managing the materials.

In academic libraries two forces combine to make subject expertise part of the job requirements. Academic libraries as hybrid education/research libraries often have specialized collections as well as users who are experts in their fields; therefore, it seems reasonable to try to find librarians who are also subject experts to facilitate the question and answer negotiation with the users. The second factor impelling subject specialization is the emergence of faculty status for librarians. If librarians are to be faculty, they will be expected to manifest the same levels of scholarity required for their teaching colleagues; if a PhD is not required, at least additional graduate study as evidenced by the subject master's degree is often an entry level requirement. Requiring additional subject preparation has the added benefit of reducing the number of applicants who will need to be screened for a librarian's position when there is a tight job market and there are many more applicants than jobs.

LIBRARIAN TECHNICIANS

Increasing job specialization has created several dilemmas in the library milieu. Within the ranks of the librarians it has caused a degree of compartmentalization; so that, many librarians are perceived to be "reference" librarians or "technical service" librarians. In addition to distinctions of function, there are also distinctions by work place, "school" librarians, "academic" librarians, "public" librarians, and now "free lance" librarians. This differentiation is further compounded by the structure of the organizations themselves; librarians are not secretaries are not clerks are not technicians. North American librarianship has not yet fully adapted to the different roles and functions of professional and non-professional librarians. While it is clear that a technician or a library assistant is not a reference librarian, this distinction is not apparent to many users.

If to work in a library is to be a librarian, all library staff are librarians, and to work outside a library, e.g., in a community information centre or as an information broker, is not to be a librarian regardless of one's professional preparation. The visibility and glamor of the extra-library jobs further distances the information specialist from the librarian and bolsters the perception of the librarian as a technician, a view often held in developing countries as well as developing markets for library service in business and industry in North America.

The information specialist model often involves a division of labor between an information specialist and the librarian. In this view, the librarian is responsible for the activities of acquiring and organizing documents and the information they contain. The information specialist is charged with providing the access and dissemination roles between the collections and the users who have information needs. The coordination of storage and retrieval functions implicit in the reference librarian model is absent. The selection function or collection development may be variously shared between the librarian and the information specialist, but the librarian is viewed primarily as support staff, the curator of the collection. The increasingly technological nature of modern society compounds the problem further.

TECHNOLOGY IN INFORMATION TRANSFER

New technologies, especially the computer, have added a new variable to information mediating. Online data bases are providing access to bibliographic data inside libraries and out. These data bases can be accessed by the user from a terminal at his desk. End-user searching is still being debated, but the increasing number of non-bibliographic data bases coupled with word processing technologies with the ability to down-load data into a personal document file clearly signal changes in patterns of information processing. Current trends in the development of artificial intelligence and expert systems have lead to the speculation whether the computer can in fact replace the human information mediator. If technology can provide the end-user with the knowledges which were formerly provided by the professional librarian, the complete librarian is obsolete. The information specialist (who may be the user) armed with subject knowledge and expert systems embodying the keys to the organization of information will be able to gain direct and efficient access. Perhaps the reference librarian is at best a stop-gap measure to mediate information transfer until technology advances to support the original concept of direct access. Developing countries may be able to skip the reference librarian state and begin with online access; however, limited resources make this seem unlikely. In any case, professional expertise will still be needed to design and develop the systems.

THE SPECIALIST/LIBRARIAN
LIBRARIAN/SPECIALIST

In the best of all possible worlds, both knowledge of the subject and knowledge of the information system are desirable. Employers may require a second master's degree or undergraduate preparation in a particular field of study. Subject specialists soon find that knowledge of a specific subject area is not enough to be able to provide efficient information access. It would seem that the reference librarian needs subject knowledge and the information specialist needs to know how information is organized. Nevertheless, there still remains the "chicken or egg" question, which has not been adequately addressed in library literature: Is it preferable to have a person with subject expertise build on it with professional library training, or whether subject specialization should be acquired after the professional degree. The premise of the accredited library schools is that a broad base of liberal education is necessary for professional education, but in-depth subject knowledge is complementary and not necessarily prerequisite. One would hope that a library degree would facilitate the acquisition of additional expertise. In fact many librarians have become quite expert through continuing education on the job. Furthermore, there would seem to be a difference between the study of a subject per se and the study of a subject in the context of information transfer in much the same way as the study of the history of a science is not the same as the study of the science. It would be interesting to see whether further research would reveal significant differences between the librarian/specialist and the specialist/librarian.

CONCLUSION

The philosophical differences between the reference librarian model and the information specialist model are perhaps only a matter of degree. Nevertheless there seems to be an important difference in orientation. The generalist approach of the librarian is designed to meet the functional problems of the user/information interface. The approach of the information specialist views the problems from the other end since it starts with the subject. These two diametrically opposing positions in theory may be closer than one may have thought in practice. Both the reference librarian and the information specialist are trying to provide the best information access possible with the resources available. The important focus for both must be the user. Information needs of users continue. Reference librarians and information specialists continue to try to meet them.

REFERENCES

Abramov, K. I. "Library education in the U.S.S.R." *Indian Librarian* 25, no. 4 (1971) 199-200.

Alam, A. K. M. Shamsual. "Libraries and library problems of Bangladesh." *UNESCO Bulletin for Libraries* 27 (Summer 1973) 262-264.

Borchardt, D. H. & J. I. Haracek. *Librarianship in Australia, New Zealand, and Oceania*. Potts Point: Pergamon, 1975.

Byron, J. E. W. "Comprehensive and efficient? 3. Reference service." *New Library World* 86 (April 1985) 70-71.

Chandler, George. "Near, Middle and Far Eastern libraries." *International Library Review* 3 (1971) 187-227.

Cornelius, David. "Possible impact of past, present and future developments of library services in Ghana" in *International librarianship*, G. Chandler, ed. London: Library Association, 1972.

Cronin, B. "Information management." *Leads* 25 (Winter 1983) 1-2.

Day, A. E. "Hands across the sea." *New Library World* 84 (November 1983) 183-184.

Fang, Josephine Riss. *China's libraries on the new long march*. New York: K.G. Saur, 1980.

Harsaghy, Fred J., Jr. "Design for future service in a developing country." *Special Libraries* 63 (September 1972) 400-403.

International handbook of contemporary developments in librarianship. ed. by M. M. Jackson. Westport, CT: Greenwood Press, 1981.

Jackson, Miles M. "Library and information services in the Pacific Islands." *International Library Review* 13 (January 1981) 25-47.

McCarthy, C. "Paraprofessionals, student assistants, and the reference clan: An application of contemporary management theory." in *Academic libraries: Myths and realities*. Chicago: ACRL, 1984.

National Information Systems. *Library and information science manpower development in the Asian region*. Bangalore, India: Document Research and Training Centre, 1977.

Nwagha, G. K. N. "Deployment of professional librarians; a barrier to the availability of publications in a developing country." *College & Research Libraries* 44 (March 1983) 168-172.

Oguara, E. T. A. "Special libraries in Nigeria: situation and outlook in development." *Nigerian Libraries* 11 (1975) 185-212.

Patel, J. P. "International problems in the South Asian bibliographical information services." *International Library Review* 15 (January 1983) 95-103.

Scott, L. A. "School library resource centers: a comparison of the US, UK, and France in 1980." *International Library Review* 14 (October 1982) 447-454.

Sever, S. "Special libraries in Israel." *Special Libraries* 67, no. 5/6 (May-June 1976) 265-270.

Simsova, S. *Primer of comparative librarianship*. New York: Bingley, 1982.

Toward Expert Inquiry Systems

Glynn Harmon

The concept of an expert inquiry system applies in this paper to a computer system that could perform at a level which approximates that of a human expert researcher in one or a few restricted subject areas. Here, the human expert would ideally be a sophisticated and highly educated scholar, such as a Nobel Laureate. To develop such a system, the research strategies and rules (heuristics) and procedures (algorithms) of one or more scholars would be acquired and organized into a knowledge system or rule base through the use of knowledge engineering languages and other expert system tools. Once developed, such a system could serve as a consultant to guide the future research of scholars in the same or similar subject domains.

The design and use of expert inquiry systems has been implied as an ideal by information scientists and philosophers for many years. Churchman proposed in 1972 that information system design and use be structured around the parameters of cognitive or intellectual inquiry.[1] Mitroff and others have used dialectic inquiry as a basis for system design.[2] Through case studies, this writer has isolated patterns of scientific discovery and proposed that information retrieval systems and their use be based on patterns of scientific discovery, rather than so heavily on heterogeneous document representations.[3] Harter cogently argues that the "blind faith" and rigidly stereotyped "fast batch," boolean searching modes which characterize contemporary online retrieval should be replaced by exemplars of scientific inquiry and problem-solving.[4] The philosophy of inquiry and research are summarized by such works as Kaplan's *The Conduct of Inquiry*.[5] Critical reviews of information user and use studies argue for the development of information systems structured to user problem-solving logics.[6] Collectively, many of the above ideas were forerunners of what we today refer to as expert or knowledge-

---

Glynn Harmon is a Professor in the Graduate School of Library and Information Science, The University of Texas at Austin, Austin, TX, 78712.

based systems. Such systems provide much promise for actualizing the ideal of information searching and retrieval based on patterns of intelligent inquiry. The purpose of this paper is to consider a few of the problems involved in the development of expert inquiry systems, and to discuss their potential application in information retrieval. The following sections, then, discuss the nature of information needs via a cognitive model, identify four basic species of questions, and discuss the development of expert system rules to guide inquiry and search strategies.

AN INQUIRY AND INFORMATION NEED MODEL

Investigations in artificial intelligence and human information processing can serve to clarify the nature of inquiry and user information needs. Reitman, a cognitive psychologist, has stated that "from an informational viewpoint we may regard the whole problem of cognitive structure as a matter of sets of cognitive elements. . . ."[7] These cognitive elements and sets are alternatively referred to in the literature of psychology and neurology as schemata, association elements, neural engrams, or even (in their larger form) as gestalts, concepts, or images. Recent investigations in artificial intelligence refer to such cognitive elements as chunks, heuristics, production systems, or rules. A Nobel Laureate in Chemistry is said to possess, for example, from 50,000 to 100,000 chunks, heuristics, or production rules about his or her specialty.[8] Obviously, many cognate terms have been used to talk about approximately the same basic cognitive entity or its aggregates.

Sets of cognitive chunks or elements apparently serve to filter and organize new or additional inputs of information for an individual. These sets make it possible to focus on and use other elements from the massive store available in one's own memory or in external, natural or artificial memories. From this author's earlier model of information need and use, inquiry may be viewed as a series of efforts to acquire a set of needed information elements and to find appropriate set-defining and set-ordering criteria. That is, inquiry may be viewed as a task analogous to constructing a mental jigsaw puzzle. The relevant pieces (elements) need to be acquired and ordered in such a way as to build a satisfactory picture. Once a perimeter is formed, it becomes easier to fill the middle parts, because the perimeter provides picture-forming clues. Likewise, gaps in the jigsaw puzzle can be filled by extrapolating clues from the filled-in, adjacent places. Thus, an inquirer needs two basic types of information: elements or building blocks to form a concept, and organizers (theories, principles, heuristics, rules) to structure and give form to the elements. In more formal terms, the culmination state of successful inquiry can be modeled as a complete, ordered set of information elements which the user forms cognitively within his or her own domain inquiry: [a,b,c,d,e,f,g]. The information elements may themselves be sets or subsets of prior inquiries. Inquiry may be depicted as set formation and transformation, and four fundamental stages are illustrated below.[9]

Stage I: Insufficient and Unordered Information

At the onset of inquiry, a null or empty set, [], often exists. This denotes a state of ignorance. The domain of inquiry and the problem might be undefined or vaguely defined. Few, if any, informational elements are available, or if available, have not been specifically designated as relevant to the domain of inquiry. Hence, the problem is one of acquiring information rather than one of ordering information. However, once two or more information elements have been acquired, ordering problems appear. The set might be ordered differently. Two elements, for example, could be ordered in the following ways: a,d or d,a. But the number of available information elements may be insufficient to suggest an appropriate ordering or a possible definition of the set. The nature of the problem is still unclear.

Stage II: Insufficient but Ordered Information

A number of information elements have been tentatively designated as relevant to the inquiry. The number of elements is sufficient to establish set ordering relations and to imply the bounds of the cognitive set:[a,d,e,g]. The task becomes primarily one of acquiring more information. The magnitude of the ordering problem increases with the number of available information elements. But as more and more elements are ordered, gaps and new needs are identified.

Stage III: Sufficient but Unordered Information

As information acquisition continues, a sufficient number or even a surplus of information elements become available: [a,x,f,c,d,e,b, g,k]. At this point the bounds of the set become more and more apparent and may be delimited as the information elements are permuted. Informational gaps may be seen. However, a state of disarray still exists, and the task is to seek organizing principles and theories.

Stage IV: Sufficient and Ordered Information

The elements are reconstellated until a satisfactory image or cognitive set is obtained: [a,b,c,d,e,f,g]k,x. The bounds of the set have been delimited so that the redundant or irrelevant information elements k and x may be excluded from the set or discarded. Once the cognitive set is established, it may be elaborated, refined, or challenged by the initial inquirer or by other inquirers. With the acquisition of new information or the revival of such previously excluded elements as k or x, the cognitive set may be restructured or decomposed. If the set is decomposed, inquiry might then revert to stages II or III or in some cases, to stage IV. The cycle of information acquisition and ordering is then wholly or partially repeated in order to form a new cognitive set.

In summary, inquiry may be viewed as a cyclic process involving both the acquisition and ordering of information. Through this process, the changing information need configuration influences the nature of the questions generated. In turn, answers to questions modify the information need configuration as shown in Figure 1.

The model in Figure 2 magnifies the above user information need configuration to represent the four basic stages of inquiry. Inquiry may progress to or revert from any one of the four basic stages to any other. For each stage, a corresponding specie of question would probably be generated.

EXPERT INQUIRY: AN EXAMPLE

To take an example of expert inquiry, Nobel Laureate Wolfgang Pauli, stated that he had been strongly influenced in formulating his discovery in atomic physics by the concept of Rydberg (1890), Zeeman (1896), Bohr (1913), Sommerfield (1916), and Lande (1921). Despite the availability of these concepts, or cognitive elements, his results were inconclusive. After much trial-and-error, Pauli stated:

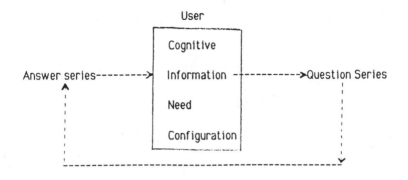

Figure 1 Information need configuration

	Unordered Information	Ordered Information
Insufficient Information	I	II
Sufficient Information	III	IV

Figure 2   Information need configuration during various stages of inquiry

At this time (1924) a paper of the English physicist, Stoner, appeared which contained . . . the following essential remark: For a given value of the principle quantum number is the number of energy levels of a single electron in the alkali metal spectra in an external magnetic field the same as the number of electrons in the closed shell of the rare gases which correspond to this principle quantum number.

On the basis of my earlier results on the classification of spectral terms in a strong magnetic field the general formulation of the exclusion principle became clear to me.[10]

Thus in 1925, Pauli was able to state the famous exclusion principle in atomic physics. He had been exposed to a concept which organized and complemented the set of cognitive elements that he already possessed. The four hypothetical stages of inquiry can be illustrated by using years to denote key cognitive elements or concepts:

Stage I   Insufficient and unordered information: [1921,
               1890,....]
Stage II   Insufficient but ordered information: [1890, 1913,
               1921,....]
Stage III   Sufficient but unordered information: [1890, 1913,
               1921, 1896, 1916, 1924]
Stage IV   Sufficient and ordered information: [1890, 1896,
               1913, 1916, 1921,1924] = 1925

It was obviously necessary for Pauli to synthesize these available concepts and to find a principle to organize them. At different points in time, however, the inquiry task was different for each scientist. Rydberg framed the seminal concept, the others elaborated on it, and Pauli put the pieces of the puzzle together.

INTELLIGENT INQUIRY: RULE BASES

The above model was developed from, and tested against, many longitudinal case studies of the scientific discovery process, including Nobel Laureate discoveries.[11] It can, therefore, serve as one basis for the development of expert inquiry systems. In expert system terminology, this model would be called a consultation paradigm, since it describes generic types of problem-solving scenarios.[12] An expert inquiry system based on a consultation paradigm should be able to elicit questions from the human inquirer, diagnose the nature of those questions, and prescribe the search heuristics to guide further inquiry. Expert systems which use rule-base programs (production systems) use an IF-THEN series of conditional statements to guide inquiry. These conditional statements take the general form of one or more IF clauses followed by one or more THEN clauses (IF premise THEN conclusion, or IF condition THEN action). Aggregates of such rules make up a rule-based system. These aggregates can consist of something like a hundred rules in a small system to several thousand rules in a large system.

A hypothetical rule base for an expert system can be illustrated by using the above inquiry and information need model. Questions generated from each stage of inquiry serves as the IF portion of the rule, while the corresponding search heuristics serve as the THEN portion of the rule. For example, in Stage I inquiry (insufficient and unordered information) the notorious "all about" question might be generated. In scientific inquiry, this sort of question might typically call for the researcher to reconstruct the history of the domain of inquiry, noting especially the initial or seminal research contribution in the area, and the subsequent landmark contributions up to the present time. Nowadays, seminal contributions tend statistically to occur from ten to fifty years prior to the culmination of inquiry in the form of a discovery. Seminal inquiries tend to frame important questions and set precedence. Subsequent landmark contributions tend to summarize smaller, prior contributions, explicate the conceptual state-of-the-art of the topic of inquiry, and modify or revise the initial or seminal contributions.[13]

The hypothetical expert inquiry system to guide Pauli in his search for the exclusion principle (see above example) would display sets of rules to guide Stage I inquiry and to deal with initial, "all about" questions. These rules might assume the following forms:

IF: Investigation is being initiated
THEN: 1. Search the prior 50 years' literature;
        2. Identify list of seminal contributions;
        3. Build chronology of landmark (heavily cited) contributions.
IF: 1. A seminal contribution is identified; and
        2. One landmark contribution is identified.
THEN: 1. Extend or modify these contributions; and
        2. Search for additional contributions in statistically likely time intervals.

The task here is to specify the domain of inquiry, its key components, and to elaborate on the problem at hand. Because there is a demonstrated statistical periodicity in the accumulation of landmark contributions, the researcher is prompted to search in the literature of appropriate time intervals.

Following Stage I inquiry, our hypothetical expert inquiry system could guide the researcher through subsequent stages. Stage II inquiry (insufficient but ordered information) could continue the task of accumulating and sifting through landmark contributions. Rules in this stage might take the following form:

IF: Seminal and two landmark contributions have been
          identified
THEN: Search the relevant literature for other contributions
          around the years 1895, 1900, 1905, 1910, 1915,
          1920, and 1925.

Again, the task here is to accumulate the major, relevant concepts
and analyze their relationships. From studies of the discovery process, the years designated for searching are statistically probable
years of landmark occurrence owing to the previously mentioned
periodicity of contributions toward a culminating discovery. The
questions generated in Stage II inquiry tend to seek additional cognitive chunks, including those which supplement, complement, or
modify the existing available chunks or fill gaps between them.

In Stage III inquiry (sufficient but unordered information) the
researcher cannot progress until findings are ordered. This stage
marks the immediate, pre-hypothesis and "information overload"
phase of inquiry. Questions generated here tend to seek principles,
laws, theories, or other insights to provide conceptual unity and
economy. The hypothetical expert system would direct Pauli to formulate a unifying principle:

IF: 1. Sufficient data are accumulated, and
          2. Progress is stymied
THEN: 1. Seek critical relationships in the system under
             study, and
          2. Search very recent literature and communicate
             with colleagues who are investigating the same
             problem.

Stage IV marks the emergence of one or more creative hypotheses which serve to organize the several major concepts into a unified
whole. Inquiry might move to a consummatory state in which all
cognitive elements are subjectively or objectively complete and
well organized, so that inquiry is either suspended or redirected.
Generally, hypotheses must be confirmed and experiments repli-
cated to the point of acceptance in the scientific community. And,
such new insights generally evoke a whole series of new questions.
Our expert inquiry system might provide such Stage IV heuristics as
the following:

IF: Hypotheses are confirmed
THEN: 1. Seek appropriate research designs for large-scale experiment to replicate the minimal experiment, and
        2. Generalize experimental findings and project implications of hypotheses to related systems and/or phenomena.

Thus, a domain-specific expert inquiry system might encourage the extrapolation of findings into unrelated realms of inquiry, and assist the researcher to seek innovative research designs.

For purposes of illustration, the above rules are simplistic and excessively general. But such rules do correspond to formalisms obtained from a number of cases of scientific discovery.[14] However, present expert systems tend to be effective only when they are highly domain-specific; that is, expert systems need to be restricted to a narrow subject area or task in order to work. Accordingly, an expert inquiry system prototype would need to be specialized in a narrow area of science or research design.[15] Last, the great impact of research cliques or invisible colleges on inquiry is well documented.[16] Expert system heuristics could prompt an inquirer to resort to other experts through informal modes of communication at critical points in the research process. Appropriate informal communication on the part of researchers is not necessarily spontaneous or assured.

ALTERNATIVE APPROACHES

Expert inquiry systems could obviously be based on approaches and rule sets other than those of scientific expert inquiry. Rules developed in library reference work involve both queries and information systems and sources. These rules apply to routine or research-oriented search strategies, elaboration of questions (reference interviews), the use of alternative subject classifications and headings, searching by form of literature, use of online systems, and resort to network resources.[17] Because many of these rules are fairly general and independent of subject or factual material, they might serve as candidate expert system rule bases. Kehoe proposes that expert system research be carried out in various online information retrieval areas: expert intermediaries; expert end users; gateway software development; bibliographic database development. Kehoe also provides a lengthy bibliography on the potential development of expert systems for online retrieval.[18] Moreover, expert system technology is expected to penetrate virtually all or most areas of knowledge or expertise over the next several years. Expert system and other artificial intelligence applications will be distributed to points of use, regardless of the types of organizations or areas of knowledge involved.

CONCLUSION

The potential development of expert inquiry systems, particularly those which address the problems of fundamental science and emulate the research strategies of expert scientists, poses many difficult but exciting challenges for investigators in these areas. First, the heuristics and other strategies of expert scientific inquiry need to be formalized. Empirical case studies of the way experts, such as Nobel Laureates, pursue their research appear to be a fruitful way to develop systems of expert rules. Rudimentary patterns of scientific inquiry reveal that such experts successively accumulate and order significant prior scientific contributions until they produce a breakthrough. Apparently, such experts pose the usual "all about" types of questions during the initial phases of their research, and then pose questions to accumulate and order cognitive chunks or elements until a satisfactory gestalt emerges. That is, their questions seek to fill gaps in their maps of scientific knowledge and to better organize or reorganize those maps. Intense research in the area of expert inquiry could provide powerful sets of rules around which to design new generations of information retrieval systems.

A second problem in developing expert inquiry systems pertains to the current need for domain specificity, or narrowness of the application subject area. Today's expert systems work best in highly specialized or restricted areas. As future generations of large, hybrid expert systems are developed, the ideal of more generalized expert inquiry systems can be approached. At present, prototypes and relatively simple systems appear to be prerequisite to the task of developing broad-domain expert inquiry systems. A third problem relates to the apparent excessive optimism which now prevails over the potential capabilities of expert systems. The great, initial enthusiasm can be expected to wane as various kinds of setbacks occur (e.g., system failures, developmental barriers, litigations, saturated markets). And, much expert system technology might become conventionalized. That is, many heuristic rules, once understood, might be reprogrammed in conventional algorithm form and absorbed into more mundane computer and library technologies.

Fourth, research needs to be conducted on how expert information professionals use systems and how they access knowledge (classifications, headings, forms) and deal with users (interviews, relevance assessment, search strategies). Such research would not necessarily be closely related to specific areas of knowledge and would thus focus on inquiry about inquiry. In these areas, research is still at a pioneer stage. Reference and online retrieval specialists are in a particularly good position to provide leadership here as well as in the more general development of expert inquiry systems.

NOTES

1. C. W. Churchman, *The Design of inquiring systems* (New York: Basic Books, 1972), pp. 1-28.

2. I. Mitroff et al., "Dialectical Inquiring Systems: A New Methodology for Information Science," *Journal of the American Society for Information Science*, 23 (November-December 1972): 365-378.

3. G. Harmon, "Information Retrieval Based on Patterns of Scientific Discovery," *Proceedings of the American Society for Information Science*, Vol. 16 (White Plains, NY: Knowledge Industry Publications, Inc., 1979), pp. 117-129.

4. S. P. Harter, "Scientific Inquiry: A Model for Online Searching," *Journal of the American Society for Information Science*, 35 (March 1984): 110-117.

5. A. Kaplan, *The conduct of inquiry: Methodology for behavioral science* (New York: Harper and Row Publishers, 1964), chapters 1-3.

6. W. Kunz et al., *Methods of analysis and evaluation of information needs: A critical review* (Munchen: Verlag Dokumentation, 1977), pp. 1-73.

7. W. R. Reitman, *Cognition and thought: An information processing approach* (New York: John Wiley & Sons, Inc., 1965), p. 91.

8. P. Harmon & D. King, *Expert systems: Artificial intelligence in business* (New York: John Wiley & Sons, Inc., 1985), p. 32.

9. G. Harmon, "Information Need Transformation During Inquiry," *Proceedings of the American Society for Information Science*, Vol. 7. (Westport, CT: Greenwood Press, 1970), pp. 40-43.

10. W. Pauli, "Exclusion Principle and Quantum Mechanics," in *Nobel foundation, nobel lectures: Physics 1942-1962*. (Amsterdam, Netherlands: Elsevier Publishing Co., 1964), p. 29.

11. G. Harmon, *Human memory and knowledge: A systems approach* (Westport, CT: Greenwood Press, 1973), pp. 19-39.

12. P. Harmon and King, *Expert systems*, 92-95.

13. G. Harmon, *Human memory*, 111-121.

14. W. Goffman & G. Harmon, "Mathematical Approach to the Prediction of Scientific Discovery," *Nature* 229 (January 8, 1971): 103-104,

15. D. A. Waterman, *A guide to expert systems* (Reading, MA: Addison-Wesley Publishing Co., Inc., 1985), pp. 139-140.

16. D. Crane, "Information Needs and Uses," *Annual Review of Information Science and Technology*, Vol. 6 ed. C. A. Cuadra, (Chicago: Encyclopedia Britannica, Inc. 1971), pp. 3-39.

17. W. A. Katz, *Introduction to reference work. Vol. II: Reference services and reference processes*. Third edition. (New York: McGraw-Hill Book Co., 1978), 2:61-108.

18. C. A. Kehoe, "Interfaces and Expert Systems for Information Retrieval," *Online Review* 9 (December, 1985): 489-505.

Public Libraries and Society in the Information Age

Arthur W. Hafner

The public library plays an important role in our democratic system, as well as in community development. This role needs to be fully understood since libraries now find themselves in a time of crisis. Funding a library, designing programs to meet community needs, and creating community awareness of the library have always been difficult challenges. These challenges persist, often appearing in new and unfamiliar contexts. Such challenges are magnified by reduced public spending, rising costs, and an economy in transition from the age of industrialization to an age of information and services. The intelligent resolution of library problems requires a clarification of the library's relationship to American goals and ideals.

Frequently, there appears to be genuine confusion as to the fundamental reasons for the existence of the public library. Some communities have a vague notion that a public library is "needed" but lack an ability to express how citizens in general benefit from library services and programs. Other communities may focus on the need to perpetuate specific library activities rather than on the more fundamental question of why the library is the appropriate agency to perform them. While libraries are generally perceived as desirable, the public library enterprise often appears to suffer from an overall identity crisis.[1] This lack of collective identity may be attributable in

Dr. Hafner is Director, Division of Library and Information Management, American Medical Association, 535 North Dearborn St., Chicago, IL 60610.

The author wishes to express appreciation to Brian Kibble-Smith, JD, AMA Division of Library and Information Management, for his contributions in preparing this paper.

The author also acknowledges Dale A. Rublee, PhD, Policy Analyst, AMA Center for Health Policy Research, and to Terry L. Austin, Carla J. Funk, and Susan Roman, Department Directors of the Division of Library and Information Management for their constructive suggestions; to Elizabeth A. Contant and Marla S. Campbell for their technical assistance; to Jack A. Hicks, Deerfield Public Library, Deerfield, IL and to C. Diane Holtz, Rye Free Reading Room, Rye, NY, for helpful comments during this project.

part to the sporadic historical development of the public library in American society. The turn-of-the-century beneficial impetus of Andrew Carnegie and other philanthropists accelerated the development of public libraries.[2] However, justification of libraries and library systems seems to have been an afterthought. Libraries today are often justified more upon their traditional community presence than upon a rational understanding of how the library contributes to the community.

The stakes for public libraries are high. Success may be defined not by expansion, but by survival. The public library that does survive will be one that is well managed, has a clear definition of its role in society, and functions effectively in the information age. Broad changes in the structure of the public library are inevitable. New approaches to public spending will combine with rapidly developing information technology to make this the most significant period of library development since the Carnegie era.

THE PUBLIC LIBRARY AS A PUBLIC AGENCY

For many cities and towns, the library is the jewel of the community. Where services are outstanding, the community has placed a high value on the library's contribution to the quality of life. Other communities, many with ample funds, are willing to exist without a library or with a library that is comparably inferior. Such communities have reached a very different judgment than have their sister communities on the value of the library.

For all libraries, however, recent budget cuts and retrenchments have been significant. Economic pressures are not new to librarians who for decades have performed an array of services with minimal resources. In fact, librarians have become so skilled at maintaining services despite budget cut that it can be difficult to clearly show that a reduction in budget results in loss of service.[3] Librarians are too frequently forced to "tighten their belts" yet again, prevented from developing beneficial services by repeated reductions. Fortunately, librarians generally avoid the unwise temptation to maintain present services at the expense of future services.

No matter how they are funded, recent budgetary problems for all public libraries are complicated by three unusual factors. First, the unprecedented size and scope of current reductions in public services reflects a new public awareness of government spending. Second, libraries have suffered from substantial cost increases, especially in publishing, energy, and labor. This is particularly a problem for libraries funded by tax levies that remain unadjusted for years of inflation. Third, librarians must cope with retrenchment during the advent of the information age, a period that ostensibly benefits library interests.

Many municipal expenditures, unlike a library, are justified on the basis of necessities such as public records administration, safety and health. This leads to a definition of some services as "essential," such as a recorder of deeds, police and fire protection, and streets and sanitation services, justifying the expenditures to support them. The question is not whether to deliver these services, but how to deliver them most effectively given the available government dollars.

This narrow focus produces a restricted definition of "essential services," inappropriate for many programs that are vital to community welfare although their value is not readily apparent. If the library is to continue its contribution to society, there must be a clear understanding within the community of how and why the library is essential in a broader sense of the term.

Still, some library advocates would argue that the library is "essential" by trying to fit it into the narrow definition. They suggest that while the adverse effects of closing a public library would not be immediately felt, its closing would eventually cause an erosion of the information base necessary for effective public participation in government. The risk in this approach to library justification is that even libraries with outstanding services may be regarded as luxuries. Without firm justification in the community for a public library at the onset, library services may be allowed to decay to the point of ineffectiveness. Similarly, repeated budget cuts may reduce library services to substandard levels. A library's contribution to the quality of life is only marginal if its information services and collections are inadequate for even the most basic community needs. In such cases, the notion that a library is "non-essential" becomes a self-fulfilling prophecy. Understanding how the library is truly essential to the community requires detailed examination of the library's role in the democracy.

THE ROLE OF THE LIBRARY IN DEMOCRACY

Generally, public libraries define their objectives as providing educational, recreational, informational and cultural services. The overriding mission of the public library is to enhance the democracy through performing these functions. The adequacy of this mission as a justification for the public library can be made clearer by examining the basis for our democracy and the spirit of Western Civilization: increased knowledge through inquiry and the free exchange of ideas.

This spirit of learning, though it transcends notions of formal schooling, is exemplified in our national tradition of liberal education. Liberal education, or instruction apart from technical and vocational training, is excellent preparation for participating in a democratic society.[4] People who are liberally educated are highly capable of making informed decisions and of acting as discerning voters. This is attributable to an understanding of issues and their broad implications through an enhanced ability to draw analogies and relate factual information to a variety of experiences.[5]

The expanded availability of all education, particularly liberal education, has paralleled the increase of democratic participation in this country. The growth of the public library system is an important historical factor in the expanded availability of education, as are the suffrage of women and the civil rights movement factors in the expansion of democracy.

An educated population is both a product of, and a reason for, the existence of democracy. Our democratic government, and our security as a nation, permits and fosters the fulfillment of the basic needs of all citizens. Our pluralistic society allows a broad range of self-expression, as long as there is not an infringement upon the rights of others. Americans, in theory, enjoy more opportunity for attaining social acceptance and self-esteem than the citizens of any other nation.

Our democracy makes possible the growth, personal development, and creative accomplishment that most Americans perceive as necessary for the pursuit of happiness. This individual freedom to live a full life is the single most beneficial aspect of American society. To insure the continuance of this freedom, the democracy itself must be preserved by the people within it. As Jefferson wrote,

> [There is] no safe depository of the ultimate powers of society, but the people themselves; and if we think them not enlightened enough to exercise their control with a wholesome discretion, the remedy is not to take it from them, but to inform their discretion by education.[6]

The library, therefore, is both an end of, and a means to, our democracy. First, the democracy makes possible the personal development that is the goal of every individual. The library assists all citizens to achieve this growth through humanistic pursuits. Second, the library, through its collections, programs, seminars, activities, and presentations, helps to provide a liberally educated population, thus insuring the continuance of the democracy.

The library, then, advances the concept of citizenship by contributing to an informed electorate and by aiding the exploration of humanistic thought through the diffusion of knowledge and the perpetuation of culture. Library collections help citizens to maintain a continuing basis of shared experiences necessary for effective learning and communication. This is why a core collection of social, historical, biographical, fictional, and academic works central to the concepts that provide the basis for our national identity can be found in virtually any public library.

It could be argued that the cultural and recreational functions of the library are simply different ways to express the library's educational role. The historical interrelationship between public education and the public library may precipitate a trend in many cities toward achieving efficiencies by combining aspects of the two systems.[7]

To justify the library on the basis of its educational function is tempting but incomplete without reference to the democratic principles that education supports. Indeed, totalitarian and autocratic governments also place a high value on education, but education is valuable only to the degree that it accomplishes the purposes of the individuals in power. Lately, however, the library has been characterized as performing an increasingly important economic function in addition to its educational, cultural, informational and recreational role.

THE PUBLIC LIBRARY
IN THE INFORMATION ECONOMY

The basis for the argument that libraries perform an important economic function lies in the shift from an industrial society to an information society. The previous major economic transition in the United States was from agriculture to industry. Industrialization increased the availability of education, especially liberal education, through greater prosperity and expanded discretionary time. Industrialization also resulted in increased access to manufactured goods and more opportunities to make a good living. On the negative side, industrialization spanned an era of dehumanized mass production. Public distrust of corporations, consumer alienation, and the complexity of society all increased during this period.

Like industrialization, the new information and service economy is responsible for its own beneficial and detrimental effects. The information economy is less labor intensive than an industrial economy. Therefore, it probably will not present workers with increased opportunities for earning a better living on the same scale as did industrialization. The information economy has created a more decentralized society, thus affecting tax bases through shifting demographics. Large, urban centers of industry are no longer reliable sources of the municipal revenue needed to drive ambitious public programs. The revenue problem is just as acute in smaller urban, suburban, and rural areas suffering from depressed local economies, inflation, the loss of federal and state subsidies, and other adverse economic impacts.

The unskilled and semiskilled workers who once enjoyed increased prosperity through industrialization now face a substantial decline of opportunity in the industrial sector. The political and economic significance of labor unions is diminishing while participation in white collar jobs is increasing. To be successful in the information and service economy requires skills and expertise that did not even exist for the last generation to enter the workforce. While there are new opportunities for success in the information economy, the costs of participating in it are high and the chances for success are narrower than they were in the past.

The social dynamics of the shift from industrialization to information will affect the library in many ways. First, the new information workforce is highly representative of the emerging electorate that will control priorities and budgets for all municipal activities. A population educated in the competitive, cost-conscious information age will examine the merits of a library program more closely than did past constituencies. The library shares a problem with many other tax-supported activities, a problem that is becoming more severe. Many citizens who do not use the library, or other public services, resent being taxed to support activities that may only benefit them indirectly through general community improvement.

Additionally, the new generation of library users is gaining daily exposure to electronic information systems and research logic now being introduced into library procedures. Remote access to information databases, the development of "user-friendly" interactive systems, and education of users in library skills is likely to expand, causing the technology gap between client and librarian to narrow. As technology is simplified and its cost reduced, the present form of user reliance upon the librarian's intuition and experience in accessing information is likely to decline.

It may be argued that most users will always prefer to allow the librarian to do their work for them. In times of extreme financial hardship, the contribution of the librarian in assisting users unwilling to do their own research could be regarded as minimal. Shifts to placing a greater burden of self-reliance upon users could lead to fundamental changes in how library services are delivered to the public, and in how library users will benefit from services.[8] Perhaps the role of the librarian will become to improve the basic processes by which information is gathered, stored, and recalled. This new role for the librarian would serve the public by expanding the world of information available.

It is a mistake to assume, however, that the shift to an information economy will automatically catapult libraries or librarians to a place of socio-economic prominence. A major obstacle to extensive participation in the information age is the public's perception of librarians in general. Though librarians have made tremendous improvements in information distribution through the innovative use of new technology, they are not yet clearly perceived as being at the cutting edge of research and information sciences. This is due, in large part, to the "uninformative and unscientific" way the term "information sciences" has been applied recently.[9]

Another obstacle faced by the librarian attempting to enter the information age is the nature of the information involved. The new generation of library users is increasingly becoming accustomed to information as a commercial decision-making tool. To this group of users, and to the commercial sector in general, useful information is characterized as data that contributes to economic achievement and commercial success. Such an attitude is a sharp contrast to the humanistic information that often forms the core of a library collection. It creates the potential conflict of library users demanding a greater emphasis on economically valuable information from a humanities-oriented library program.

Economically valuable information is invariably specialized in nature. Efficient delivery of such information often requires the formation of special libraries or other systems of organizational information management. The libraries in the best position to directly capitalize on the information economy are non-public corporate, specialized, and institutional libraries. The value of these libraries to their users or to the organization as a whole is frequently overlooked. Many such libraries are now aggressively promoting themselves. They are expanding their activities by assuming information management tasks performed elsewhere in the organization that the library staff may perform more efficiently. The public library, however, can expect its benefits from the information age to be more indirect.

Many public libraries, with a shift in focus, could become formidable competitors to special libraries and commercial brokerages in providing economically valuable information. However, this would require the long-term commitment of substantial resources to an objective fundamentally inconsistent with the library's humanistic and educational history. The library that attempts this shift invites the same degree of budgetary scrutiny and profit and loss analysis that is applied to commercial enterprises. Participation in the information-for-profit arena is further complicated by the public library's non-profit status. Additionally, the new opportunities of financial returns for libraries through information vending carry the risk of commercial failure. Commercial services that become unprofitable are quickly abandoned. A community that values its library should carefully consider whether it is willing to accept this risk, particularly if it is taken at the expense of the library's humanistic, educational history.

LIBRARY OPTIMIZATION
IN THE INFORMATION AGE

The reason for the library's existence is its contribution to the American democratic ideal. The library's mission in our democracy is to work as an agent and partner within the community to promote the quality of society and the enrichment of the citizenry. This is accomplished through programs that actively disseminate knowledge and cultural information and that provide the citizenry with an opportunity for self-development.

Few other institutions of government have such lofty goals, or are as well equipped to pursue them in such a unique fashion as is the library. Our society, however, is becoming increasingly pragmatic, interested in short-term, practical solutions to visible problems. The library could address this by emphasizing the pragmatic purposes that library information services meet. A library that supports commercial activities, engages in public service, complements the educational system, and augments public recreation is relatively easy for the community to justify on a pragmatic basis.

Pragmatic justifications, however, are an insecure foundation for the library enterprise. Such applications are rationalizations for the library, not reasons for its existence. Without a public library, it would still be possible to meet special needs with targeted alternatives similar to adopting "dial-a-ride" services rather than modifying all transit vehicles to accommodate the disabled. If the library enterprise is to grow and flourish, the community must recognize the library's contribution to democracy as a secure foundation for the library's existence.

A firm, articulable community justification for the library related to the library's role in the democracy is critical in helping library administrators to address many of the issues they now face. For example, a significant issue in the public library profession is whether to charge users for certain services. Library administrators who selectively impose charges must decide among various cost strategies. The effect of costs on the equality of information access must be considered, particularly with respect to individuals not able to pay fees for library services.[10] The answer to these and related questions of access requires finding the proper balance between commercial activity and the library's role in preserving the democracy.

Because the library must reflect the goals, needs, and values of the community, librarians are paying particular attention to identifying current and potential library users and their requirements.[11] This task is more difficult than in the past, as the user profile may change as rapidly as does the library's environment. There is a clear emphasis in current library literature and education on improved methods of library management as a way of coping with budget cuts, increasing costs, and rapidly developing information technology.

The application of modern business management techniques to library operations will help to overcome a general perception of librarians as poor managers.[12] In the past, less attention was given to principles of management in public services and programs because of the relative abundance of government funds. Strict management seemed out of place in the library due to the comparative modesty of library needs. Today, however, financial planners and review committees are prevalent in all areas of public spending. Even the most autonomous public library, with funding independent of the municipal budget, has become more accountable for its financial management. Where library trustees or other overseers are not directly elected by the public, they are appointed by elected officials who themselves are subject to constituency pressures to reduce tax burdens. Libraries are now managed with a sensitivity for the importance to the community of budgetary issues. At times, librarians are understandably reluctant to attempt the difficult task of weighing the intangible benefits of library service in quantitative terms.[13] However, it is clear that the fiscal demands on library administration are increasing and will continue to do so.

The impact that the library can have on local quality of life is apparent if a concerted effort is made by library and community planners to identify important goals supported by library activities. There are many ways to make the library an effective, visible, and direct participant in achieving community goals. For example, education apart from the formal system is becoming increasingly important. Many urban libraries are already implementing programs that promote community literacy goals. Another library opportunity exists due to the substantial growth in adult education and retraining. Workers are more frequently turning to education to become competitive for technical and service careers in the information economy. There is also a growing realization that new thrusts in out-of-classroom education are necessary to cope with the problem of hard-core poverty.[14] This latter group of citizens may become a permanent underclass unless ways are found to incorporate them into an economy that has become difficult, alien, and increasingly hostile to them. Changes in the philosophy of how to educate the population are unavoidable and contain both serious implications and intriguing opportunities for library educational services.

Another way in which librarians and the community may work together is in identifying new forms of outreach programs. Nursing homes, businesses, hospitals, and other organizations that could benefit from satellite or shared collections are now being served in many areas by innovative library programs developed in conjunction with community planners. Through entering the information fabric of the community in this and other ways, libraries can become the community information connector. The technology and expertise exist to place the library at the hub of a municipal information network. By phoning one number or visiting one location, a user could learn information about everything from local car pools to where to file a complaint in small claims court.[15]

There is also potential community benefit in using library expertise to analyze municipal functions from an information management perspective. An area ripe for library expansion is in serving the public through serving public administration. The library is in a position to create or improve municipal information databases, either by directly performing various information tasks, or by serving as a consultant in systems development. For example, library records management expertise can be applied to the proceedings of zoning boards, school boards, or other agencies. The application of library expertise to public matters and records would improve the organization of and access to information truly needed for an informed democracy. As communities realize that the public library is in the business of public information management, a range of possibilities emerge for making the library the informational nerve center of municipal administration. With this position should come the appropriate resources for the tasks, and a clearer recognition of the library as performing an essential service under any definition.

CONCLUSION

The public library has been described in many ways. Its benefits and services range from providing quality recreation to its significant educational role. The foundation of the public library concept is firmly based in American beliefs about a free society. As such, it is both a product and producer of democracy. The community, therefore, must define the library in its humanistic and democratic terms and evaluate the library's future in the information age in light of this important role.

Better understanding in the community of why the public library is an important partner will lead to a new perspective on the significance of library services and programs. As the ways in which the library contributes to community information processes are expanded, libraries will be recognized as pursuing a mission unique among the agencies of government: the improvement of the democracy through the lifelong advancement of its citizens.

NOTES

1. Colson, John C. "Form Against Function: The American Public Library and Contemporary Society." *Journal of Library History,* Spring, 1983:111-142.

2. Rogers, A. Robert & McChesney, Kathryn. *The Library in Society.* Littleton, CO: Libraries Unlimited, 1984.

3. White, Herbert S. "Library Turf." *Library Journal,* April 15, 1985:54-55.

4. Giamatti, A. Bartlett. "A Liberal Education and the New coercion." *Yale Alumni Magazine and Journal,* Oct. 1981:27-29.

5. Bradford, Dennis E. *The fundamental ideas.* St. Louis: Warren H. Green, 1986.

6. Letter to William Charles Jarvis, Sept. 28, 1820.

7. Dyer, Esther R. *Cooperation in library service to children.* Metuchen, NJ: Scarecrow Press, 1978.

8. Suprenant, Thomas T. & Perry-Holmes, Claudia. "The Reference Librarian of the Future: A Scenario." *RQ,* Winter, 1985:235-238.

9. Buckland, Michael K. *Library services in theory and context.* Elmsford, NY: Pergamon Press, 1983.

10. Estabrook, Leigh S. "The Social Scientist's Perspective." In *Financial choices for public libraries.* Chicago: Public Library Association, 1980.

11. Swisher, Robert & McClure, Charles R. *Research for decision library: Methods for librarians.* Chicago: American Library Association, 1984.

12. McClure, Charles R. "Library Managers: Can They Manager Will They Lead?" *Library Journal,* November 15, 1980:2388-91.

13. White, Herbert S. "Cost Benefit Analysis Other Fun & Games." *Library Journal,* February 15, 1985:118-121.

14. "The American Millstone." *Chicago Tribune Special Reprint* (series of editorials published during 1985 on poverty).

15. Garfield, Eugene. "Society's Unmet Information Needs." *Bulletin of the American Society for Information Sciences* 12(1):6-7, 1985.

II. INFLUENCE OF THEORY AND RESEARCH PRACTICE

In Pursuit of Windmills: Librarians and the Determination to Instruct

Connie Miller
Patricia Tegler

Filled with the visions of chivalry, heroism, and knighthood which he had gleaned from numerous romantic novels, the poor, elderly Alonzo Quixano calls himself Don Quixote and rides out into the world in search of adventure. His knightly adventures, however, as Cervantes' well-known novel so beautifully describes, result primarily from mistaken perceptions. Believing windmills to be horrible giants our misguided knight attacks, only to be lifted off his bony old horse by one of the circling arms and dropped to the ground.

Like poor, elderly Alonzo, many librarians throughout the history of American librarianship have been filled with heroic visions. Like Alonzo, these librarians have called themselves by a new name — teachers — and have ridden out to practice their profession and seek recognition. This recognition has been as much a windmill as our misguided knight's giant, and the circling arm of biblio-

Ms. Miller is Science Librarian, University of Illinois at Chicago, Box 7565, Chicago, IL 60680. Her co-author is Systems Librarian in the Chicago firm of Kirkland and Ellis.

graphic instruction has time and again lifted our teacher-librarians high into the air and dropped them to the ground. And yet, like Don Quixote, the teacher-librarians have pressed on undaunted. So undaunted are they, in fact, that they have begun to attack the recognition windmill from a new angle. Once again, victims of mistaken perceptions, they find themselves rising skyward, and subsequently dropping earthward, this time on the revolving arm of end-user training.

Frances L. Hopkins (1982), a pioneer in the recent bibliographic instruction movement, conveniently traces the hundred year old heritage of librarians' involvement with teaching. In late nineteenth century America, before Melvil Dewey's School of Library Economy which concentrated on practical training in routinized tasks, academic librarians were most often professors who headed the library part-time. These "scholar-librarians," Hopkins tells us, felt naturally inclined to teach the use of library materials. Men like historian-cartographer Justin Winsor at Harvard and student of law Azariah Root at Oberlin College are, according to Hopkins, the predecessors of modern bibliographic instructors, supplying their descendants with a "historical claim to professional and academic legitimacy" (Hopkins, 1982, 192-93).

Hopkins' historical survey demonstrates how difficult the direct connection between the "scholar-librarian" ancestors and their modern library instructional descendants has been to maintain. Something kept — and keeps — getting in the way. The growth in academic library collections created the first major obstruction. One or two Justin Winsors or Azariah Roots acting as part-time "professors of bibliography" could no longer provide adequate access to the increasingly large numbers of books and periodicals. Librarians, trained and hired to process the expanding collections, created, as "an unintended consequence of Dewey's social conscience," another important obstruction. These often mediocre graduates of library schools with undemanding admission policies simply lacked "the competence or status to teach research methods," and professor-librarians responsible for large, rapidly-growing collections and for large mediocre, clerically-trained staffs no longer had the leisure to offer instruction concerning "the methods by which a subject is attacked" (Hopkins, 1982, 193-96).

The third vital obstruction to the direct descendancy between present-day bibliographic instructors and nineteenth century scholar-librarians can be traced to Samuel Green and the Worcester

Public Library. In 1876, Green instituted formal reference service which caught on and rapidly spread, in part, Hopkins hypothesizes, because the clerically-trained librarians not competent to teach research methods were at least competent to handle patrons' information problems on demand. Hopkins believes that academic library instruction and the public library reference desk share a common aim: to foster "independent learning, free from reliance on tradition or authority." In academia, however, the goal of developing independent learners cannot be adequately met through the reference desk since reference librarians can only respond to specific questions and provide information. She feels that library instructors offer the key to true independence by teaching students "how to keep up with on-going research and how to evaluate one expert opinion in the light of others," and that simpler, less professionally rigorous reference desk service continues to deflect librarians away from their true, more complex mission as instructors of bibliographic theory (Hopkins, 1982, 194-96).

HISTORICAL INTERPRETATION

History is always interpretive, but Hopkins' survey of the historical legacy of bibliographic instruction seems to be based, like Quixote's knightly adventures, on some mistaken perceptions which crop up again and again throughout the library instructional literature. These mistaken perceptions include: (1) equating librarianship with instruction and librarians with professors; (2) equating library use with the democratic principle of independent learning; and (3) viewing bibliographic instruction as a subject rather than a process, as an end rather than as a means. The scholar-librarians, like Winsor and Root, were scholars and professors first and library administrators second. Modern day librarians descend from the clerically-trained graduates of Dewey's reformist library school rather than from historians, cartographers, or students of the law. A direct line of descent, unbroken by any obstructions, can be traced from today's information specialist back to the graduates trained to handle the information explosion of the late nineteenth century. The Winsors and the Roots have as their descendants the faculty members in all academic disciplines who carry on the vital socialization function of teaching their students, often indirectly by example, "how to keep up with on-going research and how to evaluate one expert opinion in the light of others" (Hopkins, 1982, 196).

Rather than being obstructive to the true nature of librarianship, large, expanding library collections constituted, and continue to constitute, the core of the information profession's concern. It is programs like Green's innovative reference service, which offer ways to directly link the user with the collection, that form the legitimate foundation of librarianship. A careful reading of his description of this service readily reveals that it represented considerably more than a simplistic occupation for inadequately educated employees; it offered a method for delivering information into the hands of those who need it according to individual needs (Green, 1976).

One hundred years after Green, academic librarians have failed to recognize that their mission is to provide information to those who need it. While their colleagues in special and public libraries have made information delivery a goal, academic librarians are so uncomfortable with the role of information-provider that they have developed an entire movement, bibliographic instruction, which is based on the premise that librarians are teachers. If librarianship's descendants can be traced back to Dewey's graduates trained in environments such as the Worchester Public Library to provide information, why have librarians rewritten the historical record and attempted to define themselves as teachers? Why has bibliographic education rather than information provision become the primary goal?

This redirection of goals seems to stem in part from a critical misunderstanding of education and the role of the non-teacher in the academic enterprise. Teaching is often mistakenly equated with education and hence, assigned the only significant role in the academic community. Librarians have forgotten the basic truth that "there are . . . many differing education roles in the social institution of education, and not all of the roles are teaching roles" (Wilson, 1979, 155). As long ago as 1943, Anne Boyd Roberts expressed belief in this mistaken equation when she stated that "the teaching function of reference work is as important in all libraries as the information-giving function, if we believe in the library as an educational institution." Comments such as this are misleading and ultimately dangerous for they deny the inherent educational role of the library. They contribute to a widespread failure to recognize that even libraries as collections serve an important educational function. Libraries and librarians do not need to embrace teaching in order to play a central role in academia. Nevertheless this adherence to the "teaching as education" myth continues as a basic tenet of the bibliographic instruction philosophy and has led to a misperception of the role of the librarian. Library instruction advocates have come to believe, as Anne Roberts (1980, 283) states, that the only way "to engage fully in the educational mission of . . . (the) institution" is to take on the role of the "teacher, interpreter and subject specialist."

The logical extension of the teaching-education equation is a belief (and fear) that directly providing information to students is antithetical to true learning. Many believe that "information" impedes the learning process while "instruction" enhances it. Although this view is not universally held, it has greatly influenced the bibliographic instruction movement, and to a significant degree serves as its philosophical foundation. Arguing against this perspective, Sayles (1980, 199) expresses his frustration when he states that "there is a continuous commotion about the evils of spoon-feeding, of dispensing information. We librarians are supposed to feel guilty if we *give* information to students." As an alternative to giving information to students, the instruction literature suggests that librarians in higher education should teach students to rigorously assess and understand information sources, all with the goal of making the student an "educable person" (Frick, 1975, 12). Many instruction advocates believe that directly providing information to the student undercuts this goal, for according to Frick (1982, 194), "the student who has simply been handed 'material for research' has been cheated."

While there may be times when librarians can productively contribute to the educational mission by teaching, an insistence that their role is teaching results in a double-edged loss which affects librarians themselves and the academic community in which they operate. Pauline Wilson (1979) describes the loss to librarians in terms of an organization fiction. She argues, convincingly, that librarians call themselves teachers or professors to benefit from the recognition commonly received by professionals with these names. When the sought-for recognition is, inevitably, not forthcoming ("A root cause of the lack of recognition is this: there is no basis for recognition. It is not that teachers and professors will not recognize librarians as teachers. Rather, it is that they cannot" [Wilson, 1979, 154]), one, not uncommon, response is anger and resentment toward those who legitimately hold the title of teacher. Donald Kenney (1983, 7-8), to quote an extreme example, writes that "any reference librarian who refers to faculty as good researchers is making "an astonishing statement. Often," he goes on, "faculty are the poorest models for students on conducting research and retrieving information. It is frequently the poor research methods and models established by teaching faculty that instructional librarians must try to undo." Comments such as these exhibit confusion and insecurity regarding the librarian's role. By identifying weaknesses in the methods and skills of teaching faculty it appears that instruction librarians are attempting to find educational voids that they can fill with their own expertise.

RESEARCH AND LIBRARY SKILLS

Stephen Stoan (1984) has clarified beautifully the difference between research and library skills, and by extension the roles of the scholar/teacher and the librarian, a difference which Kenney and others clearly fail to perceive. While "library information-seeking models . . . rely almost exclusively on reference tools," the citations scholars obtain come from sources like footnotes, other scholars' recommendations, browsing, serendipitous discovery, personal files, etc. (Stoan, 1984, 100-101). The failure to recognize the difference between the methods of librarians and those of scholar/teachers is ultimately damaging to the academic community as a whole. The resulting confusion centers around not simply what librarians do but what they are. By insisting that they are teachers, librarians sacrifice a sense of their own identity.

It is this lack of identity which causes librarians to lose sight of the importance of information to the process of education. It is the resulting concern for recognition which causes librarians to blur the vital distinction between dissemination of content and dissemination of information. As Wilson (1979, 155) points out, content is the province of the subject expert, the professor of chemistry, of history, or of sociology; matching relevant portions of the graphic record to users' needs is the province of the librarian. What the academic community loses when librarians insist that "instruction in the use of materials [is their] essential educational obligation" is this particular skill of matching portions of the graphic record with users' needs (Schiller, 1965, 57). There is no one else who has this particular skill, and this is important: if librarians don't actively facilitate access to the most accurate and complete information, if librarians don't anticipate informational needs and . . . respond to requests for information by providing direct answers to questions and by identifying and supplying, regardless of . . . form or location, those sources most suited to the users' requirements, these vital educational functions will simply go undone. (Schiller, 1965, 57)

The most recent manifestation of librarians' confused self-identity can be found in the end user training movement. A survey of the literature reveals how strongly the assumption that librarians are teachers with its resultant loss of identity has determined the response to end user access to online databases. Crawford (1984) begins an article in *Technical Services Quarterly* with the statement, "[t]he role of the reference librarian in academic libraries is one of teacher." Since "computers are an everyday fact of life," even found in homes and elementary schools, she concludes that "reference librarians must add the teaching of online bibliographic retrieval . . . to traditional bibliographic instruction" (Crawford, 1984, 51). Faibisoff and Hurych (1981, 352-53), in support of other authors they cite, point out "that database producers such as BIOSIS are returning to 'end user points of consumption' and are preparing programs to train and educate the end user in the searching process." "Librarians," they go on to insist, "should also play a role in this process just as they do in any form of bibliographic instruction." Richard Janke (1984, 16) from University of Ottawa, where an active Online After Six end user search service has been integrated into the reference department, warns libraries and information centers that if they fail to "offer some sort of end user searching, access to personal passwords or at least a counseling service for persons wishing to run their own searches, people will simply go ahead and get their own passwords to search on their own."

INSECURITY

Behind all of these adumbrations and bits of advice lurks an underlying insecurity: if librarians don't insert themselves into what is already an inevitable, well-advanced, and direct relationship between end users and online information these end users may completely forget librarians exist. Enormous quantities of time, energy, and pages in journals have been devoted to analyzing how librarians who have functioned as search intermediaries can remain essential in the face of the end user revolution. Many cling, hopefully and bravely, to Meadow's (1979, 52) assertion that, as end users become more experienced in online searching, a demand will be created "for the services of highly skilled professional search intermediaries to handle the 'top of the line' searches." And yet, librarians' insecurity about their continued role in end-user training and their hoped for expertise as "highly skilled professionals" contradicts totally instruction advocates' notion of the independent user.

The image of the "independent user" has long shimmered on the horizon, like Quixote's windmill, challenging librarians to don their teaching armor and charge. As the end user literature illustrates, this mystical user shimmers simultaneously as a desirable goal and as a frightening threat. Unable to resolve the "independent user" ambiguity by recognizing it for the misperception it is, librarians have invented a teaching role for themselves. By comfortably defining their primary responsibility as one of instructing patrons in the art of library use so that these then independent patrons will learn continuously and meet their information needs for the rest of their lives, librarians convince themselves that they are educationally invaluable.

The ideal of the "independent user" has it roots in democratic principles which promise opportunities for all and place great value on the self-made person. Nineteenth century liberal arts thinking serves as the primary influence with its emphasis on the realization of human potential. According to instruction proponents, both the teaching of the liberal arts and library bibliography have as their goal "increasing students' awareness of the products and processes of culture and [the development of] critical and independent thinking in preparation for lifelong self-directed learning" (Hopkins, 1983, 20). The goal of bibliographic instruction, and by extension the goal of the academic librarian, is not merely "the intelligent and effective use of libraries," as Lewis and Vincent (1983, 5) believe, but rather the development of "educable persons" (Frick, 1975, 12). The information retrieval process is correspondingly redefined. It is no longer the means to an end with that end being usable information. Rather the process itself becomes imbued with value. Bibliographic instruction is viewed as a discipline, another one of the liberal arts. This shift from BI as a process to BI as a discipline and liberal art is clear in Frick's (1982, 194) comment that the "fundamental truth" of undergraduate education is that "the manner in which you go about obtaining material for research . . . is more important in the long run than the material you obtain." According to Frick, librarians' responsibility rests with giving "students the ability to acquire their own information, thereby enabling them to become independent learners."

While the creation of independent users eager and able to define and meet their own information needs is a seemingly noble goal, it fails to account for two significant factors. First, it fails to recognize the complexity of the information retrieval function itself and the essential social responsibility that librarians have in this area. Secondly, it ignores that fact that there is little evidence that academia values the information retrieval process more than the resulting information. Herbert White (1983, 19) reminds us that

> the widespread premise that we do not help students very much because faculty do not want them helped is not really borne out by observation and experience. . . . If this were true, then faculty would to a far greater extent assure that the materials necessary for the self-education process were available, and they would coordinate far more closely with the library to map out a program of student library education for the course in question.

Faculty committed to developing the students' information retrieval skills, and creating independent library users would grade the literature search itself, rather than the resulting paper or project. Faculty devoted to teaching primarily "the manner in which you go about obtaining material for research" would exhibit considerably less concern about the quality of their institutional library's collection. As White states, ". . . for most academicians the accomplishment outweighs the concern about how the accomplishment was reached."

NEW GOALS

Having redefined the goals of librarianship, instruction advocates attempt to move academic librarianship always from information provision by characterizing it as passive and limiting. Carlson and Miller (1984, 484) typify the instruction perspective when they state that "no other approach enables the librarian to take such an active and effective part in the education role of the institution." "Teaching has done much," says Koyama (1983, 13), "to break down the passive image of the reference librarian who sits behind the desk waiting for patrons and providing service to those few who ask" (Koyama, JAL, p. 13). Kenney (1983, 7), typically extreme, describes reference service as nonacademic, "parasitic," and servant-like. "Active" teaching librarians connect passivity with the attempt to keep patrons dependent. They credit instruction with having permitted "the librarian to move away from a role of passive guardian and caretaker of the collection to that of active participant, teacher and information specialist" (Carlson & Miller, 1984, 484). Gone with instruction is the

> stereotypical prim and proper, practical-dressed and coiffured librarian of the past [who] was content to have both students and faculty dependent on her [sic] vast store of knowledge and facts tucked away in rather obscure reference sources that only she [sic] knew about. (Kenney, 1983, 7)

In her place is the "education librarian," actively involved in "information management education" which "aggressively" and "ambitiously" provides library clients with the "technology, skills, and decision making processes necessary for *independent* information retrieval and management" (Hubbard & Wilson, 1986, 15).

Certainly it is true that reference service has rarely been approached with the same degree of enthusiastic "activism" that library instruction has enjoyed. The way that the information retrieval process has been conducted has remained relatively unchanged since the days of Samuel Green. More attention needs to be devoted to exploring and expanding reference service. As White (1983, 18-19) points out, academic library operational philosophies are seldom geared toward supporting the search for knowledge, toward supporting the search for evidence to further conclusions already reached, toward "taking the burden of the work off the user's shoulders." But the label of "passive" with which instruction advocates have dismissed information provision fails to account for the fact that it is responsive. Considering the amount of space the literature devotes to methods of convincing recalcitrant faculty (and students) of the importance of bibliographic instruction and considering the commonly reported experience that only a very small percentage of end users trained to do their own searching actually continue to search on a regular basis (e.g., Buntrock & Valicenti, 1985; Walton & Dedert, 1983), this failure may be less of a dismissal and more of a defense. Unlike reference service, which directly responds to user needs and demands, bibliographic and end user instruction are generally undertaken in response to needs perceived only by librarians. The connection instruction advocates make between passivity and the ability to locate and utilize "obscure reference sources" to provide information to students and faculty ignores the reality that information and reference sources are not the same thing. The latter provides a means to obtain the former. Users look for information; it is librarians who need to know how to find the reference sources.

Extending the attack on the information provision model, Nielsen (1983, 188) equates the passivity of information provision with "intermediation" between patrons and information and claims that such an approach runs counter to "a critical social need for greater equity in the distribution of knowledge." Such ". . . attempts to foster a dependency relationship . . . between librarian and user may promise short term gain for librarianship but . . . , in the long run, [will be] counter to the interests of both librarians and users." He suggests a new role for librarians that could potentially side step both the self-image perils of the professor model and the power-hungry oppression of the specialized intermediary. Drawing on modes like the holistic health movement, models which share a "common characteristic that lies at the heart of the ideals of librarianship," Nielsen (1982, 189) encourages librarians "to rethink their relationships to nonexperts, and to work toward a sharing of knowledge rather than its opposite, the monopolization of knowledge implicit in the classic professional model." The term "disintermediation" (borrowed from the title of an article by Paul Hawken) conveniently describes this type of service in which experts give up their intermediation between information and the nonexperts who need to use it.

CONNECTION

The implied connection between "disintermediation" and library instruction is especially interesting in light of the quotations above from the end user training literature. Statements like, if librarians fail to "offer some sort of end user searching . . . people will simply go ahead and get their own passwords to search on their own" sound suspiciously power hungry. Admonitions that librarians duplicate database producers' efforts at training and educating end users by "play[ing] a role in this process just as they do in any form of bibliographic instruction" sound distinctively intermediatory. Services, like BRS After Dark or Dialog's Knowledge Index, designed specifically to connect end users directly with the information they need, do not require a librarian's intermediation. Where intermediation is essential, in complex, less user friendly services, such as CAS Online, well-planned, comprehensive, vendor-sponsored training programs introduce these services to end users and librarians alike, making extensive library-sponsored training programs unnecessary.

This does not mean that librarians cannot or should not advise users on the choice of a system or the subtleties of a search strategy, but labor intensive education programs aimed at inserting librarianship unnecessarily into a relationship between users and the information they seek neither achieves "disintermediation" nor fulfills a necessary educational function. The vendor-sponsored programs which exist emphasize basic searching mechanics. If librarians simply duplicate vendor efforts, they may do more harm than good by lending support to the widely marketed impression that finding information using computers is easy. The success of systems like INFOTRAC proves that some information can usually be found online with even the simplest approach. This apparent simplicity, however, belies the reality that computerized access developed because of information's proliferation and diversification which made it increasingly complex to locate. Computer access to information is an indication of complexity not a solution to it.

Instruction advocates have seen in increased complexity a rationale for independence. The more difficult information becomes to find, the more, it seems, users ought to be able to find it themselves. Tucker (1984, 23), for example, borrows from the educational philosophies of Ralph Waldo Emerson to argue that the "importance of independence in library research is underscored by the fact that the structure of knowledge in the subject disciplines and in bibliographic systems is becoming increasingly complex." Experienced end users, however, disagree for their significant exposure to computerized information has given them an understanding resembling that of librarians: the more layers that exist between users and information, the less likely it is that most people will find what they need on their own. Librarians' most effective response to information's complexity, and, therefore, to the widespread use of online systems, is to foster the kind of dependent awareness that one seasoned end user searcher described, to a special librarian, as characteristic of him or herself: "I know enough now to know how much I don't know and how much trouble I can get into" (Hunter, 1984, 40). Taking Nielsen's (1982) advice to "rethink their relationships to nonexperts" to heart, librarians must redirect their efforts away from teaching users how to find their own information and toward informing users about the types of information specialists can provide. Independence is valuable only to those who clearly understand its limitations.

In light of the fact that movements like holistic health place value on the sharing of information, it is difficult to argue with Nielsen's choice of models for librarianship. The way in which he appears to equate "disintermediation" and independence, however, bears closer examination. A patient treated by a physician practicing holistic health is an acknowledged expert concerning the nature of the ailment for which treatment was sought. The physician is an acknowledged expert concerning methods of treatment. Through the treatment process, these two experts exchange what they know. Each emerges from the exchange more knowledgeable than before, the physician with more understanding of ailments and the patient with more ability to care for him or herself. Neither expert can function independently from the other, their relationship, rather, is one of mutual dependence.

This same mutual dependence underlies the provision of information to library patrons, whether at the reference desk or through the process of an online search. A patron is an expert concerning his or her information need. A librarian is an expert concerning how to utilize the complex bibliographic apparatus to locate the needed information. Through the process of information provision, these two experts exchange what they know. As a result, the patron obtains more information, possibly learns more about how such information is found, and perhaps develops additional information needs. The librarian knows more about how specific needs can be met through the bibliographic structure.

MUTUAL DEPENDENCE

It is the mutually useful dependency of this exchange of expertise to which Sayles (1980, 199) refers when he points out that "librarian and patron roles are clearly defined: the former finds; the latter uses." Wilson (1979, 155) describes librarians' unique expertise as "an in-depth understanding of the graphic record as a structure, an entity," White (1983, 21-22) calls it "a knowledge of how to access [a wide variety of] literature," Shera (1955, 8) describes it as the responsibility to make available or retrievable "any document or record, for any given purpose, at any given time." It is in the context of providing information that librarians can best offer the user the expertise which is their own and best allow library users to express and to utilize the particular expertise that is theirs. It is the mutual dependency of this expertise exchange which best fosters the "disintermediation" Nielsen so strongly recommends.

By turning their attention from information provision and toward instruction, academic librarians have ultimately done a disservice to themselves and to their clientele. With much of the energy and creativity of public services staff directed elsewhere, relatively few attempts have been made to move information services beyond a traditional reliance on the reference desk. Future efforts must be directed to exploring and expanding methods of matching patron needs with the information which will meet these needs. Librarians must take seriously their mission to make available or retrievable "any document or record, for any given purpose, at any given time," and turn away from the quixotic self-deception which has characterized the profession in recent years.

Don Quixote returned home from his adventures tired and defeated and soon died, a victim of his knightly misperceptions. Ironically and tragically, before he ever changed his name, donned his armor, and mounted his bony horse, poor, elderly Alonzo Quixano had already possessed the high-mindedness, noble-heartedness, and courageous nature essential to chivalric knighthood. His most important misperception, the motivating force behind his fruitless quest, was his failure to recognize, understand, and appreciate the valuable qualities that were originally his own.

Academic librarians who call themselves teachers have, like old Alonzo, failed to recognize, understand, and utilize the skills and qualities that they possess. Overlooking their uniquely valuable ability to provide information, they have insisted that library users be educated to provide their own. Ironically and tragically, these teacher-librarians with their new names, their instructional armor, and their trusty, professorial steeds, have unwittingly "set conditions upon the direct availability of information" (Schiller, 1965, 60). The point is not that librarians should never be involved in instruction. Some people will want to do their own online searching and/or will want to become familiar with complex bibliographic and reference sources in their own and related disciplines, and some people will want librarians to teach them these skills. But defining instruction as librarians' reason for being deflects an information profession away from what it ought to be doing, what it is able to do best, and what it does better than anyone else.

Librarians must accept the truth that successful researchers, teachers, and students manage their accomplishments with little or no understanding of the organization of information. Librarians must face the reality that independently curious and knowledge-seeking individuals are characterized by an awareness that a great deal of information exists which can be located rather than by a knowledge of the mechanics of locating it. With these truths and realities in mind, librarians can abandon their pursuit of windmills and begin to appreciate, expand, and make available the valuable qualities that have always been their own.

REFERENCES

Buntrock, R. E. & A. K. Valicenti. "End-User Searching: The Amoco Experience." *Journal of Chemical Information and Computer Science* 25(1985):415-419.

Carlson, D. & R. H. Miller, "Librarians and Teaching Faculty: Partners in Bibliographic Instruction." *College and Research Libraries* 45(November 1984): 483-491.

Crawford, P. J. "Computer Searching: Teaching Patrons How To Do It." *Technical Services Quarterly* 1,no.4(1984): 51-53.

Faibisoff, S. G. & J. Hurych. "Is There a Future For the End User in Online Bibliographic Searching?" *Special Libraries* (October 1981): 347-355.

Frick, E. "Information Structure and Bibliographic Instruction." *Journal of Academic Librarianship* 1(September 1975): 12-14.

Frick, E. "Teaching Information Structure: Turning Dependent Researchers into Self-Teachers." In *Theories of bibliographic education*, edited by K. Strauch & C. Oberman, 193-208. New York: R.R. Bowker, 1982.

Green, S. S. "Personal Relations Between Librarians and Readers." *American Library Journal* 1,no.1(1876): 74-81.

Hopkins, F. L. "Bibliographic Instruction As a Liberal Art: An Application of Patrick Wilson's Theory of Pragmatic Bibliography." In *Back to the books: Bibliographic instruction and the theory of information sources*, edited by R. Atkinson, 15-30. Educational Resources Information Center (ERIC), #ED232 655, 1983. Microfiche.

Hopkins, F. L. "A Century of Bibliographic Instruction: The Historical Claim to Professional and Academic Legitimacy." *College and Research Libraries* 43(May 1982): 192-198.

Hubbard, A. & B. Wilson. "An Integrated Information Management Education Program . . . Defining a New Role For Librarians Helping End-Users." *Online* 10(March 1986): 15-23.

Hunter, J. A. "When Your Patrons Want To Search—The Library As Advisor To Endusers . . . A Compendium of Advice and Tips." *Online* 8(May 1984): 36-41.

Janke, R. V. "Online After Six: End User Searching Comes of Age." *Online* 8(November 1984): 15-29.

Kenney, D. J. "Where There Is No Vision." *Journal of Academic Librarianship* 9(March 1983): 7-8.

Koyama, J. T. "Bibliographic Instruction and the Role of the Academic Librarian." *Journal of Academic Librarianship* 9(March 1983): 12-13.

Lewis, D. W. & C. P. Vincent. "Reactions To the Think Tank Recommendations: An Initial Response." *Journal of Academic Librarianship* 9(March 1983): 4-14.

Meadow, C. T. "Online Searching and Computer Programming: Some Behavioral Similarities (Or . . . Why End Users Will Eventually Take Over the Terminal)" *Online* 3(January 1979): 49-52.

Nielsen, B. "Teacher or Intermediary: Alternative Professional Models in the Information Age." *College and Research Libraries* 43(May 1982): 183-191.

Roberts, A. "The Changing Role of the Academic Instruction Librarian." *Catholic Library World* 51(February 1980): 283-285.

Roberts, A. B. "Personnel and Training For Reference Work." In *The reference function of the library*, edited by P. Butler. Chicago: University of Chicago Press, 1943.

Sayles, J. "An Opinion About Library Instruction" *Southeastern Librarian* 30(Winter 1980): 198-201.

Schiller, A. R. "Reference Service: Instruction or Information." *Library Quarterly* 35(January 1965): 52-60.

Shera, J. "The Role of the College Librarian—A Reappraisal." In *Library instructional integration on the college level*, Report of the 40th conference of Eastern College Libraries, Association of College and Research Libraries (ACRL) Monographs #13, 5-13. Chicago: ACRL, 1955.

Stoan, S. K. "Research and Library Skills: An Analysis and Interpretation." *College and Research Libraries* 45(March 1984): 99-109.

Tucker, J. M. "Emerson's Library Legacy: Concepts of Bibliographic Instructions." In *Increasing the teaching role of academic libraries*, edited by T. Kirk, 15-23. San Francisco: Jossey-Bass, 1984 (New Directions for Teaching and Learning, no. 18).

Walton, K. R. & P. L. Dedert. "Experiences at Exxon in Training End-Users To Search Technical databases Online." *Online* 7(September 1983): 42-50.

White, H. "The Role of Reference Service in the Mission of the Academic Library." In *Reference service: A perspective*, edited by Sul H. Lee, 17-30. Ann Arbor, MI: Pierian Press, 1983.

Wilson, P. "Librarians as Teachers: The Study of an Organization Fiction." *Library Quarterly* 49, no. 1(1979): 146-162.

To See Ourselves
as Others See Us:
A Cooperative, Do-It-Yourself
Reference Accuracy Study

Eleanor Jo Rodger
Jane Goodwin

The staff, administration, and Trustees of the Fairfax County
Public Library (FCPL) believe that the public they serve should
receive the best possible library service. Evaluation of the various
components of this service is an ongoing activity, coordinated by
staff of the Office of Evaluation and Information Development.
Many aspects of the information services provided by FCPL had
been assessed in recent years. We knew how much information service was provided, by whom, for whom, and what kinds of resources were used to answer questions. The time came, then, to
answer a basic and touchy question, "How well are we handling the
questions the public asks?"

Fortunately there is a well documented, but seldom implemented,
methodology available to our profession—unobtrusive measurement of reference accuracy. Beginning with the work of Terence
Crowley and Tom Childers in the early seventies, and refined during the last decade, models have been developed for examining the
quality of reference service based on answers given to proxies assigned to initiate "typical" reference transactions. Crowley and
Childers wanted to test the relationship of reference accuracy to

Eleanor Jo Rodger was Coordinator of Evaluation and Information Development at the
Fairfax (VA) County Public Library at the time of this study. She is presently Chief, State
Network Services at the Enoch Pratt Free Library, Baltimore, MD.
Jane Goodwin is Coordinator of Evaluation and Information Development at the Fairfax
County Public Library, Fairfax, Virginia.

135

conventional measures of libraries in order to judge the value of the conventional measures in predicting the quality of the service available. Their studies, and those done since ". . . consistently show how far short of perfection public and academic libraries fall."[1] We know the dismal statistics which showed over and over again that various publics seem to have a 50-60 percent chance of receiving a complete, correct answer to questions asked at their libraries. At FCPL we assumed we were better than that—one always does! The motivations for our study were to learn if we really were better, and more importantly, to discover specific things we could do to improve our information services.

The history of unobtrusive measurement is primarily a history of studies done *to* libraries rather than *with* libraries.[2] There have been some recent more participative efforts. In a recent statewide study in Maryland, administrators of library systems agreed to have their libraries included in an unobtrusive reference test designed to improve public services.[3] However, staff of affected libraries have had limited roles in the design of such studies, and no role in their implementation. We believed that the best climate for change would be created if FCPL staff were involved in the design, data collection, data analysis, and development of recommendations from an unobtrusive reference accuracy study. The challenge was to develop a study methodology which would allow this high level of staff involvement, but which would not compromise the necessary unobtrusive nature of the process.[4]

METHODOLOGY

Decisions about the methodology for this reference accuracy study were based on a number of assumptions. First and foremost was that the rationale for conducting this evaluation study was to improve the reference service available to users of the Fairfax County Public Library. This meant that staff needed to know where the problems were in service delivery, and then needed to be willing to plan and work for improvements. To accept the study findings as valid, staff needed to believe the methodology was both fair and appropriate. Acceptance was more likely to happen if some staff participated in study planning and design.

The second managerial assumption was that whatever was found to be wrong with FCPL's reference services represented a problem for the library system, not occasions for blaming individuals whose reference transaction skills were caught by the study sample. For example, if staff members gave out-dated information it meant there was either a materials problem or a staff training problem. Both of these are system rather than individual staff member problems. Staff were assured that no attempts would be made to link individuals to particular test transactions. This understanding of where "blame" was to be placed reflected the administration's conviction about where the responsibility actually lay and helped staff to feel less apprehensive about the study.

The third assumption was that if the study were to have an evaluation component, i.e., to make judgments about the reference services offered by FCPL, clearly defined system guidelines for information services should be the standards against which performance was measured. New, staff-developed "Information Services Guidelines" had recently been introduced, making the evaluation study a timely move to see if the guidelines were understood and were being followed.

While there was substantial administrative support for the reference accuracy study, there was no new money available for this project. This meant no paid consultant could be hired, no professional interviewers could be used, and no computer time could be bought for data analysis. This severe limitation on resources, together with the previously mentioned assumption about the value of staff involvement, led us to consider doing the study with neighboring library systems, using staff from all systems as unobtrusive callers as well as study designers and date analyzers. Library systems in neighboring counties of Washington, D.C., were invited to consider participating in the study. Administrators from the Montgomery County (MD) Department of Libraries and the Arlington County (VA) Public Library indicated a willingness to explore the idea of sharing staff time and other resources to conduct the study.

While the initial impetus to cooperate came from an acknowledgement of the constraints under which the study must be conducted, it soon became clear that there were many opportunities inherent in the cooperative, do-it-yourself approach. Staff in the three participating systems serve similar clientele, but had little history of sharing problems, experiences, or resources. Involvement in the study provided many occasions for such informal sharing. More importantly, acting as unobtrusive callers would give participating staff the experience of seeing themselves as others see them. The longer the planning committee worked, the more excited we became about the benefits which would come from doing the study ourselves. The general approach of conducting a cooperative study involving staff at all stages moved from being regarded as a necessity to being considered a virtue.

THE PROCESS

A planning committee consisting of the administrative person responsible for information services and two or three additional reference librarians from each system began meeting in the fall of 1983. This committee's task was the planning and oversight of the project. The focus of the early meetings was on identifying and clarifying broad issues involved in the study.

Scope

It was decided that the study should be limited to an evaluation of telephone reference service. None of the participating libraries had sufficient staff time available to send people to other systems to act as unobtrusive walk-in library users. The study was to be conducted at the larger branch libraries in all systems. Mini branches and kiosks were excluded because their role in the systems was primarily to supply browsers with materials, not to do reference work. Since the number of participating branches varied substantially from system to system, each library agreed to contribute one unobtrusive caller for each branch they included in the study.

The planning committee decided that each system would evaluate performance of its own staff based on its existing information services guidelines, rather than spend a lot of time arguing over what was the "right" way to do reference. This meant, for example, that staff from the Fairfax County Public Library would lose points if they put a caller on "hold" for more than two minutes, since that was the limit specified in their guidelines. No such rule existed for staff from the other two systems so they would not lose points for such an action. We also agreed that each system would own its own data at the conclusion of the study. No attempt would be made to compare results. This was to be a cooperative effort, not a competitive one!

Planners were able to agree on a general framework for understanding reference service. We all affirmed that

> Good reference service is given when library users receive correct, appropriate and prompt answers to their questions, and are dealt with in a courteous, professional manner.

> The quality of reference service is a function of four variables:
> — quality/appropriateness of library's resources;
> — staffing levels;
> — staff skill in using resources available;
> — staff skill in conducting reference interviews.

The study was designed to gather information about how often good reference service was delivered, and to indicate which of the identified variables needed attention to improve services.

We decided to conduct the study for a five month period. The rationale for this fairly long testing period was that staff would probably try to be on their best professional behavior since they would know the study was taking place. Either this resolve would wear off during the early part of the study time, or the changes in behavior motivated by the test would become fixed and would become "normal" ways of providing reference service, in which case our goal of improving service would be partially met.

Each participating library would be asked twenty-five test questions during the study period, all designed to be as typical of regular patron questions as possible. Twenty-five was less a magic number statistically than it was a workable number practically.

The questions for the study were developed by the planning committee — together with right answers. The questions included fifteen ready reference questions, five in-system referrals and five that needed negotiation.

Up to four variations were developed for almost every question so staff wouldn't become suspicious about repeated identical questions. For example, one ready reference question was, "What is the current exchange rate for the English pound?" Variations requested exchange rates for the German mark, Greek drachma, French franc, and Japanese yen.

The final stage of study design was to create an assignment matrix which indicated which proxy would call which library to ask which question during which week. Attempts were made to ensure that the same question was not asked in the same system during the same week, lest the unobtrusiveness be compromised. We developed and tested call log forms. Then we were ready to begin.

IMPLEMENTATION

A joint training session was held for callers from all three library systems. Fourteen FCPL information services staff volunteers were selected as callers because we had fourteen branches participating in the study. The planning committee explained the design of the study and the goals that guided each system's participation in the project. We carefully reviewed the use of the caller's log sheets designed to record verbatim the entire telephone transaction between the caller and the library. Role playing exercises gave proxies experience using the forms and an opportunity to ask questions about problems that arose during the practice. The joint training also encouraged a spirit of cooperation among proxies as they talked with their colleagues from the other participating libraries.

FCPL coordinated the sending of weekly letters to proxies with assigned questions. Several guidelines provided the framework for scheduling callers and questions:

- No proxy was assigned to call his/her own system. Whenever possible, the same question was asked of all branches of a system by the same proxy. This insured some uniformity in the way questions were asked throughout a single system.
- Each proxy asked as few different questions as possible. Our proxies were information services staff working in participating libraries and we wanted them to be familiar with as few of the questions as possible.
- A proxy was assigned no more than three calls per week to be made within seven days of receiving the assignment letter. The scheduling matrix gave each caller some free weeks over the five month period.
- All responses were sent to FCPL to coordinate and hold until the calling was completed. When all calls were finished in

mid-July, 1984, their own transaction logs were sent to each participating library system for coding.

When the calling was completed, a joint training session was held for the coders of the response sheets. The planning committee had researched the correct answers and sources to all questions used for the study. Based on their library's procedures for handling reference questions, staff from each system were taught to code the data from the transaction logs for accuracy, correct procedure, and transaction atmosphere. Six information services staff coded the 350 FCPL responses. To insure as much consistency as possible, an individual coder handled all answers to a single question. The FCPL coders worked together so that problems could be resolved quickly and uniformly.

FINDINGS

Accuracy

We found that FCPL information Services staff do very well answering ready reference kinds of direct questions, less well responding to questions that need escalation. Surprisingly, we did not answer most of the questions about FCPL services correctly or completely.

Based on FCPL's "Information Services Guidelines," the following four point accuracy scale was used to judge the correctness of answers given to the questions:

4 — Correct answer with source cited or appropriate referral made

3 — Correct information but no source cited

2 — Partially correct answer but incomplete

1 — Wrong information — for any reason

Table 1 summarizes FCPL's accuracy performance during the study.

Using the verbatim records of the calls, we were able to analyze the kinds of errors made. Many of the incomplete answers were given to escalator questions that needed negotiation to determine the information really wanted by the caller. An example of this kind of question would be, "Can you find me a telephone number in Colorado Springs?" Staff should escalate, asking for precisely what number the caller needed. The caller would respond, "I need to call the United States Olympic Committee headquartered in Colorado Springs." The staff generally answered the initial question with a negative answer about the lack of a phone book for Colorado Springs without asking the caller for more information. After discussing the query with the caller, the staff person would have discovered the need for a number that could be found in various association directories.

The other major group of incomplete answers were given in response to questions about services and resources offered by FCPL. Examples of these questions are, "Can I get films at your library?" and "Do you have the Federal Register?" Staff tended to respond "yes" or "no" directly to the question without giving the caller more information about the service or providing an appropriate referral.

The proportion of "wrong" answers was small. Table 2 shows that staff failed to deal with the question in twelve transactions. This kind of error usually results from poor skills in conducting the reference interview. Other kinds of errors accounted for only six percent of the responses. This small percentage did not seem to indicate any special attention was necessary.

A branch could score 100 points if all 25 questions were answered completely and correctly. System wide, the average FCPL branch score was 77 points, with a range of 64 to 90 points among the branches. The median score was 78 points.

Calculated for the system as a whole, the average score per question was 3.09 based on the four point accuracy scale. An average score per question ranged from a high of 3.6 to a low of 2.56. The median of these branch average scores per question was 3.12.

Table 1

Accuracy Summary

Accuracy of the Answer	Accuracy Code	Number of Responses	Percentage of Responses
Correct/complete with source	4	196	56%
Correct/complete without source	3	18	5%
Incomplete	2	104	30%
Wrong information	1	32	9%

Table 2

Analysis of Errors for Questions Coded "Wrong"

Error Type	Number of Responses	Percentage of Total Responses
Did not deal with the question	12	3%
Incorrect referral	6	2%
Unnecessary referral	5	1%
Old information	5	1%
Wrong information	3	1%
Question misunderstood	1	1

Transactional Atmosphere

A second part of the Cooperative Reference Accuracy Study dealt with the transactional atmosphere or ambience of the interaction between the caller and the staff person. The planning committee began with a definition of good reference service which included a specification that users be ". . . dealt with in a courteous professional manner." We wanted to evaluate informational transactions in light of this conviction about good service.

On the log sheets, callers were asked to evaluate three factors about the telephone call.

1. How easy it was to understand the staff person on the telephone.
2. Their perception of the librarian's level of attention to their question.
3. The manner of the staff person in handling the call.

We found that 89% of the time FCPL staff were easy to understand. Callers rated the staff that initially answered the telephone in the branch as well as the staff that dealt with the question. To rate the librarian's level of attention to their call. Proxies used a three point scale. For 82% of the responses, callers indicated that staff seemed to have given a high level of attention to their question.

Callers were offered these seven phrases to describe the manner of the librarian who actually responded to their question:

1. Professional – courteous, friendly
2. Professional – courteous, reserved
3. Brusque, terse
4. Critical
5. Confused, uncertain
6. Distracted
7. Other – please specify

While there was no preferential ranking of behaviors indicated by the order the phrases were listed on the form, the first two were considered acceptable while the others were not. As shown in Table 3, 86% of the callers judged the librarian's manner to be professional, courteous and either friendly or reserved.*

MANAGEMENT RESPONSE TO FINDINGS

The results of FCPL's participation on the Cooperative Reference Accuracy Study were shared with staff in several ways. A full report of systemwide findings and recommendations was written by the Coordinator of Evaluation and Information Development including the questions and forms used during the study.[5] A presentation of the report was made to the Board of Trustees and to the library management staff.

A detailed report of each branch's performance was prepared for each branch manager. Individual branch results were not published. When the computer generated statistics were available, the heads of information services from all participating branches assembled to review the printouts. Perhaps the most important benefit gained from this session was to relieve anxiety among some branch personnel; the same kinds of errors were made by all branches. This also confirmed our preliminary assumption that identified problems were system problems, not individual staff problems. The branch detailed statistics verified that staff were adhering to the procedures presented in the "Information Services Guidelines."

---

*The total number of responses was greater than 350 for this measure because call-backs were coded as separate transactions.

Table 3

Manner of the Librarian

	Number of Responses	Percent of Responses
Professional--courteous, friendly	216	61%
Professional--courteous, reserved	88	25%
Brusque, terse	15	4%
Critical	0	0%
Confused, uncertain	18	5%
Distracted	5	1%
Other	13	4%
Total	355[1]	100%

[1]The total number of responses was greater than 350 for this measure because call-backs were coded as separate transactions.

The results of the study clearly indicated that we needed a concise, easy-to-use compilation of facts about services and special resources offered by the Fairfax County Public Library. The System Information File (SIF) was subsequently developed by a task force of information services staff. Copies of the SIF were distributed to branches in April, 1985.

It was also apparent from the Cooperative Reference Accuracy Study that FCPL staff needed refresher training in conducting a complete reference interview. Telephone questions are always more challenging to negotiate than face-to-face transactions. When talking with a telephone library user, staff do not have the body language clues to follow that are a part of a face-to-face transaction. FCPL has acquired the Library Video Network training tape. *Have We Answered Your Question?* to use with staff. The Regional Information Services librarians prepared a study guide to accompany the video that emphasizes aspects of the reference interview that need particular attention among staff in this system. FCPL staff have difficulty remembering to conclude reference transactions with a closure question or statement such as "Have we answered your question?" or "Is there anything else that we can help you find?" We find it awkward taking time to ask the patron to determine when the transaction has been successfully completed when there are several other library users waiting for help with their questions. We continue to search for ways to help staff conduct a complete reference interview.

A third result of FCPL participation in the Cooperative Reference Accuracy Study is the continuing effort to review and, when necessary, revise the "Information Services Guidelines." Written by information services staff in 1983, the guidelines were new and fresh in the minds of staff when the Accuracy Study was conducted. As we stated above, the results of the Accuracy Study demonstrated that staff conduct reference transactions in accordance with the guidelines. In the past few months the Regional Information Services Librarians have visited all FCPL branches to discuss the guidelines. These interviews have served to remind the staff of procedures and have resulted in suggestions for changes in the guidelines. With continued evaluation and review, the guidelines will remain timely and useful.

CONCLUSIONS

The cooperative approach to unobtrusive measurement of reference accuracy worked extremely well for the Fairfax County Public Library. With no new money and a fairly small investment of staff time we were able to obtain a clear and helpful picture of the telephone reference service we were providing, and to know what steps could be taken to improve our performance. The greatest benefit, however, was that the cooperative effort provided the opportunity for information services staff to pose as patrons, to hear themselves as others hear them. Their experiences led to much self-evaluation. Comments like, "I never realized how awful 'bye-bye' sounds." "I now know I need to talk more slowly when patrons are trying to write down what I'm telling them," and "My, it sounds rude to say 'wait a minute' and I know I've done that," were common as librarians gathered to discuss the study. The climate for making needed changes was in place when the data analysis was completed. The administrative commitment to follow through on the study recommendations has been evident, and has led to better public service.

This approach to evaluating the quality of reference service may prove useful in other library settings. Conditions which would seem necessary for successful implementation include the presence of several libraries in a limited geographical area (or money for long distance calls!), a willingness on the part of other libraries to cooperatively plan and implement such a study, the existence of reference guidelines, and a commitment on the part of the administrators of participating libraries to use the information developed to improve reference service. With a little flexibility and enthusiasm and some basic knowledge of study design, all the other details can be worked out. Most reference librarians care deeply about providing excellent public service. Participative unobtrusive reference accuracy studies are effective tools for helping them pinpoint areas of strength and weakness so they can move closer to perfection. In the words of Terence Crowley:

> Until librarians deal effectively as a profession with the many and seemingly endless sources of error in reference work, we will remain passive observers of popular culture. Some of us will provide timely, appropriate, and consistently accurate information, but the institution in which we work will not be fulfilling its potential in the information age.[6]

NOTES

1. Terence Crowley, "Half Right Reference: Is It True." *RQ* vol. 25, no. 1, Fall 1985, p. 67.

2. Crowley, *RQ*, pp. 59-68.

3. Ralph Gers and Lillie J. Seward, "Improving Reference Performance: Results of a Statewide Study," *Library Journal,* November, 1985, pp. 32-35.

4. Thanks go to Tom Childers who was a helpful unofficial guide as we worked out the many details.

5. Copies of this full report are available. Requests for *Reference Accuracy at the Fairfax County Public Library: A Report of a Cooperative Telephone Information Service Study, 1984,* should be submitted to the Metropolitan Washington Library Council, 1875 Eye Street, N.W., Suite 200, Washington, DC 20006-5454. The cost is $8.50 per copy.

6. Crowley, *RQ*, p. 67.

Bibliographic Control
of Conservative Periodicals

H. Rorlich

Periodicals in general, socio-political periodicals in particular, have become indispensable as both teaching and research tools.

The importance of periodicals in a library is the fact they reach a broad audience while providing timely and prompt responses to specific political, social and economic issues.

A scholar, or researcher has a different approach to articles than that of other readers. In looking for library materials, scholars usually start with bibliographic references provided by monographs. General user, however, begins with indexes, or most often, resorts to the help of reference librarian.

The existence of adequate bibliographic identification resources of periodicals insures the availability and access of periodical titles to a broad audience and enhances the user's ability to solve information needs fully and expeditiously.

Periodical bibliographic control, as the identification of appropriate periodical titles, the indexing of specific information contained in a given journal or magazine, as well as the provision of descriptive bibliographic information about the title, date, volume and pagination enables the user to locate the source in which the sought after information is contained. Within this context, the abstracting and indexing services are important links in the chain of communications between the source of information—journal, magazine, newsletter or any other type of periodical—and the ultimate consumer of the information, the library user.

The author is at the University of Southern California Social Work Library, University Park, Los Angeles, CA 90007. The article is partially based on the report, *Conservative Periodicals: Where Are They*, prepared by the author for the Propaganda Research Institute, Montebello, CA, August, 1985.

OBJECTIVES

The purpose of this article is two fold. First, to assess the bibliographic coverage of a selected number of conservative journals and magazines by examining some of the well known and widely used indexes and abstracts. Secondly, to stimulate debate among editors and publishers of general reference tools and reference librarians in order to make much needed improvements in bibliographic representation of periodicals expressing conservatives' views.

Many scholars from a variety of fields and disciplines have stressed the vital importance of the availability of information emphasizing the value of indexes and abstracts for how information is used and how it comes into library or information services.[1]

In today's complex world, there is an imperious need to continuously improve communication, perhaps most of all in the political arena. Periodicals of both conservative and liberal persuasion which focus on a comparative analysis of the political and social climate are viable sources of information for readers situated at the opposite ends of the political spectrum. Rochell notes that: "given the public's need for information as a tool for survival, personal achievement, and cultural enhancement it seems obvious that information must be widely available."[2] Consequently, even the finest collection of periodicals is of little use in an academic or public library unless access to and use of stored information is facilitated by appropriate reference works.

The responsibility for selection of reference materials is usually shared by the reference librarian and the bibliographer. They select those reference aids which best identify the information output, organize and describe its content.

The indexing and abstracting works commercially produced are expected to ensure the recording of descriptive, subject, and analytical information concerning a periodical publication and the organization of that information.

SETTING

The last decade has witnessed a remarkable growth of the conservative movement which gained not only in size but also in self-awareness and political status. In 1950 Lionel Trilling, one of the America's leading intellectuals, made his famous remark that "in the United States at this time liberalism is not only the dominant but even the sole intellectual tradition. For it is the plain fact that there are no conservative or reactionary ideas in general circulation."[3]

In the 1970s, however, Trilling's remark lost its validity. A visible shift toward a more conservative political climate become evident. It was the result of often ignored or under-publicized efforts of scholars, college and high-school teachers, literary and artistic personalities, activists and average men and women. At the beginning of the '70s, quietly, in an unprecedented move, they began to share an overt sense of opposition against liberal tendencies of the past decade.

Nevertheless, socio-political journals and magazines professing conservative ideas received little attention from the editors and publishers of indexes, abstracts, and bibliographies. In assessing the bibliographic coverage of conservative periodicals, evidence suggests, that most of the commercially produced general indexes and abstracts in one way or another still discriminate against conservative journals and magazines. Obviously, the selection of journals and magazines to be indexed or abstracted is highly subjective.

PURPOSE

The primary purpose of the research reported in this article was to examine the frequency of bibliographic identification of conservative Periodicals contained in commercially produced reference works.

The reason for undertaking the study was the existing blatant discrepancy between bibliographic coverage accorded to leftist periodicals and that of conservative press.

Radical and leftist publications are prominently and favorably featured. Conservatives' publications, however, "enjoy" a rather restrictive bibliographic access, thus being denied fair and equal bibliographic treatment.

Less than $3\frac{1}{2}$ of all conservative journals, magazines and newsletters are indexed, listed or abstracted. Since "abstracting and indexing is a key segment of the growing information industry,"[4] one would presume that index and abstract services would transcend political boundaries to provide a non-biased bibliographic guidance for all library users. The restrictive bibliographic control of the conservative press also contradicts the very Policies and Procedures of the American Bibliographical Center, which defines the major goals of A & I services as to:

> first, provide the researcher access to a comprehensive selection of periodical literature in the field. Second, to assist the researcher in deciding whether the contents of the articles abstracted should be read in full. Third, to provide summaries of ideas, concepts, and interpretations so that it is frequently unnecessary to read articles in full. Fourth, to provide a timely reference service for updating course materials and planning curricula in the field. Fifth, to provide the specialist a means of surveying literature in the field and of keeping abreast of development in other fields of interest and specialization. [5]

With few exceptions, however, conservative journals and magazines are denied the bibliographic coverage stated by the ABC's Policies and Procedures.

The recurring imbalance in the bibliographic availability of conservative periodicals neutralizes the primary purpose of general reference works which are expected to provide the user with an objective organization and description of the information content over a range of political periodicals.

METHODOLOGY

In order to assess the present bibliographic status of conservative periodicals, the following indexes, abstracts and directories were examined: *ABC Political Science and Human Resources Abstracts, Abridged Readers' Guide to Periodical Literature, Arts and Humanities Index, Ayer Directory of Newspapers, Magazines and Trade Publications.*

The Social Sciences Index, Popular Periodical Index, Public Affairs Information Service Bulletin, Readers' Guide to Periodical Literature, Standard Periodical Directory. Two other works, *From Radical Left to Extreme Right,* a three-volume work by Robert H. Muller and Theodore Jurgen and Janet M. Spahn, as well as William A. Katz's *Magazines For Librarians* were also examined as being relevant to the topic covered.

The surveyed reference works are among well-established tools in the field. They provide an authoritative outlet for the dissemination of information among a broad range of users, reference librarians, library educators, scholars, researchers and average library users.

The twelve conservative journals, magazines and newsletters chosen to investigate their bibliographic exposure in the above mentioned reference sources, vary in scope and range of conservatism with regard to political, social and moral issues. According to their profile and frequency of publication, they were divided into five separate categories.

First, includes journals and magazines dealing with long-range political, social and moral concerns, published quarterly. These were *The Journal of Contemporary Studies,* edited by Patrick Glynn and Walter J. Lammi, published by the Institute for Contemporary Studies; *Modern Age: A Conservative Review,* issued by The Foundation for Foreign Affairs under the editorship of David E. Collins; *New Guard,* edited by R. Cort Kirkwood; *Policy Review,* distributed by the Heritage Foundation, edited by Adam Meyerson, and *Public Interest,* a publication of National Affairs, Inc., Irwin Kristol, editor.

Second, includes monthly publications such as: *The American Spectator*, edited by R. Emmett Tyrrell, Jr; *Commentary* published by the American Jewish Committee and edited by Norman Podhoretz; and *Conservative Digest*, published by Viguerie Communications, edited by Lee Edwards.

Third category is represented by the well-known byweekly journal of opinion, *National Review*, edited by William F. Buckley, Jr. *Human Events*, published by Human Events, Inc., a weekly publication edited by Thomas S. Winter, belongs to the fourth category.

The fifth category includes two bimonthly newsletters: *The AIM Report*, published by Accuracy in Media, Inc., and *The American Sentinel*, published by Phillips Publishing, Inc., edited by John Seiler.

FINDINGS

The study surveyed twelve conservative periodicals for their bibliographic treatment by ten major reference works. When political views of individual editors or publishers were the sole selection criterion, library users were automatically referred away from conservative journals and magazines because these resources were discriminated against in most of the surveyed commercial indexes, abstracts, directories and bibliographies.

Most of the surveyed conservative periodicals were not given an appropriate bibliographic identification. Inadequate bibliographic description of the twelve conservative periodicals emerged as the best evidence of the biased reference treatment received by the conservative press as a whole. The exclusion of certain journals and magazines from the general indexes and abstracts hampers the efforts of library professionals who objectively evaluate the needs of their libraries. At the same time it justifies the often invoked policy of acquiring only those periodical titles that are indexed or listed in commercially produced reference works. Adequate bibliographic representation of the surveyed conservative periodicals is still to be desired.

The findings only increased dissatisfaction with the degree of identification and access to the information content contained in these periodicals.

Commentary and *National Review* were the only two of the neoconservative and conservative periodicals to get the widest bibliographic coverage. Since both publications mothered new avenues of national communication their bibliographic exposure should go undisputed. Both, Podhoretz's *Commentary* and Buckley's *National Review* were indexed by the *Readers' Guide to Periodical Literature, Humanities Index, P.A.I.S., Arts and Humanities* and *Citation Index,* and *Popular Periodical Index. Modern Age: A Conservative Review*, considered by Nash as "the principal quarterly of the intellectual Right," was mentioned in the *Humanities Index*, and received only a selective coverage in *P.A.I.S.* [6] *Human Events*, a perceptive observer of Washington political scene was totally ignored by all surveyed reference works.

Conservative Digest was listed only in the periodical Directories of Standard and Ayer. The anti-conservative attitude pervasive in the majority of index and abstract services determined the treatment of other conservative publications such as *Policy Review, Public Interest* and the *Journal of Contemporary Studies.* Their bibliographic coverage is provided only by *P.A.I.S.*, and even that being of uneven occurrence. Totally eluded were most of the conservative newsletters. *AIM (Accuracy in Media)*, for example, was not found in any of the reference works. It was tangentially mentioned in connection with its parent body the Accuracy in Media Organization, by the *Encyclopedia of Associations '85.*

The *American Sentinel* and the *American Spectator* were also "omitted" by all index and abstract services. The latter, however, was listed in *Access.*

CONCLUSIONS

It is a truism that both conservative and liberal journals and magazines are mirrors of the political reality in society. To acknowledge one and ignore the other is to distort reality. Denying free access to information limits the availability of those political periodicals which do not reflect the views and opinions of individual editors and publishers of reference works.

The arbitrary exclusion of conservative periodicals from most of the commercially produced reference materials not only hinders the access of the general users to a large segment of the political press, but it also reduces the chances for conservative publications to find their way into public and academic libraries. Without the existence of adequate, bibliographic resources free of political selectivity, libraries cannot fulfill the task of pursuing a balanced acquisition policy of current political periodicals.

Without adequate reference tools, a library cannot provide its users with in-depth reference and referral services. The need for politically unbiased selection of reference works is imperative in order to ensure that any library user may be exposed to obtain, examine and reproduce any source of political information.

Some of the blame for the inadequate bibliographic coverage of conservative publications should be accepted by the conservatives themselves for their complacency and inertia in addressing this problem. Specialized reference works indexing and abstracting conservative periodicals are yet to be published. The availability of such indexes would undoubtedly improve the overall bibliographic control and would also significantly increase the number of conservative periodicals found on the shelves of academic and public libraries.

A more sustained publicity pursued by the editors and publishers of conservative journals and magazines is needed that ultimately could convince editors of reference tools as well as librarians that conservative periodicals, as much as the liberal ones, justify the time, effort and cost of locating and cataloging them.

Should the editors and publishers of major reference services overcome personal, political and social biases, they could be instrumental in bringing about a most needed change in bibliographic treatment of conservative periodicals. By so doing they would contribute to the enhancement of the role of libraries as foci of information and maximize the social utility of the information which they store, while exposing library users to a wider and more realistic spectrum of current ideas.

Conservative press might be denounced and condemned but it shouldn't be ignored.

NOTES

1. Examples of such studies include: T. J. Allen & P. G.Gertsberger, "Criteria for Selection of Information Source," *Journal of Applied Psychology*, 52 (1968):272-279. Ann Armstrong & Judith C. Russell, "Public Access," *Information World*, 1 (October 1979):1, 11. Cheng-chih Chen & Peter Hernon, *Information seeking: assessing and anticipating user needs*, New York: Neal Schuman, 1982. Edward G. Evans, *Developing library collections*. Littleton, CO: Libraries Unlimited, 1979.

2. Carlton Rochell, "The Knowledge Business." *College and Research Libraries*, 46 (1985):7.

3. In William A. Rusher, *The rise of the right*. New York: William Morrow and Company, Inc., 1984, p. 11.

4. Harold Borko & Charles L. Bernier. *Abstracting concepts and methods*. New York: Academic Press, 1975, p. 3.

5. American Bibliographical Center. *Policies and procedures*.Santa Barbara: Clio Press (n.d.), p. 1.

6. George H. Nash. *The conservative intellectual movement in America since 1945*. New York: Basic Books, 1976, p. 145.

The Use of Bibliographic Tools by Humanities Faculty at the State University of New York at Albany

Susan S. Guest

INTRODUCTION

In 1980 at a conference on humanities information research held in Sheffield, England, Maurice Line, Director-General of the British Library Lending Division, commented in his closing remarks that "the reason for conducting information research is to improve information services." However, he went on,

> we have very little knowledge of how to optimize library collections in the humanities, very little idea of the relative virtues of open and closed access, big and small collections, and only vague indications of the value of exposure and browsing. . . . We know no more about the way in which people . . . obtain their references — from other researchers, from library catalogues, from bibliographies, from abstracting and indexing services or from references at the end of monographs and journals.[1]

In a 1982 review of the literature on information needs of humanities scholars, Stone summarized the outcome of research efforts to date: (1) they view the library as a "laboratory"; (2) they tend to work alone; (3) they do not delegate literature searching; (4) they require a wide range of materials and are particularly dependent on

Susan S. Guest, MLS, School of Information and Library Science, State University of New York at Albany.

primary sources; (5) retrospective coverage may be more essential for the humanities scholar than access to recent materials; (6) monographs are more important than journals; (7) browsing is a vital stimulus to research activities.[2]

These findings make evident the ways in which humanities research is different from that of the natural sciences where much of the work is done within a shared and precisely defined topical area and where, as a consequence, information needs are highly focused. Natural scientists build on prior work; their research is highly dependent on the work of others and therefore they must have continuous access to research findings concurrent with or antedating their own. Their forum is primarily the journal. Currency—keeping up with the latest findings and work-in-progress—is very important. Social scientists rely on monographic and periodical literature to an equal extent.[3] By contrast, humanities scholars are not dependent on the latest publications in their field; the materials they consult do not become less relevant over time; nor does research necessarily evolve from prior research efforts. Shifts of interest are more the rule, with periods or works being reanimated by a discovery or a new perspective.[4] For the humanities scholar the direct encounter and sustained interaction with primary sources is indispensable for the production of insights and ideas, and therefore information retrieval becomes a crucial task in itself but often more in the nature of an undefined odyssey. Northrop Frye has characterized this tension between the humanist and the information systems of libraries by saying that "the resources of the modern library imply that the scholar already knows what he is looking for and this may not be the case."[5] This explains the humanist's unwillingness to delegate searching. Smith, in a 1980 paper, makes an interesting point on this matter. She maintains that while the evidence for a phenomenon may be in the literature, the explanation for it is not and that only someone steeped in the sources has the imagination and the background to generate one.[6]

Despite important groundwork on the information needs in the humanities more research is needed on these requirements and the degree to which libraries are presently organized to satisfy them. Science, by contrast, has been closely scrutinized over the last several decades and researchers have been similarly attentive to the Social Sciences, most notably, the Information Requirements of the Social Sciences (INFROSS) project operated by the Bath University Library Group in England.[7] One area that has not been sufficiently examined is the reasons underlying the pattern of usage of bibliographic tools by workers in the humanities. There is some evidence that humanities scholars seldom use these tools.[8] But what accounts for this pattern of (alleged) non-usage? Does it have to do with the library itself or the condition of the bibliographic tools themselves? Are secondary services inadequately provided in the library, or are they adjudged to be incomplete or unsystematic by humanities workers? Is the problem one of ignorance: humanists are simply unaware of the secondary services that once known and used would be of significant relevance to their work? If these factors alone accounted for the pattern, then library systems would long ago have corrected for them resulting in increased usage of bibliographic aids by humanists. That this has not happened suggests that it is the nature of the humanities disciplines themselves, and their distinctive research methods, that are the main reasons why humanities scholars are relatively indifferent to a library's reference services. It is this idea that is tested in this research project by means of a survey of humanities faculty at the State University of New York at Albany (SUNYA).

METHOD OF INVESTIGATION

The questionnaire design is based on that used in the Information Requirements of the Social Sciences (INFROSS) Project which has become, in effect, a generic model for survey instruments also utilized in research into the information habits of humanities scholars. This allows comparability with the findings on the information "style" of social scientists as well as results from other studies of humanities scholars. In addition, Skelton has summarized data on the information gathering patterns of scientists and contextualized them against the INFROSS conclusions so these may be drawn on to lend further cross-disciplinary contrast.[9] Because of the replication of the questionnaire items in other survey instruments, extensive pre-testing was not considered necessary. However, a small number of questionnaires were administered in person to ensure that the instructions were clear. Subsequently the remainder of the questionnaires were sent to faculty in the College of Humanities and Fine Arts at the State University of New York at Albany.

The sample was drawn by making a list arranged by department of faculty in Humanities and Fine Arts, and starting from a random starting point every other individual in each department was selected. The departments surveyed were Art, Classics, English, French, Germanic Languages and Literatures, Hispanic and Italian Studies, Linguistics, Philosophy, Slavic Languages and Literature, and Women's Studies. It was decided to exclude Music and Theater on the grounds that these are, to a great extent, disciplines in which performance rather than scholarship is emphasized and, as a consequence, the role of bibliographic tools is necessarily either minor or negligible. Historians have been the focus of several other studies investigating information gathering practices in the humanities. But, as historians are formally housed in the College of Social and Behavioral Science at the State University of New York at Albany, the institutional designation was followed. The resulting number of faculty to be surveyed was sightly. The response rate was thirty-nine questionnaires returned, or forty-nine percent. (In tabulating the results, however, five questionnaires were disqualified because they were answered by social scientists with joint appointments in Women's Studies.)

A cover letter was included with each questionnaire as well as an addressed envelope to return it in. Response time was approximately three weeks. The rate of returns was highest towards the end of the first week and then slowed to a trickle.

The best response came from the Department of Classics (seventy-one percent), and the poorest from Hispanic and Italian Studies (twenty-five percent). Faculty at the rank of professor were more apt to reply, forty-five percent, than associate professors, thirty-six percent, or assistant professors, nineteen percent. It should be noted that, overall, departments in the College of Humanities and Fine Arts are top heavy with senior faculty.

DESCRIPTION OF THE QUESTIONNAIRE

The first part of the questionnaire asks for background data from the respondent: age, sex, date and type of terminal degree, academic department affiliation, and rank. This information discloses certain characteristics of the sample and allows a dimensional analysis of several variables.

The next section deals with the respondent's research activities. A short description of the most recent research project is requested, followed by a series of questions which probe where and how researchers obtain information. (It was thought that if these questions were asked in terms of a recent or current project, this would elicit a more accurate reconstruction of information seeking practices than if the inquiries were posed in a less concrete, uncontextualized form.) There is a query regarding the expected or completed outcome of the research. The relative importance of the library as opposed to personal or other information resources is explored in another item. There is a question regarding the need for or significance of current materials in the pursuit of research interests. To what degree relevant or suggestive information can be acquired from chance encounters as well as an attempt to measure the part (if any) of browsing in the reference gathering process, is the focus of further questions. In another question respondents are requested to rank in order of importance items relating to specific information sources used in their present research project as well as for staying current on developments in their field. Then, in an attempt to gather more data on the ranked responses on bibliographic tool use, respondents were asked to identify from a list of titles which sources they specifically consult. This compilation was not intended to be exhaustive or definitive but rather suggestive and respondents were encouraged to append any sources of importance to them which were omitted. (Listing some sources rather than leaving it wholly to respondents to enumerate what they used seemed a surer way to elicit a more complete response. Title recall can be spotty and/or faulty in the absence of some aid or prompt to memory. On the other hand, a complete enumeration of "core" reference tools runs the risk of evoking merely an assent of recognition rather than an indication of real use.)

The last section of the questionnaire concerns the extent to which humanities faculty used online search services. The questions attempt to determine the degree of satisfaction with the results; what component in the overall information seeking strategy the online search constituted; and whether the outcome was felt to be indispensable or readily discoverable in other sources.

The questionnaire did not contain any open-ended questions except for the description of the research project and the "other" categories in several questions where respondents could append an option that had been omitted. The rest of the answers involved either one or two words or a check against the appropriate choice, or rank ordering items on a list. Frequencies and percentages were hand tabulated. Some cross-tabulations were attempted but in the case of comparison of items by discipline, the number of responses in each were unfortunately too low to be meaningful.

ANALYSIS OF DATA

The greatest response to the survey came from faculty at the full professor level, aged 51-60. There were no responses in the youngest (21-30) age category which is perhaps not surprising given the paucity of junior faculty positions in most departments in the College of Humanities and Fine Arts. Women comprised forty-one percent of the sample, and of these, twenty seven percent returned a questionnaire.

In terms of recency of academic training, twenty-seven percent obtained their last degree within the past ten years; newer degrees were not very prevalent; nine percent were five years or less. The majority were trained in the subject they subsequently taught although twelve percent had degrees either in interdisciplinary studies or the social sciences. The largest number of respondents came from the English department, which was the biggest unit sampled.

How humanities scholars pick up references to information relevant to their research interests and for keeping abreast of developments in their discipline and what these practices reveal about the incidence of use of bibliographic tools was a principal interest of this investigation. Respondents were asked to rank listed methods in order of usefulness (Table 1). The high reliance on bibliographies and references in books and journals coupled with infrequent recourse to indexing and abstracting services make it clear that unsystematic practices predominate. Making methodical searches of the literature as a prelude to a research effort and regularly examining abstracting and indexing tools to keep informed about current work is not at all common. The concept of the invisible college is most often associated with scientists but considering the high ratings given to contact with colleagues and the importance of conferences and meetings, it would appear that an informal network of sorts plays a considerable role in the way these respondents acquire information. To those who value more immediate information channels,

TABLE 1

METHODS OF OBTAINING INFORMATION IN RANK ORDER

	Research Project	Keeping Up
Bibliographies/references in books/journals	1	2
Book reviews	2	1
Conversation/correspondence with colleagues	3	3
Conferences/meetings	4	4
Specialized bibliographies	5	5
Library catalog	6	7
Abstracts and indexes	7	8
Searching library shelves	7	7
Publishers/booksellers catalogues	8	6
Consulting librarian	9	9

informal contacts and conferences provide a quick transfer of information not possible with documentary sources.

In the sciences, preferred methods for locating references are personal recommendation, chance, and abstracts and indexes (the latter for keeping up rather than retrospective searching) in that order.[10] Social scientists (not including historians) are dependent on citations in books and journals, personal recommendations, and abstracts and indexes.[11] Historians also turn to citations in books and journals, then book reviews and specialized bibliographies. Historians, unlike either humanities scholars in this study or social scientists, rate collegial contact very low.[12] The importance of book reviews to humanities scholars and historians as opposed to abstracts may be explained by the fact that items in a review are generally more contextualized than a description in an abstract and this would be an important aid in evaluating the relevance of an item.

As an information resource, librarians were rated at the very bottom of the list by respondents which was true also in the studies of scientists, social scientists, and historians. It may be that it simply does not occur to researchers to consult a librarian except on procedural matters. A perception of the library as a supplier of already identified information rather than as a means by which to identify it[13] may account for the low incidence of contact with librarians. Most likely, however, it is that academics believe a librarian does not know the way around their part of their subject and is not an appropriate person to consult. And since the use of bibliographic tools is not regarded as important by researchers, the notion of a librarian accessing information on a topic s/he probably knows little about, using a means which is scorned by the researcher, is not likely to suggest itself as a viable form of assistance. In the University Library, the subject bibliographers are not very evident, tucked away as they are among the stacks. An interview with the humanities bibliographer at the University Library disclosed that she has held the position for over a decade and feels sufficiently well acquainted with the research interests of the faculty that frequent contact is not a priority. No regular current awareness service is offered beyond a circulating list of recent library acquisitions.

The results of an inquiry as to which bibliographic finding aids were turned to in pursuit of a research effort shows a minimal to low-moderate use. The more general guides were consulted on a cross-disciplinary basis while recourse to the more specialized indexes and bibliographies focused on specific subjects was confined to researchers in those subjects. The most heavily used guide was the *MLA International Bibliography* (forty-eight percent), followed by the *Arts and Humanities Citation Index, Index to Book Reviews in the Humanities, MLA Abstracts,* and *Year's Work in Modern Language Studies* (twenty-eight percent respectively). Respondents were invited to add titles they used which were not listed and a number mentioned a variety of sources, including RILA (Repertoire international de la literature de l'art), NUC (National Union Catalog), some indexes to periodical literature, and a number of specialized bibliographies. None of the given sources were felt to be at all relevant by respondents in the Classics Department; of those written in, *L'Annee Philologique* was most frequently cited.

The research efforts of the respondents seemed to be generally of three types: historical, critical, or theoretical, with the majority being critical. Very few people were at work on several projects simultaneously nor was there much evidence of eclecticism of research interests. Most seemed to be employed on "mainstream" research tasks. One respondent stated that he wasn't engaged on any research at all. Conference papers (thirty-seven percent) and then journal articles (twenty-seven percent) were the most frequently reported examples of completed work, while authored books (thirty-two percent) and journal articles (twenty-eight percent) were stated to be the most likely outcome of the research. Not listed but mentioned were contributing a chapter to a book, a festschrift article, guest lectures at universities, and talks to women's groups (Table 2).

In terms of location of information, it appears that most respondents (eighty-five percent) rely on their personal collections as the major resource for information that is relevant to their research. This finding is strongly supported by other studies which make it clear that the primary factors determining where researchers turn for information are the accessibility, ease of use, and familiarity of the information source, and it is therefore not surprising that personal collections are the most heavily exploited source of information by the State University of New York at Albany humanities faculty. Studies have shown that personal collections are preferred by researchers even when they perceive other sources of information as being of potentially greater significance or utility. In other words, because of the convenience and familiarity of their personal collection, researchers will tend to forego using other information sources because of the costs involved.[14] Soper found, in a study of personal collections, that the preponderance of citations in the published work of a group of scientists, social scientists, and humanities scholars were to materials they personally possessed rather than to those in an institutional library collection.[15]

TABLE 2

OUTCOME OF RESEARCH

Outcome	% Likely to Result	% Already Completed
Thesis for higher degree	2	3
Book of which you are an author	32	12
Editor/translator of another's work	7	12
Other publication edited	7	-
Journal article	28	27
Conference paper	20	37
Other	4	9
Total	100	100

The SUNYA humanities faculty however, reported that the next most heavily used channels of information were the University Library collection and the University Inter-Library Loan service (seventy-four percent for each category) corroborating the importance of the library to humanities scholars which has been a finding of some other investigators. [16]

There was little recourse by this faculty to the personal resources of colleagues (thirteen percent) or to public libraries (twenty-one percent). With a major research library at their disposal people probably assume that the smaller public library is unlikely to have what is unobtainable in their institutional collection. This may not always be the case. For example, fiction collections at the main public library branch may very well be more current and inclusive than their counterparts in a university collection. Soper found an exceedingly low use of inter-library loan, particularly among scientists and social scientists; humanities scholars were more likely to have recourse to it. [17] This would conform to the general picture of the humanities scholar as one who requires a wide range of materials. [18] Soper additionally found that the personal collections of natural scientists and social scientists contained a high proportion of materials also held by their institution's library whereas this was not true of humanities scholars. [19] Convenience is evidently not the sole motive behind the personal collections of humanities scholars whose need for all sorts of disparate materials precludes the luxury of a collection which primarily duplicates items available in the university library. Corkill and Mann noted some respondents in their study stated that they did not expect their university libraries to collect the rather esoteric items they needed for their work. [20] Other sources mentioned by respondents in the present survey included site visits, interviews, correspondence, and libraries and special collections elsewhere in the United States and abroad (Table 3).

The results in this study tend to support those uncovered in the survey of humanities scholars by Corkill and Mann [21] and from the Information Requirements of the Social Sciences (INFROSS) project [22] that persons with the largest personal collections are also the heaviest users of libraries while those with small personal holdings tend to shun formal information channels.

The SUNYA humanities faculty who described their research as being more theoretical in nature were more likely to indicate the library's importance to them than those engaged in more applied work (Table 4). Other findings—one from a study of social scien-

TABLE 3

LOCATION OF INFORMATION

Location	% Not Important	% Important
Personal collection	15	85
University Library	26	74
University ILL service	26	74
Public Library	79	21
Archives	75	25
Unpublished papers	63	37
Colleague's collection	87	13

TABLE 4

LOCATION OF INFORMATION BY TYPE OF RESEARCH

Location	Practical/Applied	
	% Not Important	% Important
University ILL service	23	77
University Library	32	68
Public Library	75	25
	Theoretical	
University ILL	33	67
University Library	–	100
Public Library	83	17

tists and another of historians — indicate that the information needs of researchers employing a quantitative methodology rather than more traditional methods of research were more readily satisfied by library holdings just as were those in search of methodological or conceptual information rather than historical or descriptive materials.[23] Unlike the Information Requirements of the Social Sciences (INFROSS) project findings, this survey discloses that the older, more experienced researcher uses the library more rather than less than the other age groups (Table 5).

In reply to a question regarding the importance of recently published materials to their research, respondents resoundingly indicated both books and journal articles were of considerable importance, with a slight edge to journal articles in the "very important" category (sixty-three percent to fifty-eight percent for books) (Table 6). Recent journal articles have hitherto been characterized as the mainstay of scientific research. Humanities scholars have been thought to be more reliant on books than journals[24] and on retrospective rather than current coverage.[25] Humanities research, unlike science, is not cumulative and does not proceed by building on pre-

TABLE 5

IMPORTANCE OF LIBRARY BY AGE

	% Not Important			% Important		
	Public Library	Univ. ILL	Univ. Library	Public Library	Univ. ILL	Univ. Library
21-30	-	-	-	-	-	-
31-40	92	50	17	8	50	83
41-50	75	20	80	25	80	20
51-60	73	14	14	27	86	86
61-70	33	-	33	67	100	67

TABLE 6

IMPORTANCE OF RECENT MATERIALS

	Books	Articles
Not Important	3	6
Slightly Important	7	6
Moderately Important	32	25
Very Important	58	63
Total	100	100

vious knowledge. A definitive work may be quite old, and while recent interpretations can be important to scholars, they cannot rely on someone else's version of a primary source but need to experience it first-hand themselves. In light of the fact that half of the research projects of the respondents deal with topics dating from the eighteenth century and earlier, this finding is unexpected. Social scientists and historians have typically been thought to rank currency higher than humanities scholars do. Table 6 suggests it may be otherwise.

A question regarding the incidence of accidental discoveries of information attempted to assess, among other things, what role browsing plays in obtaining references. There has been some speculation in the literature that given that the humanities are primarily book-oriented disciplines, purposeful or casual scanning of library shelves or in bookstores, for example might be a primary means for locating relevant references or provide a stimulus for research ideas. Table 7, together with the item "searching library shelves" in Table 1, shows that browsing among books in either an unfocused or purposeful way is not felt to be of crucial importance. Seventeen percent said they often discovered material in this fashion, while fifty-five percent indicated that only occasionally did they do so. The respondents did not seem to be great frequenters of bookstores either. More references seemed to be obtained by scanning the jour-

TABLE 7

ACCIDENTAL DISCOVERY OF INFORMATION

	Rarely or Never	Occasionally	Frequently
Browsing library shelves	28	55	17
Scanning current periodicals	–	54	46
Spotting something else while looking up a reference	7	60	33
Receipt of offprints	54	31	15
In bookshops	57	29	14
Conversations with colleagues	18	53	29
Keeping up with accessions to University Library collection	57	32	11

nals. Forty-six percent said they did so frequently. With the high demand for the most recently published materials, journals probably provide a good source of current articles and book reviews of just published works. That colleagues rated rather low (twenty-nine percent) as sources of fortuitous information compared with the high ratings in reply to the question which asked for information sources to be ranked in order of importance is somewhat surprising but perhaps can be explained by respondents making a distinction between a purposeful and accidental context; finding the former more reliable but the latter of only occasional and uncertain utility.

The last part of the questionnaire dealt with the use of online search services. These were taken advantage of by twenty-four percent of the respondents whose research topics had in common an historical or factual focus rather than a critical/descriptive one. No one relied on the service to the exclusion of other channels. Neither was there unreserved enthusiasm over the results except in one case. Fifty percent, however, felt they were moderately satisfied and had uncovered citations they would not have come across by other means.

CONCLUSIONS

The character of humanities research which emerges from this study does not conform entirely with its depiction in the literature. Older researchers were found to use the library more rather than less. Journals were of considerable importance as a source of current materials. Recency of both books and articles was stressed, yet the majority of the research projects of respondents were not on contemporary topics.

In other respects the findings confirm earlier ones. Most people rely on their personal collections as a resource for information, followed closely by the holdings of the University Library and the Inter-Library Loan Service. Dependence on the library did not vary for those with more theoretical research interests as contrasted with those in which an applied emphasis dominated. Contact with colleagues was important as an information source to respondents but only in a structured, purposeful context. They did not appear to expect much from less focused interaction. Resort to librarians was exceedingly minimal. This may be due, in part, to lack of effort on the subject bibliographer's part to initiate frequent contact as wide-spread ignorance regarding the services a librarian can provide is very common.

Bibliographic tools were fairly seldom used, a finding that may be explained by general lack of familiarity, but is also consistent with the expressed need for currency by respondents. Printed guides are not able to be absolutely up-to-date whereas journals containing both articles and reviews are much more contemporaneous sources. Likewise collegial exchanges are apt to expedite the transfer of more recent information than documentary sources. That humanities scholars prefer reviews to bibliographic guides as a means for ferreting out citations is consistent with the noted need to confront the materials of research as directly as possible; a review gives much more contextualized information than an annotation or an abstract. Some investigators, however, believe an unfamiliarity with bibliographical sources to have ominous implications for students; that teachers have to provide guidance on the acquisition, rather than merely the manipulation of information. [26]

A low use of bibliographic aids may also be explained by the standards of documentation of research adhered to by humanities scholars. Exhaustive, retrospective coverage is not so important or relevant in an area where knowledge is not cumulative. Indeed it has been argued elsewhere that it is not really relevant in science either where secondary accounts condensing prior research efforts would be more to the point and that exhaustive bibliographic coverage is merely a cherished notion of librarians, but, in such quantities, of little real use to researchers. [27]

Indifference to bibliographic tools is only partly a matter of the distinctive research methods of the humanities scholar at SUNYA. These methods — the need to confront materials as directly as possible, the standards of documentation in humanities scholarship — are certainly one cause of this indifference; but other factors, which are not unique to the humanities but seem to operate across disciplines — unfamiliarity with bibliographic tools and a stated need for current materials — also explain the low use made of such tools. The provision of bibliographic tools by library systems (and publishers) has probably been too wholesale in terms of quantity and rather insensitive, with respect to quality, to the real needs and practices of researchers.

NOTES

1. Line, M. B., "Concluding Observations" in Stone, S., ed., *Humanities Information Research: Proceedings of a Seminar*, Sheffield, CRUS, 1980, BLR&DD Report No. 5538, pp. 91-96.

2. Stone, S., "Humanities Scholars: Information Needs and Uses," *Journal of Documentation*, December 1982, pp. 292-313.

3. Skelton, B., "Scientists and Social Scientists as Information Users: A Comparison of Results of Science User Studies with Investigation into Information Requirements of the Social Sciences," *Journal of Librarianship* 5, No. 2 (April 1973), pp. 138-156.

4. Garfield, E., "Is Information Retrieval in the Arts and Humanities Inherently Different From That in Science? The Effect that ISI's Citation Index for the Arts and Humanities Is Expected to Have on Future Scholarship," *Library Quarterly*, 50(1), 1980, pp. 40-57.

5. Frye, N., "The Search for Acceptable Words," *Daedalus*, 102(2), 1973, pp. 11-26.

6. Smith, C., "Problems of Information Studies in History" in: Stone, S., ed., *Humanities Information Research: Proceedings of a Seminar*, Sheffield: CRUS, 1980, BLR&DD Report No. 5588, pp. 27-30.

7. Skelton, p. 154.

8. See Line (ref. 1) and Stone (ref. 2).

9. Skelton, p. 147.

10. Ibid, p. 147.

11. Ibid, p. 147.

12. Stieg, M. F., "The Information Needs of Historians," *College and Research Libraries*, 42(6), 1981, pp. 549-60.

13. Smith, p. 29.

14. Allen, T. J. & Gerstberger, P.G., *Criteria for Selection of an Information Source*, Cambridge: MIT, 1967.

15. Soper, M. E., "Characteristics and Use of Personal Collections," *Library Quarterly* 46, No. 4 (October, 1976), pp. 397-415.

16. Stone, p. 300.

17. Soper, p. 411.

18. Stone, p. 296.

19. Soper, p. 413.

20. Corkill, C. & M. Mann, *Information Needs in the Humanities: Two Postal Surveys*, Sheffield: CRUS, 1978, BLR&DD Report No. 5455.

21. Ibid, p. 30.

22. Line, M. B., "The Information Uses and Needs of Social Scientists: An Overview of INFROSS," Aslib Proceedings, 23(8), 1971 (Aug.), pp. 412-34.

23. See Vondran, R., Jr., "The Effect of Method of Research on the Information Seeking Behavior of Academic Historians," Dissertation, University of Wisconsin-Madison, School of Library Science, 1976.

24. Stone, p. 296.

25. Ibid., p. 296.

26. Smith, p. 29.

27. Wilson, P. & M. Farid, "On the Use of the Records of Research," *Library Quarterly*, 49(2), 1979, pp. 127-45.

III. THEORY

Application of the Finite Difference Calculus to the Observation of Symbol Processes

Charls Pearson

Much of the present development of mathematics was originally motivated by its applications to problems in the physical sciences; in fact, the golden age of mathematics was the eighteenth century while the revolution in the physical sciences was still taking place. The physical scientists very early learned to appreciate the interrelation between mathematical methods and observational methods. This may be said to have originated with Galileo who developed averaging methods in order to produce precise measurements with the crude instruments available to him.

Another golden age of mathematics is coming. It will be motivated by the application to problems in the semiotic sciences. But first, semiotics must make a science of itself with precise theories and rigorous experimental methods. The present paper precedes any

Dr. Pearson is at the Catronix Corporation, 3272 Browns Mills RDSE, Atlanta, GA 30354.
An earlier version of this paper was presented to the SIG/ES session on "The Role of Mathematics in Semiotic Observations," at the Fourth Annual Symposium on Empirical Semiotics held in conjunction with the Sixth Annual Meeting of the Semiotic Society of America in Nashville, Oct. 3, 1981.
This work was supported in part by grant #IST-7827002 from the National Science Foundation, Division of Information Science and Technology. I would also like to thank my colleagues Pranas Zunde, for his intellectual stimulation and challenge, and Vladimir Slamecka, for his continuing support and encouragement.

of this development with a simple example of how a presently existing branch of mathematics may be used to model observations in experimental semiotics.

This paper demonstrates that the calculus of finite differences may be used to model and describe observations of symbol processes. The clearer insight into symbol processes thus gained enables further refinements to the methods of observation which sharpen the observations themselves. This is the first known attempt to apply the calculus of finite differences to experimental semiotics.

The Vocabulary Growth Rate curve for natural language has never been observed because of the low precision of classical counting procedures and the large measurement noise introduced by these procedures. These faults are due to the observation methods themselves and do not depend on whether the observations are carried out manually or by computer. However, Type-Token curves, Rank-Frequency curves, and Number-Frequency curves obtained with classical counting instruments are displayed in Figures 1, 2, 3, 4, and 5. Even here the measurement noise and lack of precision are evident.

By using the finite difference calculus to model the Vocabulary Growth Rate independently of its observability and to show the relation between the Vocabulary Growth Rate and Type-Token relation, insight is obtained that was used to redesign the classical counting methods. The resulting invention, the Echelon Counter, enabled measurement of the Vocabulary Growth Rate for the first time, as well as improved measurements of the Type-Token function.

While the paper demonstrates a point in mathematical semiotics, it uses an example from the experimental paradigm of Type-Token measurement. It is set within the linguistic-conceptual paradigm of Pearson's Language of Menetics and the theoretical paradigm of Pearson's Universal Sign Structure Theory.

A mathematical relation is obtained for the Type-Token relation which satisfies all the known boundary conditions exactly and describes the measured values approximately.

INTRODUCTION

The potential for applying the calculus of finite differences to experimental semiotics may be adumbrated by its recent applica-

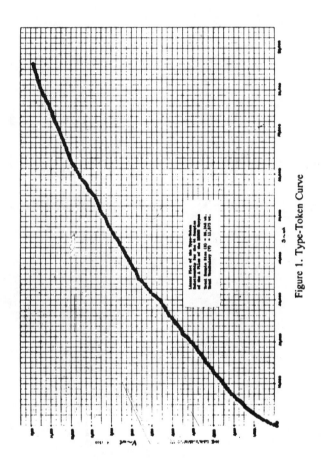

Figure 1. Type-Token Curve

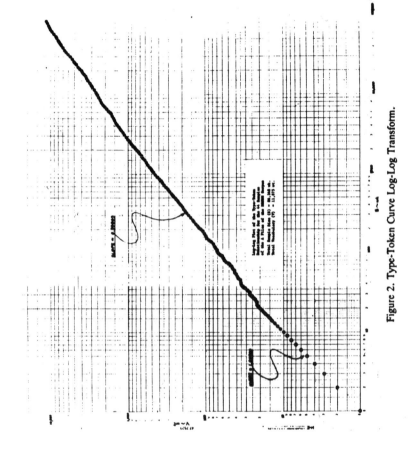

Figure 2. Type-Token Curve Log-Log Transform.

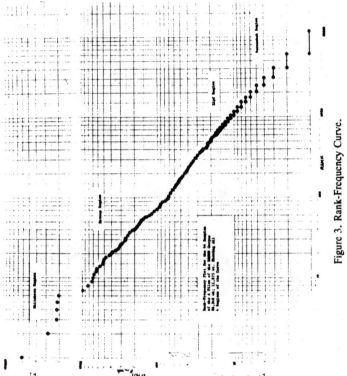

Figure 3. Rank-Frequency Curve.

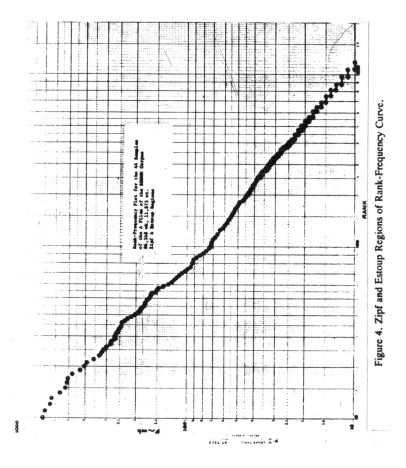

Figure 4. Zipf and Estoup Regions of Rank-Frequency Curve.

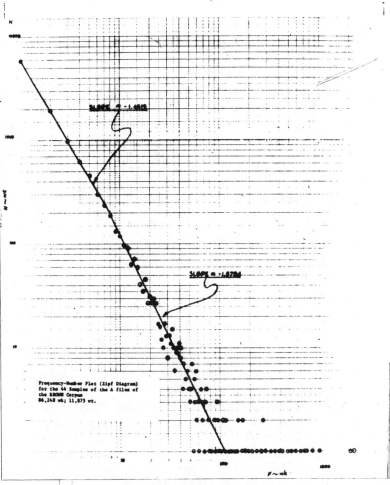

Figure 5. Number Frequency Curve.

tions to problems in some of the other semiotic sciences such as economics, psychology, and sociology. Introductory textbooks usually cover such topics as the difference calculus, the sum calculus, and finite difference equations. The calculus of finite differences is the study of the general properties of the difference operator, Δ.

Given a function **f(x)** we may define the *DIFFERENCE OPERATOR*, Δ, by

$$\Delta f(x) \equiv f(x + h) - f(x) \tag{1}$$

where **h** is some given number usually positive and called the *DIF-FERENCE INTERVAL*. If in particular **f(x)** = **x** we have

$$\Delta x = (x + h) - x = h \tag{2}$$

or

$$h = \Delta x \tag{3}$$

A geometric interpretation of Δ is given in Figure 6.

We note immediately the very strong analogy between the definition of the difference operator and that of the derivative operator from the differential calculus.

$$\frac{df(x)}{dx} \equiv \lim_{h \to 0} \left\{ \frac{f(x + h) - f(x)}{h} \right\} \tag{4}$$

This analogy is very pervasive and powerful. Many of the methods of the finite difference calculus have familiar analogs in the classical differential calculus although the methods themselves are grounded on drastically different underlying theories and usually have drastically different results. For instance, the basic concepts of the differential calculus are "real-valued measurements," "continuum of the system of real numbers," and the "limit operation." The corresponding basic concepts of the finite difference calculus are "counting processes," "discreteness of integer numbers," and "summation operations." Also corresponding to the integral of a continuous polynomial function $\int \mathbf{x^n dx}$ we have the summation of a discrete factorial function $\Sigma \mathbf{x^{(n)}}$, with

$$\int x^n dx = \frac{x^{n+1}}{n+1} + C \tag{5}$$

where **C** is a constant, usually determined by boundary conditions, and

$$\sum x^{(n)} = \frac{x^{(n+1)}}{n+1} + C(x) \tag{6}$$

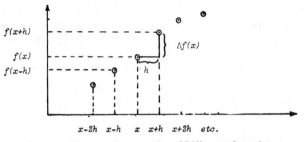

Figure 6. Geometric Interpretation of Difference Operation.

where $C(x)$ is a periodic constant, again determined by the boundary conditions of the problem. A periodic constant has a constant value for integral values of **h**. The trick, therefore in taking advantage of this particular analogy is to be able to transform back and forth between polynomial function x^n and factorial function $x^{(n)}$ and to be able to translate between periodic constants $C(x)$ and ordinary constants C. Similar tricks abound for utilizing the various other analogies between the two subjects.

The calculus of finite differences is therefore useful for modeling and describing discrete phenomena and discontinuous processes. Such for example are symbol relationships and the observation of symbol processes.

THE FINITE DIFFERENCE CALCULUS

Having defined the difference operator Δ by eq. 1, we may now list the general rules of the finite difference calculus.

$$R1: \quad \Delta[f(x) + g(x)] = \Delta f(x) + \Delta g(x) \qquad (7$$

$$R2: \quad \Delta[\alpha f(x)] = \alpha \Delta f(x) \qquad (8$$

where α is a constant.

$$R3: \quad \Delta[f(x)g(x)] = f(x)\Delta g(x) + g(x+h)\Delta f(x) \qquad (9$$

$$R4: \quad \Delta\left(\frac{f(x)}{g(x)}\right) = \frac{g(x)\Delta f(x) - f(x)\Delta g(x)}{g(x)g(x+h)} \qquad (10$$

Those of you familiar with the differential calculus will immediately notice the resemblance between these rules and the general rules of differentiation. In which case you might also recall there was a fifth rule of differentiation as follows:

$$D[f(x)]^m = m[f(x)]^{m-1}Df(x) \tag{11}$$

where **m** is a constant.

This rule does not carry through exactly to the finite difference calculus as do the other rules of differentiation. In order to perfect the analogy we define the *FACTORIAL FUNCTION* by

$$x^{(m)} \equiv x(x-h)(x-2h) \ldots (x-[m-1]h) \tag{12}$$
$$m = 1, 2, 3 \ldots$$

consisting of **m** factors. The name "factorial" is motivated because in the special case **x = m, h = 1**, we have

$$m^{(m)} = m(m-1)(m-2) \ldots 2 \cdot 1 = m! \tag{13}$$

i.e., factorial **m**. In order to make this analogy as complete and systematic as possible and to simplify the resulting calculations, we define

$$x^{(0)} = 1. \tag{14}$$

Also for negative integers we define

$$x^{(-m)} \equiv \frac{1}{(x+h)(x+2h) \ldots (x+mh)} = \frac{1}{(x+mh)^{(m)}} \tag{15}$$
$$m = 1, 2, 3, \ldots$$

With our treatment of factorial functions complete we may now list the differences of some special functions:

$$1. \Delta[c] = 0 \tag{16}$$

2. $\Delta[x^{(m)}]$ $= mx^{(m-1)}h$ (17

3. $\Delta[(ax+b)^{(m)}] = mah(ax+b)^{m-1)}$ (18

4. $\Delta[b^x]$ $= b^x(b^h - 1)$ (19

5. $\Delta[e^{ax}]$ $= e^{ax}(e^{ah} - 1)$ (20

6. $\Delta[\sin ax]$ $= 2\sin(ah/2)\sin a(x + h/2)$ (21

7. $\Delta[\cos ax]$ $= -2\sin(ah/2)\sin a(x + h/2)$ (22

8. $\Delta[\ln x]$ $= \ln(1 + h/x)$ (23

Note the obvious similarity between these differences and the derivatives of the same functions.

We now prove eq. 17 both as an example of how to prove difference relations in general and as an example of the usefulness of our recently introduced factorial function. Applying definitions 12 and 1 we have

$$x^{(m)} = x(x-h)(x-2h) \ \ldots \ (x-[m-1]h) \qquad (24$$

$$(x+h)^{(m)} = (x+h)(x)(x-h) \ \ldots \ (x-[m-2]h)$$

$$\Delta x^{(m)} = (x+h)^{(m)} - x^{(m)} \qquad (25$$

$$= (x+h)(x)(x-h) \ \ldots \ (x-[m-2]h)$$

$$- x(x-h)(x-2h) \ \ldots \ (x-[m-1]h)$$

$$= [(x+h) - (x-[m-1]h)](x)(x-h)$$
$$\ldots \ (x-[m-2]h)$$

$$= mhx^{(m-1)} \qquad (26$$

In order to apply these tools to solving problems it is necessary to be able to pass back and forth from the differential notation to the difference notation. Since the one analogy we have developed in detail relates derivatives of power functions to differences of factorial function, it enables us to develop a notation for passing back and forth between power functions and factorial functions. This makes use of factorial polynomials. From eq. 12 we find on putting **m** = 1, 2, 3, . . .

$$x^{(1)} = x$$

$$x^{(2)} = x^2 - xh$$

$$x^{(3)} = x^3 - 3x^2h + 2xh^2 \qquad (27$$

$$x^{(4)} = x^4 - 6x^3h + 11x^2h^2 - 6xh^3$$

$$x^{(5)} = x^5 - 10x^4h + 35x^3h^2 - 50x^2h^3 + 24xh^4$$

etc.

If **p** is any positive integer, we define a *FACTORIAL POLYNOMIAL OF DEGREE* (**p**) as

$$a_0 x^{(p)} + a_1 x^{(p-1)} + \ldots + a_p$$

where $a_0 \neq 0$, $a_1, \ldots, a_p$ are constants. From eqs. 27 we see that a factorial polynomial of degree (**p**) can be expressed uniquely as an ordinary power polynomial of degree **p**. In fact if one is a master of many mathematical models he may recognize the numerical coefficients appearing in equations 27 as the Stirling Numbers of the First Kind, s^n_k where we define a *STIRLING NUMBER OF THE FIRST KIND* recursively by

$$s^{n+1}_k = s^n_{k-1} - ns^n_k \qquad (28a$$

with

$$s^n_n = 1, \quad s^n_k = 0 \qquad for\ k \leq 0,\ k \geq n + 1 \qquad (28b$$

$$where\ n > 0.$$

This allows us to simplify the transformations of eq. 27 by using the Stirling Number notation as follows

$$x^{(n)} = \sum_{k=1}^{n} s_k^n \, x^k \, h^{n-k} \tag{29}$$

Conversely any power polynomial of degree **p** can be expressed uniquely as a factorial polynomial of degree (**p**). We write the first few:

$$x = x^{(1)}$$

$$x^2 = x^{(2)} + x^{(1)}h$$

$$x^3 = x^{(3)} + 3x^{(2)}h + x^{(1)}h^2$$

$$x^4 = x^{(4)} + 7x^{(3)}h + 6x^{(2)}h^2 + x^{(1)}h^3 \tag{30}$$

$$x^5 = x^{(5)} + 15x^{(4)}h + 25x^{(3)}h^2 + 10x^{(2)}h^3$$
$$+ x^{(1)}h^4$$

etc. From this example we see that power polynomials can be expressed uniquely in terms of factorial polynomials by

$$x^n = \sum_{k=1}^{n} S_k^n \, x^{(k)} h^{n-k} \tag{31}$$

where the S_k^n are *STIRLING NUMBERS OF THE SECOND KIND* defined recursively as

$$S_k^{n+1} = S_{k-1}^n + k S_k^n \tag{32}$$

with $S_n^n = 1$, $S_k^n = 0$ for $k \neq 0$, $k = n+1$ where $n > 0$.

This completes our short introduction to the finite difference calculus except for one special relation from the sum calculus that will be used in section 6. For completeness, we now state this special result without proof.

$$\sum x^{(-1)} = \sum \frac{1}{x+h} = \frac{\Gamma'(\frac{x}{h} + 1)}{h \, \Gamma(\frac{x}{h} + 1)} \tag{33}$$

The function on the right of eq. 33 is called the *"DIGAMMA FUNCTION"* and is denoted by $\Psi(x)$.

SYMBOL PRODUCTION PROCESSES

One of the obvious areas in which to attempt to use the finite difference calculus as a mathematical model is in the study of symbol production processes, for the reason that symbol production is by nature a discrete process. One can produce a one or two-word text, but not a one-and-a-half word text. It is meaningless to conceive of a one-and-a-half word text. It must be either one word long or two words long because symbols are produced, and exist, discretely. One subject of current interest in information science includes a constellation of different relationships and symbol production processes, all intertwined in what may be called the "Type-Token System for Words in Natural Language" or "Type-Token Constellation" for short. These include Zipf's Number-Frequency law also known as the Zipf Integer effect, the Rank-Frequency Law of Words and Holophrases which is also known as the Law of Zipf and Estoup, the Type-Token curve as a function of sample size, the Type/Token ratio also as a function of sample size, the Vocabulary Growth Rate curve, and many others. You saw examples of some of these earlier. In addition, several of the useful regularities of information engineering and library management, such as Lotka's law and Bradford's law, are closely related to the Type-Token Constellation. We will now apply the finite difference calculus to the study of the Type-Token relationship.

Because the ordinary Type-Token relation is not statistically independent, it cannot be described using the methods of statistical estimation. In addition present methods of measurement yield too much measurement noise and too little precision for statistical estimation methods to be useful even if they were valid (Pearson,

1976). For this reason information scientists in Georgia Tech's SemLab searched for a type-token relationship in which the data would satisfy the statistical independence requirements rigorously. The search led to a little-studied relationship called the Vocabulary Growth Rate. This is defined as the rate at which new vocabulary items, measured in word-types (wt), enter the sample with respect to the increase in size of the sample, measured in word-tokens (wk) (Pearson, 1980). The relative frequency of new words in the nth position of a sample is *logically* independent of the relative frequency of new words in any of the other words positions. It turns out that the statistical dependence of the data in each of the other type-token relationships arises because each of these other relations depends on the Vocabulary Growth Rate in a way that destroys independence of the measurements. In addition, and in compensation perhaps, this dependence is such that each of these other relations can be derived from the Vocabulary Growth Rate. For instance, the Type-Token relation can be expressed as

$$T(K) = \sum_{S=1}^{K} VGR(S) \qquad (34$$

where **T(K)** is the number of types in a sample expressed as a function of the sample size **K**, and **VGR(S)** is the Vocabulary Growth Rate expressed as a function of the sample size **S**. This allowed us to concentrate our experimental investigation on observations of the Vocabulary Growth Rate and later obtain each of the other relations by means of the finite difference calculus.

However, there is a good reason why the Vocabulary Growth Rate relation has been little studied: it has never been observed. Therefore semioticists do not have even a vague intuition as to an approximate mathematical form for describing this relation. Therefore, although this relation has been mentioned in the literature, nothing substantive has been learned about it.

The reason the Vocabulary Growth Rate curve has never been observed before is because of the lack of precision of all previous instruments for measuring type-token phenomena. The value of the Vocabulary Growth Rate for any sample size **S** is a real number between 0 and 1. All previous instruments for measuring type-token phenomena, including instruments employing digital computer techniques, use methods based on raw counting procedures which are precise to the nearest whole integer and whose values therefore increase by either 0 or 1 at each step. Therefore the Vocabulary Growth Rate was completely hidden between the cracks of the instrumentation.

MATHEMATICAL DEVELOPMENTS

The mathematical relations which model the empirical relations of the Type-Token Constellation are related by statistical sampling theory, statistical averaging theory, and the calculus of finite differences. Given an assumed form for the underlying theoretical distribution of the Vocabulary Growth Rate curve, the model of a single measurement of the curve can be obtained by sampling theory. From this a Vocabulary Growth Rate Number-Frequency curve can be obtained by finite differentiation and the general form of the observed Vocabulary Growth Rate curve can be obtained by averaging theory.

From the assumed theoretical distribution of the Vocabulary Growth Rate, the underlying theoretical distribution of the Type-Token curve can be obtained by Stieltjes integration which reduces in this case to a simple summation. From the theoretical distribution of the Type-Token curve, the mathematical model of a single measurement of the curve can be obtained by sampling theory. And again, from this a Type-Token Number-Frequency curve can be obtained by finite differentiation and the general form of the observed Type-Token curve can be obtained by averaging theory.

From the theoretical distribution of the Type-Token curve, the underlying theoretical distribution of the Rank-Frequency curve can be obtained by a Stieltjes transform which reduces in this case to a summation transform, or what may be called a finite difference transform. Again, from the theoretical distribution of the Rank-Frequency curve, a single measurement of the curve can be obtained by sampling theory. And again, from this a Rank-Frequency Number-Frequency (or Zipf's Number-Frequency) curve can be obtained by finite differentiation, and the general form of the observed Rank-Frequency curve can be obtained by averaging theory. However, because of the relationship between the transformed variables, the general form of the Rank-Frequency curve is exactly the same as a single measurement of this curve.

Certain key relations can be set out in advance. For instance, the theoretical form of the Type-Token curve **T(K)** can be determined from the assumed form of the Vocabulary Growth Rate curve **VGR(S)** by indefinite summation as follows:

$$T(K) = \sum_{S=1}^{K} VGR(S) \tag{35}$$

Also noting that max **R** = **T** and that the sum over all types of the frequencies for each type is just the total number of tokens, we get:

$$K = \sum_{R=1}^{T(K)} F(R) \tag{36}$$

which is to be solved for **F(R)**. This last may be seen more easily with the aid of the following diagrams, where $\sum_{R=1}^{T(K)} F(R)$ is the area under the curve of Figure 7, and **K** is the horizontal coordinate of Figure 8.

In the case where the Rank-Frequency curve is hyperbolic, Zipf (1938) obtained the Rank-Frequency-Number-Frequency relation:

$$N = \frac{C}{(F^2 - 1/4)} \tag{37}$$

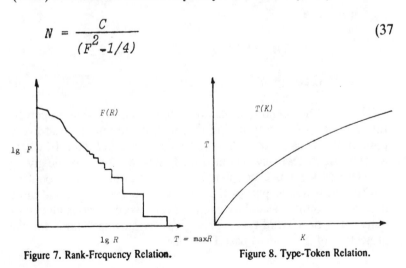

Figure 7. Rank-Frequency Relation.   Figure 8. Type-Token Relation.

by carrying out the finite differentiation as follows: let the rank-frequency curve be given by the hyperbolic relation

$$R = \frac{C}{F} \tag{38}$$

Then the number of types of the same frequency is given by the requirement for integer occurrences,

$$N = R' - R'' = \frac{C}{F - 1/2} - \frac{C}{F + 1/2} = \frac{C}{(F^2 - 1/4)} \tag{39}$$

where **F** can assume only integer values, as can be seen by the diagram in Figure 9.

Derivation of number-frequency curves for the Type-Token relation and the Vocabulary Growth Rate relations is similar.

Arbitrary constants which appear in these equations are to be evaluated by means of the known semiotic boundary conditions as set forth in Pearson (1976).

$$\mathbf{T(0)} = \mathbf{0} \tag{40}$$

$$\mathbf{T(1)} = \mathbf{1} \tag{41}$$

$$n \geq m \rightarrow T(n) \geq T(m) \tag{42}$$

$$n \text{ finite } \rightarrow T(n) \text{ finite} \tag{43}$$

These last two conditions can be combined into one more powerful condition by simply noting that both conditions hold at every point of the Type-Token relation. This is shown in Figure 10 where we suppose that we have counted the first **m** wk. of a sample giving us **T(m)** as the wt. encountered up to this point. If we count an **additional n** wk. as part of the same sample, we cannot add more than **n** wt. to the vocabulary even if every word-token is an occurrence of a **new** word-type. This gives us an upper limit for the projection of **T(m + n)** past **T(m)** of

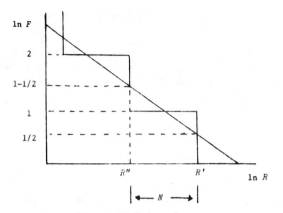

Figure 9. Zipf Integer diagram.

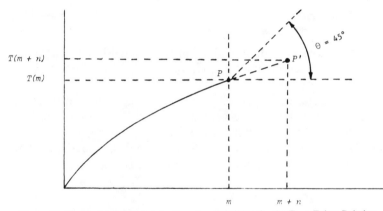

Figure 10. The Restricted Monotone Boundary Condition for the Type-Token Relation.

$$T(m + n) \leq T(m) + n \qquad (44$$

which is represented in Figure 10 by the dotted line at $\Theta = 45°$ projecting from **P**.

On the other hand we also see that even if all of the new word-tokens are occurrences of word-types already encountered in the sample up to the **m**th token, we cannot decrease the number of word-types already encountered. This gives a lower limit for the projection of **T(m + n)** past **T(m)** of

$$T(m) \leq T(m + n) \qquad (45$$

which is represented in fig. 10 by the dotted horizontal line projecting from **P**. Since the actual observation **P**, must lie between these two extremes and can take on either limit, both conditions must hold simultaneously, giving:

$$\forall (m, n \in N) \; : \; T(m) \leqslant T(m + n) \leqslant T(m) + n \qquad (46$$

where **N** is the set of natural numbers; i.e., the non-negative integers. This is the restricted monotone condition and from it we recapture both eq. 42 and eq. 43 as well as another important condition

$$0 \leqslant T(n) \leqslant n \qquad (47$$

by substituting **m** = 0 and applying condition 40. This is the first time the restricted monotone condition has been stated for the Type-Token relation.

In summary, the Type-Token Constellation consists of three theoretical distributions; three general observable relations; and three number-frequency, or individual relations: each trio consisting of one each for Vocabulary Growth Rate, Type-Token, and Rank-Frequency. These nine relations form a mathematically consistent system.

THE ECHELON COUNTER AND THE FINITE DIFFERENCE MODEL

With this much as a preliminary model and using the improved understanding of our observational limitations that it yielded, we invented an instrument for counting types and tokens, called an Echelon Counter, that yielded a much higher precision and noise suppression. The Echelon Counter was described in detail in patent disclosure and its design and performance was reported publicly in Pearson (1980). A comparative example of results of measuring type-token data with classical counting instruments and with the Echelon Counter is shown in Figures 11 and 12. Using the Echelon Counter, the Vocabulary Growth Rate data was clearly observable and in preliminary studies, $\Delta T / \Delta S$ appears to be approximately

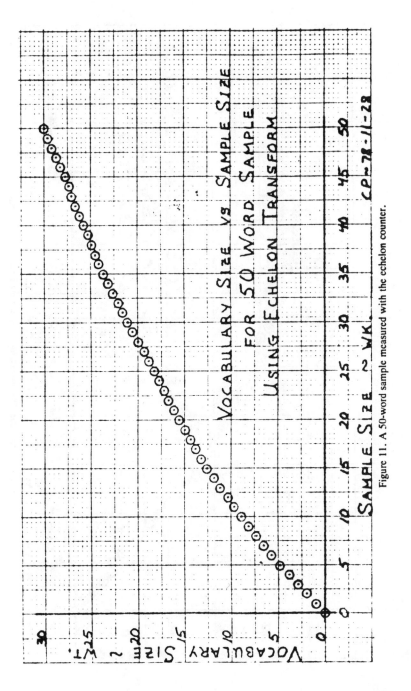

Figure 11. A 50-word sample measured with the echelon counter.

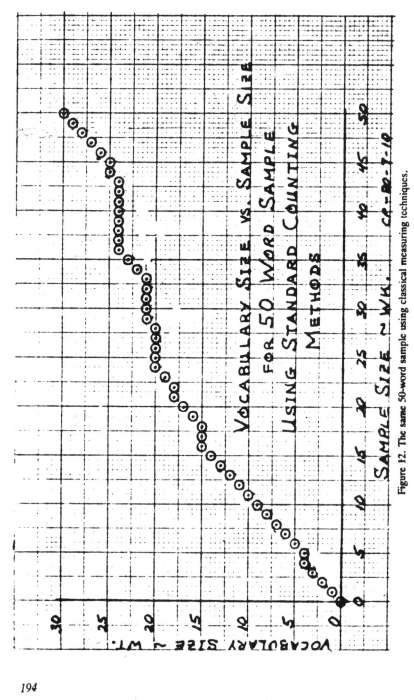

Figure 12. The same 50-word sample using classical measuring techniques.

equal to $(S+1)^{-1}$; using this and the fact that the spacing between text sample sizes is

$$\Delta S = h = 1 \text{ wk}, \tag{48}$$

we get

$$\Delta T = (S + 1)^{-1} \tag{49}$$

From this we get by Stieltjes integration

$$T(S) = \sum_{i=1}^{S} \Delta T = \sum_{i=1}^{S} (i + 1)^{-1} = \sum_{i=1}^{S} i^{(-1)}$$

$$= \frac{\Gamma'(S + 1)}{h\Gamma(S + 1)} + C(S) \tag{50}$$

$$= \Psi(S) + C(S)$$

where $\Psi(S)$ is our old friend the digamma function from eq. 33.

Let us now attempt to evaluate $C(S)$ by applying the boundary conditions eqs. 40, 41, and 46. For $S = 0$ we have

$$\frac{\Gamma'(1)}{\Gamma(1)} + C(S) = \frac{-\gamma}{1} + C(S) = 0 \tag{51}$$

yielding

$$C(S) = \gamma(S) \tag{52}$$

where δ is Euler's Constant

$$\gamma \approx 0.5772 \ldots \tag{53}$$

and $\delta(S)$ is appropriately called a *"Periodic Euler's Constant."*

We have now used up all of the undetermined factors in the solution but still have two boundary conditions left to satisfy. How shall we take care of these? Let us see what still needs to be done to satisfy them. Let us calculate $T(1)$, we have

$$\frac{\Gamma'(2)}{\Gamma(2)} + \gamma(2) = \frac{1-\gamma}{1} + \gamma = 1. \tag{54}$$

In other words, the second boundary condition is already satisfied by our solution, merely by its form. Likewise the digamma function is monotonically increasing for all positive values of **S** in a restricted way that satisfies eq. 46 thus guaranteeing the satisfaction of the last boundary condition **merely by the form of the solution.** It should be emphasized here that this is the first proposed form of the Type-Token relation that satisfies all three boundary conditions by any means, let alone by its form alone. This is a significant achievement for the finite difference calculus. We thus have our final relation

$$T(S) = \Psi(S) + \gamma(S) \tag{55}$$

CAVEATS

It must be emphasized in the strongest terms that eq. 55 is not our final proposal for the Type-Token relation. It is our final step in this motivation of the semiotic usefulness of the finite difference calculus and with its achievement we certainly have accomplished that; however, there are still many problems associated with eq. 55 that remain to be cleared up by detailed investigations. For one thing, this development takes into account neither the peculiar nature of individual languages nor of individual authors, both of which are known to affect the Type-Token relation. Nor does it take into consideration the grammatical constraints of natural language as opposed to a random string of words. In addition for all values of **S** greater than 1, the function produces too small a value. For instance,

$$T(2) = \frac{\Gamma'(3)}{\Gamma(3)} + \gamma(3) \simeq 1.512 \tag{56}$$

a value which is approximately 0.48 wt too small; and 0.48 wt is easily detected by our present instrumentation. It is suggested that the proper Type-Token relationship may be given by a sum of terms

$$T(S) = \Psi(S) + \gamma(S) + L(S) + G(S) + A(S) \qquad (57$$

where **L(S)** is a term determined by the particular language, **G(S)** is a term determined by the grammatical constraints of the language, and **A(S)** is a term determined by the particular author. If this were the case, the present analysis has succeeded in isolating the first two of these terms.

SUMMARY

The finite difference calculus allows us to obtain the Type-Token relation in terms of the Vocabulary Growth Rate as

$$T(K) = \sum_{S=1}^{K} VGR(S) \qquad (58$$

with boundary conditions given by

$$T(0) = 0 \qquad (59$$

$$T(1) = 1 \qquad (60$$

$$T(m) \leqslant T(m + n) \leqslant T(m) + n \qquad (61$$

If **VGR(S)** is close to $(S + 1)^{-1}$ as appears to be the case in our initial measurements then the Type-Token relation can be expressed as

$$T(S) = \Psi(S) + \gamma(S) \qquad (62$$

However, it is more likely that there are several additional terms to account for the individual language, author, and grammatical constraints and the expression may be more like

$$T(S) = \Psi(S) + \gamma(S) + L(S) + G(S) + A(S) \qquad (63$$

In any case it is obvious that the finite difference calculus is an exceedingly powerful tool for the study of symbol production processes.

NOTES

1. Pearson, C. "Quantitative Investigations into the Type-Token Relation for Symbolic Rhemes." *Proceedings of the Semiotic Society of America*, 1(1976), 312-328; ed. Pearson, C. & Hamilton-Faria, H.
2. Pearson, C. "The Echelon Counter: A New Instrument for Measuring the Vocabulary Growth Rate and the Type-Token Relationship." *Proceedings of the ASIS Annual Meeting*, 17(1980), 364-366.
3. Zipf, G. K. "Homogeneity and Heterogeneity in Language." *Psychol. Record*, 2(1938), 347-367.

Contemporary Trends in Applied Metatheoretic Research: A Case Study About Information Metatheory: A Fragment

Nicolay Stanoulov

If any theory is "the general or abstract principles of a body of fact, a science, . . . " and/or "a body of theorems presenting a concise systematic view of a subject" then its supporting human activity is the concerned research as an "investigation or experimentation aimed at the discovery and interpretation of facts, revision of accepted theories or laws in the light of new facts" (Webster's New Collegiate Dictionary). There are many substantial grounds — historic, dynamical, as well — for theory changes in the sense of its evolution. The article is concerned with a sketchy only description of a methodological apparatus revealing the logical transition of an existing theory from one to other its kinds bearing on a well grounded deductive method. The theory itself is an informal one (T_i) — classical information theory of C. Shannon (1948). A near-formal information-theoretic axiomatic system T_a should be first created from T_i, and next an information metatheory T_m as a new informal subject.

Such a successive conceptual approach seems a venturesome attempt. As known, metatheories have been formulated mainly for formal mathematical theories but not for informal ones. And it is the

The author is Head of Systems Science Div., Central Laboratory of Control Systems, Bulgarian Academy of Sciences, Sofia 1113, Bl 107, P.O.B. 79 Bulgaria.

transition of mathematics to metamathematics as an outstanding example that manifests itself such an evolution (or "dynamic optimization") in the methodology of natural science. There is nowadays a tendency in it, cybernetics as well, to formulate metadisciplines. Well known is the axiomatic trend in general systems theory, as well as in modern theoretic physics.

The deductive theory T_a published elsewhere (N. Stanoulov, 1982) roughly follows the metamathematical paradigm. The significance of such a deductive approach lies in defining the subject matter, as well as explicating its features, and forecasting new ones. The solution of such basic problems cannot be carried out by the T_r owned means. It is hardly acceptable that this study should follow without fail the stereotype of metamathematics (S. C. Kleene, 1952) nor is it beyond debate as to its rigidity or to its thorough validity.

The author is fully aware that such a subject is difficult for understanding in some places. All the more so that it is admittedly a concise presentation. It turned out unattainable to avoid somewhat "heavy" mathematics burdened additionally by some professional jargon. I dare to advise a part of the readers to skip over these places and hope that the overall idea will be quite well grasped. The interested readers may consult the referenced literature for more details.

COMMUNICATION – WHAT ABOUT?

A well recognized fact is that our civilization is based on communication (R. Bellman, 1975). First conceived in "pure" T_1-sense the ideas and apparatus of Shannon's theory penetrated into the area of other sciences. This expansion is generally accepted with interest even enthusiastically, though the results obtained do not always correspond to the desire and efforts spent.

Common communication is like a "constraint" (relation) between "message sent" and "message received" (R. C. Conant, 1976), thus demonstrating the relationship of two such representatives of information "objects" (IOs) constituting any statistically analyzable network of information transfer called an information system (IS). Because of the additivity of the information-theoretic measure of rates of constraint, it is possible to make constructive conclusions about the decomposition of the whole system, as well as its hierarchy.

One may claim that such a conceptual view also holds within systems in science and life, besides ISs. This seems true if such systems possess an intrinsic part responsible for the information activity, i.e., for the interactive behavior of its IOs.

Dynamic Evolution of Information Theory — What May Be It?

Though deductive investigations for T_i exist they refer, on the one hand, to its "classical" content and differ, on the other hand, to the extent of elaboration, for example, from theory of groups, theory of natural numbers in mathematics, etc. No attempts to formulate so far a formalized T_i are known, i.e., to attach to its elaborated axiomatic system T_a appropriate logical means. Thus, we can put T_i on the "initial" step of the hierarchical scale of the theory generalization, T_a will fill in then the next step, and the last step will be T_m in which T_a should be described and possibly examined with respect to the information phenomena. T_a- and T_m- constructs yield novel results for the principal properties of any IS, and give a precise definition of the concept of information itself. Figure 1 shows imaginatively the dynamic evolution of the information-theoretic structures. To exactly build T_a like many classical mathematical theories seems impossible. The dynamic evolution described runs in "normal" (i.e., progressive) time. If needed, time reversibility may be perceived only psychologically, and retroacted as an actual and inescapable return from "future" knowledge (T_m, T_a) or even such a "present" one (T_i to a "past" knowledge — historic "traces" (T_m, T_a, or T_i).

About an Information-Theoretic Axiomatic Systems

Existing T_a (N. Stanoulov, 1982) comprises logical operators, modal logical operators for necessity and possibility, predicates, functional and individual symbols, variables, primary terms, constant relation R of rank 2, identity relation, etc. Three auxiliary definitions for IO types are introduced on modal-logic bases — IOg, IOd, IOc labelled in T_i as source, destinator (receiver), and communication channel, respectively. Nonempty sets My, Z, Mx, their ordered multiplets (Z,Mx), (My,Z), and (My,Mx)~(My,Z,Mx) built by the dyadic relation $R = (R1,R2, \ldots)$ stand for the terms in T_a (~is a sign for equivalence). They form IOs and ISs in T_i. As shown in T_a the essential IO types are IOg~My, IOd~Mx, and

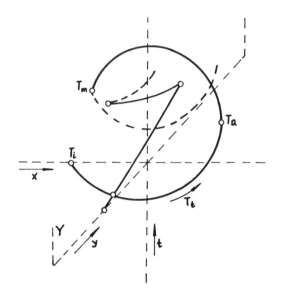

FIGURE 1. Serpentine curve (T_t) approximating the dynamics of the theory change; T_i is the informal theory, T_a is the axiomatic system for T_i, T_m is the metatheory for T_a; t is the time parameter, x is the specific parameter of the scientific investigation, y is the intensity parameter of such an investigation. Y is the conceivable plane separating the informal and formal studies

Ioc~(My,Z,Mx) representing nonempty sets of "outputs," "inputs," and "states," respectively, in T_a. All mentioned above and next on representations, however, appeal by no means to any intuitive feeling — in the sense of T_i — of the formalism adopted in T_a.

Finite sequences called formulas may be composed of the elements of T_a. A class of such formulas called axioms are also introduced: existence axiom (A1), communication axiom (A2), R-properties axiom (A3 — transitivity, symmetry), information metrics axiom (A4). For symbolical formulation of them two specific kinds of natural language propositions are introduced for IOg, IOd, respectively.

Some T_a-owned term interpretations in T_i may be possibly used as far as they refer to the metric space of the Ti-messages, e.g., the discrete entropy H of IOs, the upper bound for exchange of messages (that is, the capacity of IOs). Ascribing certain quantitative specifications to distinct IOs other formulas can be deduced from the axioms interpreting thus the primal content of the basic theorems in T_i for discrete noiseless and noisy channels, the so called correction theorem, as well. The axioms enable further more other interesting inferences to be made not known in T_i. So, according to A2 the correction channel may be connected in a manner (see Figure 2) distinct from the correction theorem. The "observer" is included now serially in IS acting (i) to forecast the messages m_y of IO_g, and (ii) to use this forecast to correct the receiving messages $m_x \neq m_y$ so that the originally transmitted m_y again appear as IS output. This scheme has advantages over the classical one and is well spread in communication practice.

SOME SPECIAL PROBLEMS IN A METATHEORY

A procedurally justifiable evolutionary approach should comprise such problems as consistency and completeness of T_a. In a speculative discourse one can argue that the consistency of T_a is resolved unpretentiously at once if he takes it "on trust" (M. Loéve, 1960). It will be, however, more satisfactory if letting E be a formula in T_a with $\neg E$ its negation. Now if E is true in T_a then $\neg E$ can be there neither true nor a consequence of E. Drawing on "utilitarian" reasons (S. C. Kleene, 1952) the system of axioms A1−A4 in T_a would be complete if it gives "everything necessary" for some purpose. If these reasons refer to the relation R(My,Mx) then the axiomatic system in T_a should be taken as complete.

On the Information Metatheory

The formulation of T_m bears exclusively on the issues of T_a. Similar studies so far available refer solely to abstract specification of the properties of data types (see, e.g., J. V. Guttag & Horning, 1978; D. J. Moore & Russel, 1981). According to metamathematics only finitary methods should be adopted in T_m. That is, roughly speaking, all constructs have to relate in it to statements with real informal content. An article concerning T_m in more detail will be submitted for presentation, as the author hopes, in 11th International Congress on Cybernetics, Namur (Belgium), August 1986.

A metaanalysis of the properties of IOs is first made by introducing a new set of dyadic relations IR $\subset C_R \cup C_W$ for the sets and the multiplets in T_a. C_R is an outer term ordering of My and Mx, as

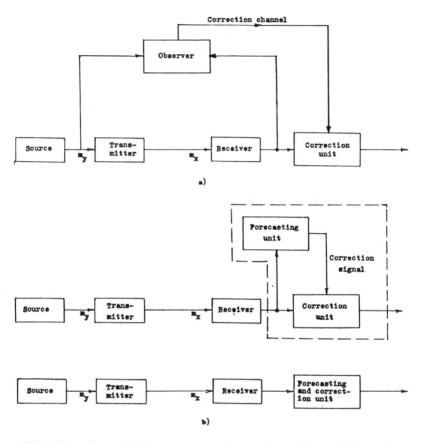

FIGURE 2. a. Communication system corrected according to Shannon's information
theory
b. The same communication system corrected according to the information-theoretic axiomatic system

well as (My,Mx) by means of R (see T_a) while C_W is an inner term
ordering of My, Z, Mx (Mn,Z), as well as (Z,Mx) by means of a
dyadic relation W, WxR. Then

$$M_0 = \{m_0 : m_0 \in M_0^* \cap IR\}, M_0 \subset M_0^*$$

is the *object variety set* in T_m. M_0^* stands for the set of all terms in
T_a.

Several corollaries explicate the informativeness of various IR-orderings of Mo-objects in T_m. Figure 3 visualizes some IOs kinds with R-, W-, as well as Ir-orderings.

Any multiplet (conjunction) of IOs submitted to R-ordering forms a IS. Any conjunction of two different IOs with only one R-ordering forms an elemental IS denoted as ^eIS. Conversely, a composite IS (^cIS) is formed at least through two R-orderings (Figure 4). ^eIS and ^cIS may have an arbitrary number of W-orderings. Some IR-conjunctions are simultaneously ISs (Figure 3).

The necessary existence condition for any IS is given through the presence of different IOs in it while the concerned sufficient condition is given through the presence of R-ordering of such IOs as stated in a theorem. The decomposition approach in general systems theory (M. Mesarovic, 1964) demonstrates brilliantly the role the IR-components play for identifying the properties of IO and IS (Figure 5). Thus, R is responsible for the mutual boundedness of M_o-conjunctions while W reveals their internal dynamics to transition from/to Z to/from My or Mx (see Figure 3). According to the decomposition theorem the discrete metatheoretical model of IS (or IO) simply becomes MyW_1ZW_2Mx provided that W is the product of subrelations W_1 and W_2 (Figure 5).

The object variety elements of M_O are mutual correlative parts, is also stated. That is, an arbitrary IS may become IO within an IS (different from the originally one), or an arbitrary IO within an IS may become another IS. Hence, the metalanguage of T_m comprises some systems-theoretical means. More generally, introducing IR-ordering in T_m yields proving strictly metatheoretical statements which are only intuitively true in T_i. Formulating T_m enables also to bring a well argued classification of all IOs.

Let's introduce now in a similar to M_0 manner an ordering of the own elements of the terms My,Mx,Z (called shortly alphabets), IOs, too, as follows:

$$M_i = \{ m : m \in M_i \cap \beta_M \}, \; M_i \subseteq M_i$$

M_i^* stands for the set of all conjunctions of the elements-letters of any alphabet. β_M is the set of all rules-syntaxes governing over the letters. M_i is called *information variety set*. For more correct specification the m-conjunctions of M_i^* are denoted by m_y, mx and mz.

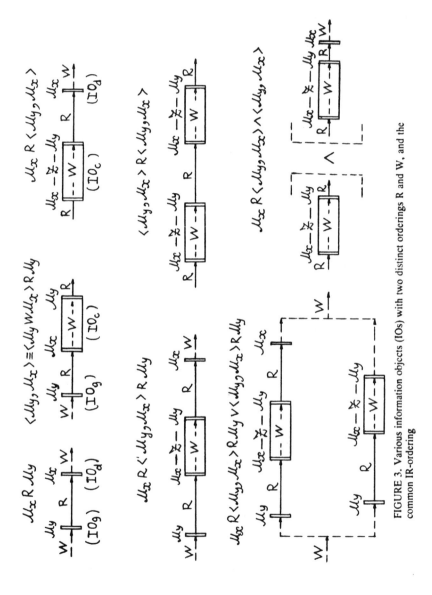

FIGURE 3. Various information objects (IOs) with two distinct orderings R and W, and the common IR-ordering

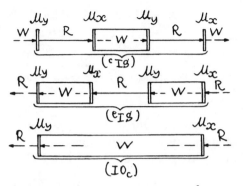

FIGURE 4. Formation of various information systems (ISs) ^{c}IS : elemental IS; ^{c}IS : composite IS

They are elements of My, Mx, Z, respectively, along with their syntax BM. As clearly seen, the BM-elements are not from the R or W type.

Any IO possessing both Mx (input) and Mn (output), that is, IO~IOc is called intermediate IO. Any IO having only My or Mx is called terminal IO. The former may be noiseless or noisy. Now each IO_c-type channel interpretation in T_i may be explicated. Introducing the lead and lag operators $D-\Theta$ and $D+\Theta$, respectively, the terminal IOs may also be explicated very effectively (Θ is the lead or lag time, arbitrarily small or large depending on the existence period of IS and its IOs). Hence, an appropriate metatheoretical insight to the IO definitions in T_a is given. Attaching time parameter to intermediate IOs, in addition, they turn into terminal IOs. That is, the most general variety object $m_0 \in M_0$ is IO_c. IO_g, IO_d and IO_c form a complete (or canonical) totality of IOs comprising all five groups of known IOs (see, e.g., I. G. Wilson, M. E. Wilson, 1965).

The availability of IR-ordering for the elements of M_0^* specifies from metainformation viewpoint a correspondence between the terms Mx and My pertaining to IOs. It seems as if this correspondence conveys (or maps) "something" by the aid of R from one to another IOs in an arbitrary IS. Let this famous "something" be presumably called information without appealing to any known paradigm. Now introducing various kinds of algebraic morphisms (homomorphism and isomorphism, as well) one can specify uniquely any mapping of an element, e.g., IO_g~My into/onto another element IO_d~Mx via a noiseless or noisy channel. Based on such results one may identify with certainty any correspondence between m_y and m_x by a definitive function h of My into Mx in

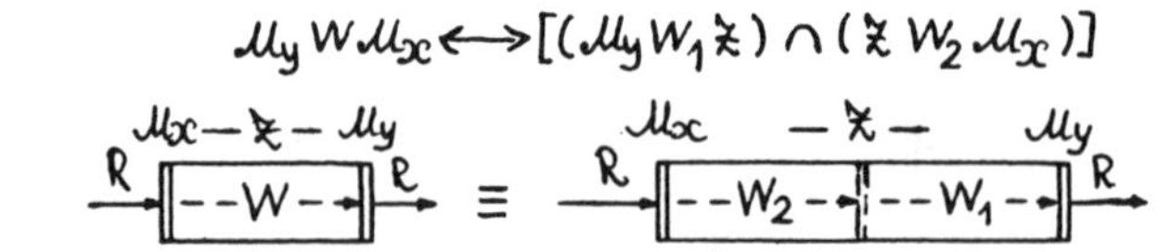

$$\mathcal{M}_y \, W \mathcal{M}_x \longleftrightarrow [(\mathcal{M}_y W_1 \check{x}) \cap (\check{x} W_2 \mathcal{M}_x)]$$

FIGURE 5. The decomposition approach in general systems theory and its interpretation in information metatheory

such results one may identify with certainty any correspondence between m_y and m_x by a definitive function h of My into Mx in arbitrary ISs possessing any number of IOs and various kinds of morphisms.

The physical (model-based) implementation of any mapping utilized may be performed by an information process: as follows. Let T be a shift operator. Then,

$$Tm_y = \left\{ m'_y(i) \right\}_{-t}^{+t}$$

where $m'_y(i) = m_y(i+1)$, $Tm_y = T(My \cap \beta_{My})$. Obviously, $m_{y(t)} = h(m_y) = m_x$ with $t > 0$ being a finite number time parameter. As all morphisms are transitive T carries the "model" m_y of the information ("something"!) of IO_g to the left after certain time units. Finally, this model becomes $m_x = h(m_y)$. That is, it reaches IO_d, or in other words, IO_d receives the information of IO_g.

INFERENCES ABOUT INFORMATION THEORY PROVOKED BY ITS METATHEORY

Following the axiomatics in T_a the IR-ordering may be interpreted as performance of the basic destination of any IS in T_i. The exchange of information as an interaction-communication (conceived in a broad sense, social, as well) is the main motive and organizational force for current information science and its practice. The rigorous assertions, as well as the IR-ordering ensure the physical validation and implementation of IS via models and do not contradict the causality principle.

The revealed IO-models with time parameter attached to them have, or may have in author's view, incentive power for further semiotical development in T_i. Besides the "classical" IOs (ideal-noiseless, corrupted and partially transforming ones described in T_m) some of the distorted and fully transforming IOs may be promising for semantic and pragmatic studies in T_i.

An interesting though speculative as yet problem consists in attempting to apply such a T_m to other scientific issues. Common for most of them is the exchange of "something," performing correspondences between inputs and outputs (e.g., transport problems).

Yet more speculative seems the application of the T_m-model to life sciences, e.g., biology etc. First of all it must be emphasized that this model, and especially its logical hierarchic levels — formal, metatheoretical, as well, should be at first glance only descriptive in nature. The normative life sciences are obligatorily informal, and it is not as yet any allusive tendency to other expansions. For the societal systems the tendency at least is to absolve the truly significant issues affecting them — the meta-like ones — from any formal problem-solving matter. But who may emphatically abstain somebody to taste the "forbidden fruit"? The outlined evolutionary approach might be a "know-how" for a theory change! It enables at least to discuss ways for theory change. Thus, for example, S. Watanabe (1975) suggested a model of scientific evolution. It was slightly readjusted in (N. Stanoulov, 1982) according to the metatheoretical study initiated in T_a and briefly mentioned here. The interested readers may direct themselves to these references.

CONCLUSION

Formulating a near-formal logical foundation and revealing meta-informally the basic information phenomena may facilitate the scope for deeper penetration of classical information theory T_i in various human activities. The advocated and only briefly described here logical transition T_i - T_a - T_m is, to our knowledge, a unique case study still spreading its impact plausibly beyond over information science itself.

Of course, it would be highly unrealistic to expect that any scientific evolution should follow all the stages of the theory change discussed, nor can one imagine when the limits of this evolution will be attained. However, the subject matter proposed exhibits the closest connection between a theory and the related research for deeper insight into its essence and evolutionary change.

REFERENCES

Bellman, R. "Communication, Ambiguity and Understanding." *Math. Biosciences*, 26, 1975.

Conant, R. C. "Laws of Information Which Govern Systems." *IEEE Trans. on Systems, Man, and Cybernetics*, SMC-6; April 1976.

Guttag, J. V., J. J. Horning. "The Algebraic Specification of Abstract Data Types." *Acta Informatica*, 10, 1978.

Kleen, S. C. *Introduction to metamathematics*. New York: Van Nostrand, 1952.

Loéve, M. *Probability theory*. New York: Van Nostrand, 1960.

Mesarovic, M. "Foundations for A General Systems Theory." In *Views of general systems theory*. New York: Wiley, 1964.

Moore, D. J., B. Russel. "Axiomatic Data Type Specifications: A First Order Theory of Linear Lists." *Acta Informatica*, 15, 1981.

Shannon, C. "A Mathematical Theory of Communication." *Bell Systems Technology Journal*, 27; 3,4, 1948.

Stanoulov, N. "An Evolutionary Approach in Information Systems Science." JASIS, September, 1982.

Webster's New Collegiate Dictionary. Springfield, MA: G. & C. Merriam Co., 1979.

Wilson, I. G. & M. E. Wilson. *"Information computers, and system design."* New York: Wiley, 1965.

"On Fire or on Ice": Prefatory Remarks on the Library in Literature

INTRODUCTION

According to Eco (1984b:3), the title of a text is often a key to its interpretation. However true that may be, the reader runs the risk of either misinterpreting the title or being intentionally mislead by the author. The title of this paper is intentionally enigmatic and is intended to cause consternation, especially the prepositional phrase "on fire" (that force which all librarians and literati fear and/or welcome). The reference to fire and its binary opposite "ice" will become clearer in this text.

I take as my theme the image of the Library in literature. It is my contention that there exists a discourse of the Library—a way of speaking which possesses distinct characteristics. For instance, the Library is often associated with or actively portrayed in a fantastic manner. There is ample evidence to suggest that the fantastic is a distinct characteristic of the literature of the library. The destruction of the library (a recapitulation of the burning of the Library of Alexandria) is a major legendary and symbolic motif in the western writing about the library. Finally, the destruction of the library is interpreted in this paper as both a curse and a blessing (hence my title).

At the very least there is something about the portrayal of the Library in literature which should give us pause—to examine with a critical eye.[1]

The author is Librarian, Career Development Center Library, SUNY-Albany. Address all inquiries to Daniel Peter Walsh, 11 Sunny Crest Dr., Carmel, NY 12203.

211

Only a handful of scholars have considered the Library in a critical or semiotic manner. A search[2] revealed a distinct paucity of works in this potentially rich area. What does exist is among the most stimulating, thought-provoking and controversial criticism written today. The Library, that venerable human institution, is apparently ripe for decentering.

The Library has been deployed as trope (figure of speech) for a very long time, perhaps as long as libraries of any size have existed. The analytical tools which enable us to regard the Library have reached an important stage[3] (using the convenient Ramist ploy) of development, especially in the past ten years with the work of the post-structuralist critics both in the United States (namely Jonathan Culler, Eugenio Donato and Robert Scholes) and elsewhere (in France: the late Michel Foucault, and Jacques Derrida, in Italy with Umberto Eco).[4] The next few years promise to be pivotal in terms of new developments in literary criticism and the critique of the Library.

Happily, there is no lack of texts that contained some reference to the Library. I have, chosen the most representative, though many texts are not included due to considerations of space or availability.[5] Inclusion is based simply on their appeal, both public and private, and the degree of "literariness" they display (naturally they also make considerable reference to the library). We detect "literariness" in a text when communication loses its simplicity and becomes "multiple or duplicitous" (Scholes, 1982:21). Thus, "literariness" is essentially another way of saying that a text is rich in meaning. "Text" also requires some clarification. "Text" is usually defined as a set of signals, conveyed through some medium, from a sender to receiver organized by a particular code or set of codes. The receiver sensing the presence of a text, interprets it according to the available and appropriate code(s). Furthermore, a distinction between open and closed is often drawn — an open text is one that is open to interpretation though related to certain generic norms, a closed entity or work implies a set of signals which is closed and self-sufficient.

All of the texts considered in this paper are for the most part open and therefore subject to a number of interpretations. The idea of intertextuality, in which texts speak of other texts, which speak of other texts and so on is manifested throughout this paper, and the texts it attempts to analyze and decenter. Not only do new texts incorporate old ones (with their meanings retained) but old textual elements appropriated with new meanings. This concept attributed to Julia Kristeva, Roland Barthes, Umberto Eco and others refers to the common principle that just as signs refer to other signs rather than directly to things, texts refer to other texts. Therefore, an intertext can be conceived of as a text or number of texts lodged or embedded within another, affecting meaning, whether the author is aware of it or not. Intertextuality will take on even greater importance below when discussed with regard to the Library – the harbinger of intertext (Scholes, 1984:145, 149).

THE TEXTS – NARRATIVES AND BASIC SEMIOTIC ANALYSIS

As previously mentioned, selection of the source texts is based on aesthetic appeal and a vivid description of the Library within the text. Observations regarding the Library, patrons or aspects of Library operations, are also taken into account. There is a discourse of the Library, a way of describing and evaluating the production of which is governed by rules of exclusion and inclusion. The major binary forms will emerge during the analysis of the texts.[6]

As Undank (1979:64) points out "texts speak of possible worlds and of possible ways of orienting one self in those worlds." The novel is a machine for generating interpretations (Eco, 1984b:2). One could say that each text what ever the genre is a machine that, with a little prodding will generate any number of interpretations, each validated by the text we are interpreting.

The following texts will be considered: *The abortion: An historical romance 1966* by Richard Brautigan, "Public facilities" a short story by Bette Howland, "The Library" a poem by Timothy Steele, *Titus Groan* – Volume One of *The Gormenghast Trilogy* by Mervyn Peake, *Bouvard and Pecuchet* by Gustave Flaubert, "The Library of Babel" a short piece by Jorge Luis Borges, and finally, *The name of the rose* by Umberto Eco.

I will divide the texts according to the binary opposition fire: ice – fire stands for the blaze of intertextuality and the actual fire, recapitulating that great loss/gain, the burning of the Library of Alexandria. Ice stands for the scintillation of texts which by one reason or another do not "blaze"; they are frozen, the intertextuality is suspended.

ICE

The Abortion: An Historical Romance 1966

Brautigan's (1971) famous text describes a most unusual Library located in the city of San Francisco. There are no borrowers, patrons bring hand crafted books of their own making: personal books, bizarre books, books that no one will read. No one lingers long at Brautigan's Library except the Librarian who is quite literally at the patrons disposal (he lives on the premises) twenty-four hours a day. The Library stays open so that any patron can wander in and deposit a book. The Librarian follows a standardized procedure for every new book. When the patron brings in a book, the Librarian enters the book's title and its author in "The Library Contents Ledger" (a pun on the Library of Congress Listing?), the book is "welcomed" and then the patron is given the privilege of placing it on a shelf anywhere in the Library. The patrons are an odd assortment indeed, mainly the very young and the very old, the disenfranchised, the rejected. Some of the books and the comments they engender are enlightening:

> *Love Always Beautiful* by Charles Green. The author was about fifty years old and said he had been trying to find a publisher for his book since he was seventeen years old when he wrote the book.
> "This book has set the world's record for rejections," he said. "It has been rejected 459 times and now I am an old man."
> *Sam Sam Sam* by Patricia Evens Summers. "It's a book of literary essays," she said. "I've always admired Alfred Kazin and Edmund Wilson, especially Wilson's theories on *The Turn of the Screw*." She was a woman in her late fifties who looked a great deal like Edmund Wilson.
> *Pancake Pretty* by Barbara Jones. The author was seven years old and wearing a pretty white dress.
> "This is a book about a pancake," she said.
> *Bacon Death* by Marsha Peterson. The author was a totally nondescript young woman except for a look of anguish on her face. She handed me this fantastically greasy book and fled the library in terror. The book actually looked like a pound of

bacon. I was going to open it and see what it was about, but I changed my mind. I didn't know whether to fry the book or put it on the shelf.

Being a librarian here is sometimes a challenge. (Brautigan, 1971:26-31)

There is not the degree of intertextuality that is present in the other texts we will look at — these texts or rather works can with the exception of *Sam Sam Sam* stand alone. They refer only to themselves, at least as far as we can tell. This library does not "glitter and disappear" — it is "ice," it glitters but does not disappear, it does not burn. While it of course never completely evades the all pervasiveness of the intertext, there is an effort towards decentering the prevailing conventions.

The Librarian is trapped (or is the Library a sanctuary?), he loves his books, although no reference in ever made to him reading them. He maintains "professional" bearing, dutifully taking care of the books in his charge and then, when the library is full, seeing to the removal of the overflow to a series of hermetically sealed caves in a remote part of northern California where they are seen to by a fantastic character named Foster (who battles among other things "seepage"). This whole section of the novel is strongly evocative of the Plato's Parable of the Cave.

The Librarian (as with Brautigan's other novels, this is a first person narrative) recounts the history of the Library (he is the 36th Librarian) which summarized begins in New York (although this is shrouded in uncertainty), this is evident by the signifier "there are a lot of old Dutch books," then it moved to St. Louis, and then to San Francisco in the 1870s. Apparently, the Library was not destroyed during the earthquake and fire of 1906, in which "it didn't lose a book." Thus, there is not the usual recapitulation of the Great Fire of Alexandria. This Library is more like that of Borges' Library of Babel, it is immutable, not easily destroyed.

The rest of the novel is devoted to the Librarian's romance with a despondent, desperate woman named Vida, cursed with an unearthly beauty. Over the course of time, she becomes pregnant and the two decide to have an abortion. A good deal of the text describes their trip to Tijuana for the abortion (a sign for such activity, within the cultural context of California of the 1960s), and the loss of the Library during his absence to an older woman who chides him for leaving it with the reprobate Foster, and takes over his position as Librarian. Because of the Librarian's kindness and poetic sense, he becomes a "hero of Berkeley."

Brautigan informs the reader that "This novel is about the romantic possibilities of a public library in California." The text is about just that, but much more; it is a unique blend of satire, the surreal, and the erotic. There is a pleasure the Librarian derives from his position, and from the presence of the texts in which he is surrounded. There is a section where he "reads" the woman's (Vida) body – thus, the woman as text. The key binary elements at work in the text are: Creation:destruction; man:woman; order:disorder; attention:neglect; personal:public; seen:unseen; wanted:unwanted; and, ugliness:beauty.

Brautigan decenters the concept of Library, raises the products of the patrons to a privileged state, regardless of style, content, the identity and fame of the author and so on. This position is the result of the temporal context of the work, i.e., the radical 1960s of California where all institutions and conventions were turned upside down. The text also speaks about the proliferation of texts, at times the Library becomes full and must be emptied, instead of destroying the books, they are consigned to a place never seen, only referred to. We are only left to imagine the vast, preserved, unread immutable, contents of the caves. There is a minimum of order, no shelf lists, no circulation of books – though it is by definition a Library. There is a mysterious organization referred to as the American Forever, Etc. which runs the Library by supplying a modicum of funding, which is negligible.

Creation of unwanted offspring is metaphorically, symbolically, in sense to books which no one will read, they must be consigned someplace, taken care of in some way. The unborn child is the result of a creative act, however misconceived – as are the works, unwanted by their authors – given, with relief to the Library. Space does not permit as full an analysis as the text demands. However, it is clear that the text is extremely complex from the number of binary oppositions which taken together constitute a partial semiotic system. There are contradictions, and ambiguities in the text which are not resolved – are the books consigned or are they destroyed by neglect in the caves? There is also a strong statement against bibliomania, Vida on three occasions tells the Librarian that he is wasting his life among his books and that he must leave the Library for the outside (phenomenological) world. There are a number of questions which continue to haunt me, do we have a parody of Borges Library of Babel, satire of the public library — knowledge in general?

There is an elaborate intertext lurking beneath the surface of Brautigan's text. Since his death in 1983 he has been described as too rooted in the 1960s to appeal to more modern readers. Perhaps now he will be appreciated for the craftsmanship he displays in *The abortion* and his other equally intelligent works.

Public Facilities

Bette Howland's (1978) "ethnographic" text regarding a Chicago branch library known as Borglum and the various points of interest of the neighborhood and inhabitants is interesting for a number of reasons. One is the disjointed, discontinuous narrative style she employs, the other is the wonderful detail which infuses her account of winter life in a poor rundown ethnic neighborhood.

In her Library the patrons often know more about the holdings than the employees. However, they do not create texts from the texts and works they peruse. The Library is used as an "alternative to idleness." One could add that the state of idleness is never transcended. In this Library the most popular texts are the medical dictionary (which is kept locked in a case when not requested by patrons), The Wall Street Journal, Standard and Poors and Barons. Borglum is the kind of place where patrons tell staff to maintain the rule of Silence. One can infer from the descriptions of the patrons and staff that they all are in poor physical condition and look as if they were all shot from a cannon through a Salvation Army window. Eccentricities are overlooked:

> Our business was books; [in italics] checking them in, stamping them out. Cataloging. Shelving. Minding our own business. At Borglum the level of tolerance for individual extremes was very high. (Howland, 1978:79)

Her Library patrons are attempting to come to grips with their problems, yet employ the library voyeuristically, peering into the medical topos or the financial topos — dreamers impotent to do anything. Books have taken on a greater dimension than real life.

Personal and place names have special significance (Eco 1984a:154) from a semiotic viewpoint, often they contain clues to characters identities adding to the semantic reserve of the text and rounding out interpretations. Furthermore, names can suggest the mythological nature of a text "by fixing in an image or a pun the character from the start, without any possibility of conversion or change." Some of the names in Howland's text are quite revealing:[7]

> Borglum (the Branch name), "bore" — (weary, ennui, "a dull time") + "glum" — (sullen, gloomy, dark).

> Mrs. Speer (the head librarian) — her name is that of the infamous nazi architect; it is also (OED) the branch of a deer's horn, "to look into, to ask"; her character is autocratic, prone to phobias, precise yet gets nothing accomplished. Her mission is to "protect the public from itself."

> Bee Bee (a staff member) — this young woman reads at work — something expressly forbidden, (OED) "Bhi" (Aryan) means "to fear" (lit. "quivering"), always worried, furtive that her clandestine reading will be discovered (as will her courtship with a local man) will be found out — thus she is always high strung and nervous. She hides books in her library locker, quite ironic that "The worst thing that you can hide in a library" is books. "The clandestine had a natural appeal for Bee Bee." (ibid. 85)

There are a number of binary oppositions which make up the structure of this short story: ennui:tirelessness; clean:dusty; circulation:stagnation; boom:bust; rich:poor; efficiency:inefficiency; main branch:Borglum and so on.

At one point in the text the author contrasts the main branch with Borglum. Borglum is as worn out looking as the neighborhood in which it is located. The head librarian has refused to catalog and place in circulation all the recent acquisitions, everyone seems lackadaisical, weary (with the exception of a few stalwarts, yet they are powerless). The books are in deplorable condition: "bindings loose, pages ripped out, pictures defaced, mustaches, pubic hair, scratched in ball point pen etc." (ibid. 81). The staff attitude is summed up in the following excerpts:

> There were two schools of philosophy in the public library. One was that it existed for the sake of circulating books. The other was that it existed for the sake of preserving them. (ibid. 80)

Why catalogue? Why file? Why put books on the shelves? Why send them off to meet their fate—abandon them to the inevitable? Why start the whole damn thing all over again? She was weary of it all, the endless cycle, dreariness, decline, destruction. (ibid. 84)

The Main Branch is described thusly:

> . . . Board of Directors, meetings downtown . . . the lime-stone white elephant on Michigan Boulevard? Guards, uni-forms, badges posted everywhere; at the turnstile entrances, outside the public lavatories, on marble staircases with high carved mottoes. MCMXL . . . PRO BONO PVBLICO . . . (ibid. 80)

The two are placed in polar opposition to each other, the Main Branch is privileged, public relations conscious, it is the Library with intertextuality and the burden of Western civilization. Borglum is frozen, there is a minimum of intertextuality, the poor are concerned with survival, "high carved mottoes" signifies the luxury of privilege the presence of which is inscribed everywhere to be read by those who cannot decode the symbolic trappings and further reinforces the meaning for those who can. The patrons of the Main Branch respond to this environment in expected fashion, they have meetings, produce texts and so on. The patrons and staff of the Borglum branch respond in a more elemental, ontological manner:

> Funny things go on in libraries; everyone knows that. It's got something to do with all those stacks; shelves and shelves of weighty books. Reason is a passion; an instinct, a drive. It's not so strange if citizens respond in its temples with primitive gestures; flashing switchblades, unzipping flies. (ibid. 80)

I find irksome Howland's global reference to "Libraries," I think her description fits the Borglum Branch not the Main Branch. The knowledge that the Borglum patrons seek has direct relevance to their lives—especially for those using the medical dictionary, their needs are the most personal. The knowledge is too important to write about, it must be supplemented with experience. They have more at stake than the privileged Main Branch patrons. Furthermore, they are not hesitant to inscribe, mark their fleeting presences on the texts they borrow. Therefore, the Borglum Branch presents something of a problem it is moribund, yet more alive in another sense then the sterile, elitism of the Main Branch. Finally, the Borglum Branch is slated for remodeling. It is not to be torn down (and not recapitulate the Library of Alexandria destruction) but "only remodeled, surrounded" (ibid. 80). This Library scintillates, but is frozen; there is a minimum of intertextuality.

FIRE

"The Library"

Timothy Steele's poem "The Library" is an auspicious place to begin this section. His brief text is very rich in meaning; however, the dominant themes expressed in binaries are: past:present; calm: storm; nature:culture; and hoard:discard. The poem is a personal reflection on the modern twentieth century with its ironic juxtaposition of past and present, books — the design of which has not changed in a thousand years, share the same topos as micro-computer databases, and "tattle-tape."

The poet reflects on this blend of technologies, of past and present. His search for materials amid the tremendous profusion of texts, even with the marvels of library automation conjures up intertextual images to express his doubts and suspicions — "I feel I'm playing Faustian video games." He places little trust in the fragile system, the recurring use of the image of the hot wind (Santa Annas) and the autumn leaves warn that the wind from the desert could come (perhaps in a different form) and sweep it all away. The wind awakens the ancient memory of the burned Library of Alexandria. The hoardings of (Squirrel-like) modern Man are at least safe from partial catastrophe. The poetic narrator settles on the rituals of check-out time and the instinctive hoarding of a squirrel in the conclusion of this somber, self reflective poem:

> The frail must, in fair times, collect and store, and so amid swirled papery debris, The squirrel creeps nosing round, compelled to hoard by instinct, habit, necessity. (Steele, 1983:129)

Humans are frail creatures, "compelled to hoard by instinct, habit and necessity," whom without culture, as manifested in the Library would probably not survive. The changing of the seasons, symbolizing the blind forces of nature would not notice the loss in any case.

Titus Groan: Volume One of the Gormenghast Trilogy

"To tell a story," Eco (1984b:23) tells us, "you must first of all construct a world, furnished as much as possible down to the slightest detail." Mervyn Peakes' masterpiece *The Gormenghast Trilogy* is an indicate, wonderfully atmospheric world which brings to mind an intertext consisting of Dickens, Lord Dunsany, and Poe, with Lovecraft thrown in for good measure. The text vividly relates the recent history of the infinitely immense Castle Gormenghast and its various inhabitants, especially its rulers, the Groan family and its assorted retainers, servants and others. The narrative is quite involved and suffice to say it is the recounting of the birth, coming of age, flight and prodigal return of Lord Titus Groan.

Titus rebels from the claustrophobic world of Gormenghast — a world governed by textual instructions in the form of ritual procedures which must be followed exactly to the letter. He flees the Castle for the ontological surety of first hand experience. He later returns disillusioned, for the comparative safety and predictability of the text.

The Library

Located in a vast, infrequently traveled region of Castle Gormenghast, it is a long two tiered building with several entrances. The Library is for the sole use of Lord Sepulchrave (Titus' father), a devout lover of books (also perpetually melancholy). It is Sepulchraves' private and only preferable realm, and if not for the elaborate ceremonies it is his duty as Lord to perform, he would remain there all the time in order to avail himself of "his only pleasure — books." Approximately 100,000 books comprise the Library holdings, many of the them written by the past Earls of Gormenghast; it abounds in literature, essays, and poetry.

Peakes description of the Library is so lovingly drawn that I feel compelled to reproduce it at least in part:

> The room was lit by a chandelier whose light, unable to reach the extremities of the room, lit only the spines of those volumes on the central shelves of the long walls. A stone gallery ran around the library at about fifteen feet above the floor, and the books that lined the walls of the main hall fifteen feet below were continued upon the high shelves of the gallery.
>
> In the middle of the room, immediately under the light, stood a long table. It was carved from a single piece of blackest marble, which reflected upon its surface three of the rarest volumes in his Lordship's collection. (Peake, 1968:216-217)

The place in the text which concerns us involves Lord Sepulchrave, and several key characters including the infant Titus himself. Steerpike, an extremely ambitious young manservant wishes to establish himself in a higher position in the highly ritualized and hierarchical social and political life of the Castle. By various machinations he has attained the exalted position of assistant to the Master of Ritual, an ancient wizened creature named Sourdust, but he wants more.

By burning the Library and arriving just in time to save the occupants (Sepulchrave, Countess Gertrude, Titus, his nanny, his sister and Sourdust) and he will increase his prestige and thus raise his standing. If Sourdust should die, so much the better.

Steerpike cleverly prepares the Library for incineration by employing an elaborate arrangement of oil soaked rags distributed behind the book lined shelves. He is inhuman in his attention to detail. He goes so far as to enlist the aid of the two senile twin sisters — Cora and Clarice of Sepulchrave — who have been neglected by the "court" to help him carry out the deed. The dialogue he has with them prior to the Burning is instructive:

> [Steerpike] "And now you must tell me, dear ladies, what is your brother's main interest?" They [the aunts] went on smoothing their knees. "Is it not literature?" said Steerpike. "Is he not a great lover of books?" They nodded. "He's very clever," said Cora. "But he reads it all in books," said Clarice. "Exactly." Steerpike followed quickly upon this. "Then if he lost his books, he would be all but defeated." "If the center of his life were destroyed he would be but a shell."

"As I see it your Ladyships, it is at his library that our first thrust must be directed." (Peake, 1968:273)

When Steerpike commits his arsonist deed, only Sourdust – the Librarian and Master of Ritual is killed, overcome by smoke. The rest are saved by Steerpike. Sepulchrave goes mad when his Library is destroyed, his visage is characterized by a "sick sliding smile" (which recalls a statement made by Gibbons to be discussed below) and eventually dies a suicide, killed by owls. The poor ruined Library is described in highly imagistic language:

> the smoking shell of Sepulchrave's only home. The shelves that still stood were wrinkled charcoal, and the books were standing side by side upon them, black, gray and ash-white, the *corpses of thought*. (emphasis mine, Peake, 1968:34)

The segment of Peake's text that I have just presented consists of the following binaries: pragmatic:ethereal; privilege:underprivilege; book experience:life experience; and destruction:creation. The Library is for the exclusive use of the Lord, thus following the tradition of the privileged state of learning and the text.

Steerpikes' destruction of the Library could not have been accomplished had Sepulchrave been more aware of everyday life in the Castle. He is a bookman, the Library held a dire and fatal importance for him. "The Library appeared to spread outward from him as from a core" (Peake, 1968:217). Sepulchrave is a sufferer from book melancholia,[8] which can be cured only through "fire" – an act of ridding oneself of books. He has the weight of 100,000 books simultaneously comforting/appalling him. At one point in a rage over being "infantile" about expressing ordinary human affection toward his young son Titus: "He flung the book from him and then immediately retrieved it, smoothing its sides with his shaking hands" (ibid. 245).

He is ambivalent about his library, because, within each literati is the knowledge that they are not living life, but experiencing a simulcrum of it. Edward Gibbon's famous utterance (quoted in Thiem, 1979:510) regarding the burning of the Library of Alexandria is appropriate to Sepulchrave's response ("sick sliding smile") to the burning of his Library: "a philosopher may allow, with a smile that [the Saracen destruction of theological controversy] was ultimately devoted to the benefit of mankind." According to Gibbons' research the only texts left in the Library of Alexandria were ponderous, useless things, thus the smile signifies the pleasure of seeing the follies of the past burned. The Great Burning recapitulated in Peakes' novel will be discussed in the conclusion. The intertextuality of Peakes' text is rich in the core literature of the West.

Bouvard and Pecuchet

Gustave Flaubert's classic work recounts the misadventures of two office clerks who having received a substantial inheritance set out to appropriate vast areas of experience and knowledge. All their efforts are ill-conceived, and ill-fated; they are obsessed with "wanting to conclude" epistemological questions of shifting quantity and to boot must contend with a society which is duplicitous at best.

At one point in the story, the two bachelors attempt to acquire and copy every printed article they come in contact with, until it occurs to them that knowledge about a subject does not immediately give competence in that area. For instance, all the book-knowledge one can absorb will not guarantee a perfect harvest (or a harvest at all for that matter). The two fail at everything they try but their efforts are so charming, hilarious, and poignantly human that one cannot help liking them.

Donato's (1979) comments regarding Flauberts' text are so telling and complete for the purposes of this paper that any addition is unnecessary. Flaubert's text is the product of the Library, it contains self-reflexive comments on the Library while it appropriates it. Intertexuality, it would appear, begins in the novel with Flaubert's text. It is obvious from the reading Donato performs that Flaubert is a linguistic nihilist, and that he offers a scathing critique of representation with his Bouvard and Pecuchet (ibid. 217). As Donato explains:

> If the Library makes Bouvard and Pecuchet possible, in no way does it provide it with a privileged origin which might guarantee the mimetic or representational veracity of fiction or the capacity of the world to fictionalize itself in an unequivocal fashion. What the Library imposes on the two unfortunate heroes of Flaubert's novel is the impossibility of reaching its order, its totality or its truth. (ibid. 216)

We, the author, the characters, the readers are all doomed to wander in a labyrinth much like that in Borges' Library (which will be considered next). The author, furthermore, is reduced to the status of scribe, no privileged origins. Without the publication of Bouvard and Pecuchet; Borges' Library of Babel would be impossible. It is perhaps the first novel which is overtly intertextual, "it is a book constructed out of fragments of other books; the book presupposes, then, the Library as its genetic memory" (ibid. 216).

Finally, a few comments from Flaubert on his "meanderings through the Library" are of considerable importance for what follows:

> I'm aghast at what I have to do for Bouvard and Pecuchet. I read catalogues of books that I annotate. . . . I am sir, inside a labyrinth! . . . I have gotten indigestion from books. . . . I burp in folio. . . . Reading is an abyss; one never gets out of it. I am becoming as dumb as a pot. (ibid. 214-215)

Additionally, Flaubert in his companion "volume" to Bouvard and Pecuchet The Dictionary of Received Ideas has two entries that further reinforce his feelings regarding the novel:

> Book: "Always too long, whatever the subject."
> Library — "Always have one at home, especially if you live in the country." (ibid. 296, 315)

Perhaps the effort of intextualizing a novel is damaging to the health because Flaubert died before the text was finished.

Library of Babel

Jorge Luis Borges, in his well known "Library of Babel" depicts a coolly surrealistic landscape which is simultaneously a parable and a symbol. To Borges the Library stands as a symbol for the universe, complete with scholars of various persuasions arguing about its shape and structure. There is no entrance into this Library — it is closed to the "outside," there is no "outside," only the Library.

There are several organizing principles of the Library: (1) The Library is eternal. (2) The number of orthographic symbols is twenty five, repeated randomly which proves "the formless chaotic nature of all books." (3) Architecturally organized according to a complex geometric form.

The Library denizens hold various beliefs regarding its existence, physical laws, and history. Of the denizens, there seem to be at least a few differentiations: Librarians tantamount to mayors, "Inquisitors" ("official searchers") "who are always exhausted," "Purifiers" ("Weeders") whose job is to eliminate useless works (they are the book burners, "their ascetic, hygienic fury is responsible for the senseless loss of millions of books" (Alexandria recapitulated).

Those who mourn the "treasures" (the burning of the Library seen as "fortunate misfortune"; ridicule book-knowledge) overlook two notorious facts. "One, the Library is so enormous that any reduction undertaken by humans is infinitesimal. Two, while "each book is unique, irreplaceable, but (inasmuch as the Library is total) there are always several hundreds of thousands of imperfect facsimiles of works which differ only by one letter of one comma" (Borges, 1977 [1962]:85). There is even an equivalent to the Grail called "The Man of the Book" — "the cipher and perfect compendium of all the rest, "it is analogous to a god." As Borges points out the quest for this ideal has spurned on the minions of this world:

> Thousands of covetous persons abandoned their natal hexagons and crowded up the stairs, urged on by the vain aim of finding their Vindication. These pilgrims disputed in the narrow corridors, hurled dire maledictions, strangled each other on the divine stairways, flung the deceitful books to the bottom of the tunnels and died as they were thrown into space by men from remote regions. Some went mad. (ibid. 85)

The tale is a parable of our own world. We know this because of the cultural codes implicit in the text—which constitute the texts reference to things already "known" and codified by a culture. Traditional realism of which this text is an example, despite its odd appearance is defined by its reference to what is already known. The axioms and proverbs, the short hand of communication, of a culture or subculture constitute already coded bits upon which a novelist and writer of the caliber of Borges may rely (Roland Barthes quoted in Scholes, 1982:97-100). Thus, when Borges states that books in the Library "in themselves mean nothing"; he is drawing on the knowledge already deployed in the reader regarding the importance of context. He is also drawing on the almost innate fear that grips a patron when all the books of a library are beheld.

The Library is perfect in its holdings, all languages are present, yet there is much dross:

> Everything is there: the minute history of the future, the auto-biographies of the archangels, the faithful catalogue of the Library, thousands and thousands of false catalogues. . . . (ibid. 86)

The intertextuality that Flauberts used with such success, is turned on its ear. For every statement of truth the Library contains, there are thousands of refutations. The Library is immutable in contradiction. No possibility of ridding ourselves of this synergistic monster exists:

> Perhaps I am deceived by old age and fear, but I suspect that the human species — the unique human species — is on the road to extinction, while the Library will last on forever: illuminated, solitary, infinite, perfectly immovable, filled with precious volumes, useless, incorruptible, secret. (ibid. 87)

In Borges hands, the Library, usually a staid and comfortable place becomes a "fantastic and terrifying labyrinth of paper" (O'Sullivan, 1984:75). O'Sullivan whose text demystifies Borges and to a large extent much of the existing material regarding the Library from a post-structuralist perspective goes on to point out that:

> Having himself worked in the Argentine National Library, Borges is well aware of the almost gothic horror which faintly illuminated and seemingly endless rows of shelves are capable of evoking. (ibid.)

Borges' metaphors suggest "exteriority" of texts — libraries, books, encyclopedias and dictionaries. Exteriority refers to the idea that instead of studying the core meaning of a text (logocentrism) for the primal oral moment, we should instead examine the discourse itself, "its appearance and its regularity, that we should look for its external conditions of existence, for that which gives rise to the chance series of these events and fixes its limits" (Foucault cited in O'Sullivan, 1984:74).

Michel Foucault was concerned with the Library in his later writings (prior to his death in 1982). It is Foucault who inspired the idea of the conflaguration of intertextuality that characterizes the Library thusly:

> Libraries simultaneously repel and attract, disclose and obscure, promise knowledge and yet oftimes yield only confusion and ignorance. Intertextuality usurps extraverbality, the Library replaces rhetoric, and we are left to deal with a world of infinite self-referentiality, of perfect repetition and actuality. (ibid. 75)

Additionally, by "on fire" as Foucault and O'Sullivan aver, they mean that texts can extend the space existing books can occupy; hides, displays; can "cause them to glitter and disappear." Hypertextuality characterizes the Libraries of Borges, Eco, Peake, and Steele: it is a condition of proliferation, "of bound volumes extending beyond themselves seemingly to infinity" (ibid. 76).

"The shelves" in the Library of Borges are arranged "in an indefinite, perhaps infinite, number of hexagonal galleries" and these are reflected in a mirror by the entrance (note this same apparition in Eco's text to be considered next) way which only increases the sense of vertigo by insinuating that the Library may indeed be "limitless and periodic." We must remember that mirrors suggest questions of mimesis and representation mirrors are real objects that merely suggest representation. Thus, we see in the Library, discourse and duplication, the Library and the Mirror.

According to Roland Barthes (cited in O'Sullivan, 1984:78) every text is the intertext of another text, this much has been stated in the preceding pages. However, he makes a distinction between text and work which has profound implications for the Library. A text is a category which "traverses and transgresses traditional hierarchies and generic divisions." A work on the other hand, "sits on the Library shelf, occupying a specific book space, while the text is plural intertextual — not defined by, nor confined to the various myths of filiation source, origin, genius and influence."

O'Sullivan summarizes the semiotics of the Library of Borges and its philosophical implications in the following:

Discourse cannot be forced into continuums of unity and/or similarity and we are left to contend with the metaphor of the Library and all its attendant characteristics—*plentitude, serialization, the exteriority of language, the infinity of words* (ibid. 78, emphasis mine)

Borges' libraries are merely maze-like suggestions of infinity, housing finite beings reading by incessant and insufficient light. . . . He presents us with the horrible fancy of the library, the vast contradictory library, whose vertical deserts of books run the incessant risk of metamorphosis which affirm everything, deny everything, and confuse everything like a raving god. (ibid.)

The Name of the Rose

All the textual forms covered thus far may be found in Eco's famous best selling novel of medieval Europe. It is the culmination of the intertextuality of the Library. Eco points out that: "to tell a story you must first of all construct a world, furnished as much as possible down to the slightest detail" (Eco, 1984b:23).

He has largely succeeded in creating such a world. However, what kind of world is it? Is his text a representation of a medieval world; a medieval world seen through the eyes of a late twentieth century scholar; or a contemporary account masquerading as a "medieval tale"? Perhaps all these views are tenable to a certain degree. What is most fascinating is the knowledge that Eco is fully aware of the preceding ideas especially intertextuality. He read and reread many texts written during and about the medieval setting in which he places his tale: he is familiar with the Library: "the Library is a great labyrinth, a sign of the labyrinth of the world. You enter and you do not know whether you will come out" (ibid. 55). Shades of Borges! (And shades of many other texts, obscure and otherwise are present in Eco's text.) There is an enormous intertext[9] lurking in Eco's text, some of the features of which will be discussed below.

Eco's text is incredibly rich, and offers clues to its own construction and interpretation.[10] The remainder of this section is influenced by his own statement regarding interpretation: "Books are not made to be believed, but to be subjected to inquiry. When we consider a book, we mustn't ask ourselves what it says but what it means"

(Eco, 1983:316). All the master tropes are represented in the text, metaphor, metonomy, synecdoche and above all irony.

The Library of the monastery is located at the uppermost floor of a huge building within the monastery walls known as the Aedificium. Access to the Library is restricted, only the Librarian is permitted to go there. The Library is huge, with many thousands of volumes. There is an elaborate filing system which orders the collection, but it is a secret to everyone but the Librarian. The holdings of the Library are presented in a bound volume. The Library is defended like a fortress. The Aedificium is honeycombed with secret passages, it is a labyrinth. The Library is a maze, based on complex geometric forms especially the pentagon and the heptagon, with mirrors, soporifics and vision producing substances to further confuse intruders. "Someone puts magic herbs there during the night to convince importunate visitors that the library is guarded by diabolical presences" (Eco, 1983:175).

One possible reading of the Library of Eco is that it is employed metaphorically as a symbol for the contemporary Library. There is the seeming confusion (as well as order), the privilege of the institution and its holdings, and its huge, unmanageable size. Furthermore, the Librarian often presents a formidable visage, together with his/her seemingly miraculous knowledge of the alchemical filing systems. Humor is introduced by the use of mirrors (recall Borges, his text constantly recurs), and soporifics and hallucinogens recall the both Borges and Flaubert. The "diabolical presences" may call to mind the weight of all the entombed souls, the murmuring voices of dead author-functions.

Semiotic coding of Eco text involves the following binary oppositions: privileged:deprived; known:unknown; creation:destruction; presence:absence; finite:infinite, and so on.

For example, a metonymic expression is created when William and Adso proceed from the unknown (mystery) to the known (de-mystery) at the conclusion of the text when all is revealed, terrible as that may be. The one instance of the library in Eco is synecdotal — it conveys some sense about all Libraries, it is a metalibrary. The finite/infinite binary is expressed innumerable times in the text, and signifies the rapture of monastic life as much as it does the realities of life everywhere, and the survival of the Library.

In many places in the text, Eco permits the characters to speak, quite contemporarily of semiotic and post-structuralist issues:

Adso: "Until then I had thought each book spoke of the things, human and divine, that lie outside books. Now I realized that not infrequently books speak of books: it is as if they spoke among themselves. In light of this reflection, the Library seemed all the more disturbing to me. It was then the place of long centuries old murmuring, an imperceptible dialogue between one parchment and another, a living thing, a receptacle of powers not to be ruled by a human mind, a treasure of secrets emanated by many minds, surviving the death of those who had produced them or had been their conveyors." (Eco, 1983:286)

William: "A book is made up of signs that speak of other signs, which in their turn speak of things. Without an eye to read them, a book contains signs that produce no concepts, therefore it is dumb. This Library was perhaps born to save the books it houses, but now it lives to bury them. This is why it has become a sink of iniquity." (ibid. 396)

Note the description by Malachi of the role and training of the Librarian:

He [Malachi] spoke as if discussing someone other than himself and I realized he was speaking of the office [Librarian] that at that moment he unworthily held, but which had been held by a hundred others, now deceased, who had handed down their knowledge from one to the other. (Eco, 1983:75)

It is enough for the Librarian to know them [the books of the library] and know when each book came here. As for the other monks, they can rely on his memory. (ibid. 76)

The *Name of the Rose* is many texts, it is an exegesis in semiotics, an attempt to represent the medieval world of the monastery — it is first and foremost, a murder mystery. Without going to great lengths to recount the plot, the key to the resolution of several grisly, bizarre murders rests somewhere on the shelves of the Library. William of Baskerville (recall Sherlock Holmes, Doyle) and his Watson, Adso of Melke must enter the Library, an act clearly against the rules of the place (note the emphasis on "rules" and "order"), and decode the maze and find the text.

William figures out the riddle of the Library by viewing it from outside. "The Library is constructed according to a celestial harmony to which various and wonderful meanings can be attributed."

At one point in their efforts to unravel the secrets of the Library the pair are lost, wandering aimlessly through the Labyrinth (recall Borges).

The most fascinating aspect of Eco's text is the Burning of the Library at the end of the book. The Library becomes the symbol of the Great Disaster, like the Titanic, it is swollen with hubris, doomed by its own overwhelming Presence to destruction. Also typical of disasters is the cavalier attitude expressed by the participants.

As Adso points out, "the Library could not be threatened by any earthly force, it was a living thing. . . . But if it was living why should it not be opened to the risk of knowledge" (Eco, 1983:185-186).

In this passage is expressed the idea of privilege and underprivilege and the inevitable transformation which occurs in the text. The knowledge is hoarded by the monks, access is restricted by a number of devices which ironically result in its downfall.

The fire which burns the Library is accidental though occurs at the moment of the greatest unmasking i.e., the discovery of the murderer.

> Everything happened in a few moments as if for centuries those ancient pages had been yearning for arson and were rejoicing in the sudden satisfaction of an immemorial thirst for ecpyrosis. (ibid. 483)

> William realizing we would not be able to put them [burning books] out with our hands decided to use books to save books to save books.

The effort failed, it only produced more sparks. This statement is so ironic that its meaning needs no gloss to make it public.

> The Library had been doomed by its own impenetrability, by the mystery that protected it, by its few entrances. (ibid. 489)

The Library which seemed so solid revealed its weaknesses, cracks:

the walls corroded from within the crumbling stones allowing
the flames to reach the wooden elements wherever they were.
(ibid. 488)

The fires spread quickly to the church and then to the rest of the
Abbey, destroying it as it rightly should, for what are book men
without their precious texts.

Adso visits the ruined Abbey years later and manages to salvage a
few pages of the many thousands of destroyed texts: "at the end of
my patient reconstruction, I had before me a kind of lesser library, a
symbol of the greater, vanished one: a library made up of fragments, quotations, unfinished sentences, amputated stumps of
books." As one of the monks put it: "We live for books. A sweet
mission dominated by disorder and decay" (ibid. 112).

> "Perhaps you do not know, or have forgotten, that only the
> Librarian is allowed access to the Library." It is right and
> sufficient that only the Librarian know how to decipher [filing
> system of the Library] these things. . . . "The books are regis-
> tered in order of their acquisition, donation, or entrance within
> our walls" (ibid. 75).

Eco's text is vitally important towards the development of a semiotic of the Library. It will continue to inspire and haunt interested
readers for many years to come.

CONCLUSIONS

Before moving on to a discussion of the work of Jon Thiem, and
the Great Burning I will briefly consider the above texts as examples of the fantastic.

According to Todorov (1975:25), text is considered fantastic
when an audience wavers between a naturalistic and supernatural
explanation for a particular phenomenon. If the text leads them to
choose the former, it falls into the class of the "strange," where the
most improbable events are discovered to have a naturalistic explanation. If a supernatural explanation is proposed, then the work falls
into a different class, the "marvelous." It is only when the audience is left suspended between the two modes of explanation that
they are in the realm of the fantastic.

The fantastic is a distinct characteristic of the literature of the Library. It can be found in varying degrees in all the texts thus far considered. We have huge, grotesquely swollen Libraries immolated, their owners consigned, mad, to a bookless world forced to experience the world directly. This condition prevails in the "Fire" texts, specifically: Eco, Peake, Steele (to a lesser degree). Borges' Library of Babel may be considered a principle example of the fantastic Library — unfathomable, monstrous, a parable, "that great libraries with their repetitious, contradictory contents are no less perplexing than the world they are meant to explain . . . configurations of hell" (Thiem, 1979:524). One can go on and on, however the main point is that the Library is, when decentered from the familiar, quite surprising, and terrible.

One fantastic element which seems to recur endlessly is the Great Burning of the Library of Alexandria. Jon Thiem (1979) has considered this historical event/archetype from a number of perspectives, many of which are applicable to the texts considered above.

Thiem considers the legendary and symbolic significance of the burning of the Library in Western consciousness. It would appear that there did exist a Great Library and that it did indeed burn at some point in history. What seems to be contested is the significance of the Burning.

Today most literati consider the loss of the Library as a great tragedy: it was not always regarded as such. Since the Renaissance, and perhaps before, the Burning has been viewed by many scholars and intellectuals ("learned antagonists of letters") as a "fortunate misfortune symbolizing the ecstatic annihilation of the memory of historical man" (Thiem, 1979:507).

Thiem traces the development of the idea of "fortunate misfortune" and the deprecation of learning as folly, as troublesome, seditious impediments to existence, through the work of authors spanning four hundred years of European literary history from Louis Le Roy (ca. 1500s) to George Bernard Shaw.

With the proliferation of the printed book many scholars began to note the incredible burden that the new knowledge brought, its periphery beyond the ken of one person. Learning was regarded as a folly, preventing people from enjoying life. Furthermore, the new inventions, i.e., gunpowder, printing press proved the Ancients were fallible, thus the destruction of the Library "affords the Moderns the opportunity to revitalize learning with new insights, new developments so that they too might enjoy great honor" (ibid. 514).

The destruction of the Library was interpreted differently in each period of European history. For instance, theistic reasons were, according to tradition, used to condone the burning, as is exemplified in the Story of Omar and the Destruction of Alexandria:

> It is said that Caliph Omar, consulted on what should be done with the Library of Alexandria, replied in these terms: If the books in this library contain things opposed to the Koran, they are bad and must be burned. If they contain only the doctrine of the Koran, burn them anyway they are superfluous. (ibid. 517)

During the Medieval Ages, the Burning was regarded as a shocking waste, a catastrophe, "to the medieval scholar, who in his bookishness prized all authors" (ibid. 512).

For Rousseau, Browne, and a number of their contemporaries considered the Library of Alexandria: "as propagator of Letters was to the past what printing is to the eighteenth century, so the burning of the Alexandrian library becomes a fugura for the abolition of the pernicious press" (ibid. 518). A common thread runs through texts of this period, that being the bulk of letters and learning ought to be destroyed in order to ensure the moral and mental well being of the people.

For the modern utopian, "the destruction of the learning of the past, of its radical revision and reduction, represents the cessation of historical process and constitutes a basic precondition for happiness and justice" (ibid. 519).

A major shift appeared around the end of the nineteenth century, instead of representing the accumulated follies of the ancients, or the stultification of western culture; the Alexandrian Library came to symbolize the historical memory of humanity. Shaw's *Caesar and Cleopatra* (1901) recapitulates or reactivates two arguments or positions used to rationalize the Alexandrian destruction: books are vanities that menace the well being of the people, the integrity of the past hinders present and future creativity (ibid. 523).

Summarizing Thiem's complex argument, the basic reasons for the symbolic manipulation of the Burning seem to be:

1. "After printing, no one man could any longer master the learning of a single discipline. For the man of letters embarrassed by the proliferation of learning, the vision of learning

destroyed or reduced at Alexandria might offer intense gratifi-
cation."
2. "Books threaten to replace or use up the prerogatives of the
world."
3. "The man of letters through his intimate relation to the books
and learning of the past, feels more sharply than others the
excess and terror of history . . . benign state of forgetful-
ness." (ibid.)

What are we to make of all this with regard to our texts? First off,
by my reading of Thiem suggests that the burning Library of Eco,
Steele and perhaps Peake "expresses the hostility to letters of a
culture dominated by electronic media" (ibid. 525). It is notewor-
thy that the authorial presence in Eco's text is a monk, deploring the
loss of the Library, yet acknowledging the necessity of the act. The
liberating aspect of the Burning did not go unnoticed by Eco.

Another curious feature of the "fire" texts is that the loss is always of gigantic proportions; Peakes' burning library is vast and the
domain of one individual. It is almost as if: "the tremendous mass
[of books] was set on fire and offered as an expiatory sacrifice to
veracity, to good sense and true taste . . . the burden of the past
acquires here an appropriate numerical value with the burning of a
huge pile of books and journals" (ibid. 519).

All the texts (including this one) seem to reflect the second point
in my extrapolation of Thiem's ideas: i.e., that books threaten to
distract our energies from more ontological concerns. In Peake,
Eco, Steel, Howland, Flaubert and Brautigan, their characters are
constantly struggling with this idea, in some cases catastrophically.

In conclusion, this paper hopefully revealed the potential richness
of the enormous amount of material regarding the Library as sym-
bol/sign and the implications of such an interpretation.

NOTES

1. See Raman Selden's thoroughly enlightening text cited in the bibliography for a comprehensive overview of contemporary literary criticism, esp. Chapters 3 and 4.
2. I am in the process of compiling an annotated bibliography of the Library in literature
and interpretive sources. A number of sources in French, German and Japanese as well as
English have been assembled, intended for a much more comprehensive and thorough mono-
graph.
3. See Robert Scholes and Edmund Leach sources in the bibliography for an introduction
to the conceptual apparatus available to the student of signification. Both books have extensive "suggested reading" sections which are annotated.
4. See Jonathan Culler in Bibliography esp. Part One.

5. A number of very interesting texts are no longer in print or were unattainable at the time of writing. In an anticipated longer version of this paper, every effort will be made to acquire them.

6. See Scholes (1982:17-21) for additional information about "literariness." See Leach (1976:12-15) for material about the characteristics and dimensions of the sign and the symbol. See Culler (1981:76-77) for definitions of the four master tropes: metaphor, metonymy, synecdoche and irony.

7. Associated meanings are for the most part derived from *Oxford English Dictionary*, see bibliography for full citation.

8. See pages iii, 400 for the despair caused by books, and p. 22 for the great proliferation of texts, p. 24 for the mischief caused by books in Burton, *The Anatomy of Melancholy*.

9. "A book is made up of signs that speak of other signs, which in their turn speak of things" (Eco, 1983:396).

10. For those few who want to read more about the creation of a best seller, Eco recently completed a brief, charming account of the arduous task (reminiscent of Flaubert's travails with *Bouvard and Pecuchet*) of putting researching and putting together *The name of the rose* (Eco, 1984b).

REFERENCES

Borges, Luis Jorge (1977). The library of Babel. In *Ficciones*, trans. and with an introduction by Anthony Kerrigan pp. 79-88. Grove Press.

Brautigan, Richard (1971). *The abortion: An historical romance 1966*. Simon and Schuster, New York.

Burton, Robert (1977). *The anatomy of melancholy: What it is, with all the kinds, causes, symptoms, prognostickes & several cures of it*. Vintage Books.

Culler, Jonathan (1981). *The Pursuit of Signs: Semiotics, Literature, Deconstruction*. Cornell University Press.

Donato, Eugenio (1979). The museum's furnace: notes toward a contextual reading of Bouvard and Pecuchet. In *Textual strategies: Post-structuralist criticism*, edited and with an introduction by Josue V. Harari, pp. 213-238. Cornell University Press.

Eco, Umberto (1983). *The name of the rose*. Harcourt Brace Jovanovich.

_____ (1984a). *The role of the reader: Explorations in the semiotics of texts*. Indiana University Press.

_____ (1984b) *Postscript to the name of the rose*, translated by William Weaver. Harcourt Brace Jovanovich.

Flaubert, Gustave (1981). *Bouvard and Pecuchet*, translated with an introduction by A. J. Krailsheimer. Penguin Books.

Howland, Bette (1978). Public facilities. In *Blue in Chicago*, pp. 68-94. Harper.

Peake, Mervyn (1968 [1946]). *Titus Groan* vol. 1 of *The Gormenghast Trilogy*. Ballantine Books.

Leach, Edmund (1976). *Culture and communication: The logic by which symbols are connected*. Cambridge University Press.

O'Sullivan, Gerry (1984). The library is on fire: Hypertextuality and the violation of generic boundaries in Borges and Foucault. *The CEA Critic* 46(3&4):72-79.

The Oxford Universal Dictionary (1955). Third Edition with Addenda. Oxford at the Clarendon Press.

Scholes, Robert (1982). *Semiotics and interpretation*. Yale University Press.

Seldon, Raman (1985). *A readers guide to contemporary literary theory*. University Press of Kentucky.

Steele, Timothy (1983). The library [poem]. *Poetry* CXLII (III): 128-129.

Thiem, Jon (1979). The great library of Alexandria burnt: Towards the history of a symbol. *Journal of the History of Ideas* 40(4):507-526.

Todorov, Tzvetan (1975). *The fantastic: A structural approach to a literary genre*, Trans. by Richard Howard, with forward by Robert Scholes. Cornell University Press.
Undank, Jack (1979). *Diderot: Inside, outside & in-between*. Coda Press.

IV. PRACTICE: ONLINE

Online Searching
and Its Place in the
Library School Curriculum

Tillie Krieger

Searching for information "online," that is, using a computer to access information that resides in a machine-readable database that may be in any location, has created yet another revolution in the operation of libraries. Earlier revolutions that have been faced by librarians were the changes resulting from going from "library hand" to printed and typed cards, the presence of telephones, the introduction of microfilms, and quite recently, the proliferation of photocopy machines.

Each of these developments brought change in both library operation and in library education.

Changes due to computer technology began to be clearly evident in the decade of the 1960s, with the development of the 2nd and 3rd generation of computers. The Library of Congress began the process of utilizing the computer for machine-readable cataloging (MARC). Materials requiring cataloging were being produced and

---

The author is on the faculty The College of Staten Island, St. George Campus, Staten Island, NY 10301.

239

acquired more rapidly than the manual methods then used could handle. In less than a decade from its beginnings in 1964, libraries were utilizing computer-produced records making use of MARC. Accessing catalog records, known as "online catalog searching" has spread from the technical service areas as many public service personnel now search for holdings in their own and other libraries.

The first use of computers for indexing purposes goes back even earlier in time. But the experiments that would eventually result in online searching were largely confined to indexing scientific data and were utilized by the government. The early contracts of Lockheed with NASA and System Development Corporation (SDC) with the National Library of Medicine (NLM), were described in the literature, but largely assumed to be beyond the needs of the majority of libraries; something to consider for the future.

Reference departments in most libraries subscribe to a large number of abstracting and indexing (A&I) services that are produced by means of computer technology. The first use made of the computer for the A&I services was in the production of the printed, or hard copies of their services. In a short time it was possible to access the tapes directly for the data they contained, first in a batched mode, and as computer technology developed, directly in an interactive mode.

Today, a wide range of materials are produced using computer technology. These include directories, numerical data, and increasingly, full-text files, all of which are accessible via computers.

This type of "online searching" is the major focus of this paper.

The ability to collect data by computer, and to access it has resulted in changes in the operation of libraries, has altered the perception of library service on the part of those working in libraries and for the public as well, and has also had a strong impact on library education.

NEED FOR ONLINE SEARCHING ABILITY

Librarians found that they could access data quickly through computer technology and that it was cost-effective. The data accessed was complex and the new tool was not simple to use. Training was required to locate the data in the machine-readable database. Who was to be trained, where the training was to be provided and what the nature of that training was to be affected both library service and library education.

The January 1986 issue of *American Libraries*, carried 28 advertisements for reference positions, and only a few of the postings did not include a requirement for the ability to do online searching. These were positions for service in oriental and latin languages, music, art, and the small public library. Of the 23 ads for reference librarians that remained, 18, or 78 percent, asked that the applicant be able to search online (also referred to as "bibliographic database knowledge," "computerized reference searching," or some variation in terminology).

Table 1 indicates the growing demand for online searching ability as shown in ads carried in the January issue of *American Libraries* from 1975 through 1986. It reflects the changes that were occurring in libraries. A complete analysis of the need for individuals familiar with online searching would require data from a number of sources.

TABLE 1

Advertisements for Reference Positions
in <u>American Libraries</u> and Requirement for
Online Searching Capability

Date of Advertisement	Number of Reference Advertisements	Number of Advertisments Requesting Online Ability	Percent
1/1986	28	18	.78
1/1985	32	22	.88
1/1984	24	14	.78
1/1983	15	11	.79
1/1982	17	13	.87
1/1981	13	9	.69
1/1980	11	6	.60
1/1979	11	3	.33
1/1978	13	9	.75
1/1977	4	0	.00
1/1976	9	1	.13
1/1975	4	0	.00
TOTALS	181	106	.69

The average is 69 percent. The percentage would be higher if public library reference positions were excluded. The year 1978 presents an anomaly as in that year the new Dallas Public Library opened and requested many new positions and a desire for online searching ability. In every year since 1981 when the average was reached, a higher percentage was recorded.

EARLY TRAINING

Bourne and Robinson[1] provide an excellent review of the education and training for computer-based reference services. The early training was provided by the search service suppliers, NLM, Lockheed, and SDC, by means of seminars and user group meetings. These training sessions were later offered at national library meetings and at scheduled workshops. Institutions, such as the State University of New York/Biomedical Communications Network (SUNY/BCY) also offered training for specific databases that were available within the institution.

Database producers, such as the American Chemical Society and BIOSIS offered training on their systems, as did ERIC when their tapes first became available in 1970. Other producers followed and have continued to offer seminars to improve searching capabilities for their individual databases, even though many of the producers provided access to their databases only via the search services suppliers, LIS (now DIALOG), SDC, and BRS.

Library schools offered training and education later. The schools often did not have the facilities, space, or equipment, nor was there faculty available to teach the courses.

Within the library schools the first discussions revolved about whether training for online access should be considered education and thus a part of the curriculum, or if it should be considered as training in a technique that might be useful in library operations, but did not belong in the curriculum.

As Faibisoff and Bennett[2] noted in 1977 at a workshop on training held prior to the 6th ASIS Mid-Year Meeting at Syracuse, there were many questions regarding what should be taught as well as how that training should be conducted.

The issues raised concerned:

The nature and comprehensiveness of educational and training programs.
The kind and amount of training found in different environments (library schools, on-the-job training, vendor services).
Problems arising from training a heterogeneous group of users.
The cost of on-line training in library schools. Constraints of time and library school curricula.
The different techniques and devices used by various groups. Skills needed for searching.[3]

The level of training provided by the search service suppliers including basic training; turning on the terminal, accessing the database and primary features of the service. Advanced training included more sophisticated search strategies, cost-effective use of the system and reference negotiation. They could not afford to teach either broad principles or database details.

Training devices and aids to help use the system effectively, as well as methods for evaluating performance were later developments.

ONLINE IN THE CURRICULUM

A number of individuals have written about the early problems encountered with the introduction of online searching into the curriculum.[4-7] The first attempts paralleled the introduction of online services in the libraries. First came the recognition that a new tool was available, then the exploration of that tool to examine its use and the need for it. This was followed by a period of study, experimentation, a determination of costs and finally the introduction of the service into practice. Exploration continues and methods of using this new tool and training others into its intricacies proceed. The database producers and search service suppliers made changes and additional databases continue to become available.

The growth in the number and variety of databases make it impossible for any class, or series of classes, in a library school program to do more than provide students with an overview of what is available along with an introduction into the protocols and methods of access.

The January, 1986 issue of the *Directory of Online Databases* reveals the growth in the number of databases and services available. (See Table 2.)

These 2901 databases cover subjects as diverse as computers, cooking, business & finance, engineering, law, entertainment, medicine, politics, publishing, commodities and careers. DIALOG divides its databases into 57 separate subject categories. (See Table 3.)

In addition to not being able to master all of these databases, there is no reason for one individual to do so. What is important is to realize they are there, and how to obtain access to any one of them should the need arise.

From the beginning faculty members and schools varied in their approach. At first faculty members emphasized the conceptual and theoretical issues of computer-based storage and retrieval, often in the context of the information science courses within the curriculum. The introduction to online searching was placed in courses relating to information science; where were Information Storage and Retrieval, Automation, and Abstracting and Indexing, where the computer as a tool was emphasized. The need in the field was increasingly for individuals who were both theoretically aware and practically capable of accessing the systems. This lead to the incorporation of online searching in the general information seeking process with such courses as Subject Bibliography, or Basic Reference. Particular types of databases such as MEDLINE, often became a part of a specialized subject course.

TABLE 2

Growth in Number of Databases and Services[8]

Directory Issue (#1)	Number of Databases	Number of Database Producers	Number of Online Services	Number of Gateways
1979/80	400	221	59	
1980/81	600	340	93	
1981/82	965	512	170	
1982/83	1350	718	213	
1983/84	1878	927	272	
1984/85	2453	1189	362	
1986	2901	1379	454	35

TABLE 3

Online Courses in the Curricula (School Bulletins)
n=61

Courses	Number	Percent	Percent Offering
Single Online Course - No Integration	23	.38	
Online Included in Basic Reference	17	.28	
Online Included in Humanities Ref.	5	.08	
Online Included in Soc. Sci. Ref.	9	.15	
Combined Humanities/Social Science Reference	1	.02	
Online Included in Science/Technology Reference	15	.25	
Online Within the Legal Reference Offered by 17 Schools	7		.41
Online Within the Health Sciences Reference Offered by 25 Schools	20		.80
Online Within the Business Reference Offered by 13 Schools	1		.08
Online Within the Advanced Reference Offered by 6 Schools	2		.333

The producers of the individual databases, such as the National Library of Medicine and BIOSIS; along with the search service providers; DIALOG, SDC, and BRS continued to provide training. Most of these efforts were directed toward the practicing librarian not at students in library schools. The search service suppliers furnished special education discounts to the library schools to assist them in training the students into their services. The database producers and the search service suppliers have remained active in extending knowledge of their products to both the library and the education communities.

Online user groups formed and provided another avenue for individuals to receive and exchange information about specific needs. Continuing education courses offered by the schools are yet another venue for librarians in the field to learn about online access to information. In the long run however, it is the library school that is to be responsible for educating the new librarian into the topic of Online Searching.

THREE APPROACHES

Schools thus far have met this challenge of introducing online searching into the curriculum in three ways. The most widespread method is characterized by Harter and Fenichel[9] as the Single Online Course. This approach provides a single course devoted entirely to online searching. In these classes students are introduced to a publicly available system, often DIALOG, SDC or BRS. The students learn about file structure, indexing languages, evaluation of databases, the pre-search interview, search strategy, Boolean logic, the mechanics of searching and the management of a search service.

The second approach introduces online searching along with a course such as Information Storage and Retrieval, or Advanced Reference. The student learns online searching along with some major part of another course and their relationship to one another is stressed.

The third is the Integrated Approach. In this approach, the student is introduced to online searching briefly, in a basic reference course or in a one-credit lab. This is followed by various elements of online searching divided among the different reference courses and the information science courses as a part of the context of each course. The approach emphasizes the contents of the databases but not the operational aspects.

In a recently published study, Powell and Creth[10] sough to identify specific knowledge needs of librarians within academic research libraries. In their study they identified 56 topics, Online Searching ranked tenth in importance.

Harter and Fenichel raise the question, "Has online searching reached a stage in library education equivalent to, say cataloging or basic reference in which it is regarded as a mandatory skill of the librarian or information specialist?"[11] In the Powell and Creth study noted above, topics such as: Knowledge of Catalog Codes/Rules ranked 12.5, Subject Cataloging, 15.5, and Subject Classification as 17th.

In both the Guy and Large[12] and the Harter and Fenichel[13] studies they pursue an answer to the question as to the place of online searching in the curriculum. Both conducted surveys. The results of both studies indicated that library educators were aware of the need to introduce online searching and were coping with a number of problems inherent in the introduction of new technology into their curricula.

CURRENT STATE

An examination of the bulletins of 61 schools of library and information science (listed in the Appendix) indicated that all included online searching instruction in their curriculum.

The number of courses in the area of online searching ranged from 0 to 5. Three schools did not offer a separate Online Searching course, integrating it into other courses. Forty schools offered a single course, thirteen offered two courses, three offered three courses and one (catholic) offered five; the number of credits ranged from 0 to 3.

The survey method of research often suffers from a lack of sufficient responses. An examination of the objective data, such as the bulletins of the various schools has other drawbacks.

The listings in the bulletins indicates a wide variation — in course titles:

Online Databases Searching
On-Line Information Systems
Online Database Searching and Services
Interactive Database Searching
Computerized Database Searching
Online Searching and Services Online Retrieval
Online Databases and Information Services

to mention just a few. Most of the titles were used by only one school. Those that were used by more than one included:

Online Bibliographic Searching
Online Information Systems
Computer-Based Information Retrieval

As a caveat it should be noted that online access may well be included in the reference courses, but relying on bulletins, rather than polling the schools, these data may be under-represented. Also, since it often takes a year or two for the bulletins to reflect methods that the schools may have in effect, and the bulletins do not indicate any experiments that may be in progress.

INTRODUCING ONLINE SEARCHING

The mixture of approaches in the schools has been a result of variations in philosophy, but it has also been due to differences in faculty, space, funds, focus, and above all, the rapid developments in the online field.

Faculty

The faculty teaching the library school courses had had no courses in online, therefore each had to be trained and to integrate this new skill into their experience. Developments were taking place rapidly, new databases introduced daily and documentation not always available. The online search services were in competition to obtain sufficient staff and train them to develop the market and provide documentation. Faculty were inexperimental status as were the practicing librarians who were performing searches. Much of the variation that currently exists in the schools was the result of the turmoil that existed a decade ago when online searching ballooned into a real service offered to the public. Schools had difficulty in obtaining adequately trained faculty for teaching a full separate course, and the faculty that had been teaching the information science courses were the most familiar with the events that were occurring in practice.

Reference instructors found that the introduction of online changed the nature of their courses. Where the A&I services had formerly occupied a part of the course, with the advent of online access they began to dominate the reference courses, rather than just being another resource.

Space and Funds

In order to teach online it is necessary to have equipment, space for the equipment, and to have telephone lines to connect with the search services. The space was usually lacking, nor was there funds for equipment, or for the materials, both the time and the paper supplies that needed to be used in order to access the databases.

Library schools for many years were relatively inexpensive departments or schools within the university. They required a faculty, usually from 7 to 9 members as a norm, they often used space within the library building and a few classrooms. The large collections required were already needed for the reference departments and while some additional funds were needed for unusual items and duplicate copies, the cost was not large.

With the advent of online systems which required terminals, phone lines, furniture and required security, administrators had to reconsider library education.

Even with the discounts graciously provided by the search service suppliers online time is expensive. Practice for several hours is needed to learn the fundamentals of accessing the system. Time is needed to become familiar with the command structure and search strategies, to make comparisons and evaluate results. The schools provide from 1 to 5 hours of time per student with additional time needed for demonstrations. The majority of students now assume that online searching is a necessity.

A number of instructors have experimented with producing databases that simulate online searches and could be accessed on the department or the university computers. These can help contain costs, but with the changes in the services occurring rapidly, they could not supplant online searching, they could only supplement it.

It is the practical work at the terminal that is needed.

The rapid changes within the field, such as those introduced by DIALOG in 1985 with its new enhancement, as well as the daily announcements of new databases means that textbooks, no matter how well done, are out-of-date when issued.

LEXIS has introduced on-line tutorials to help teach and overcome the changes in the field, but this has not yet been done by the other search services. But even when they do offer them, the costs will not disappear, they will only make it easier to keep up-to-date.

The need for increased funding came at a time when universities faced reduced income and budget cuts.

Focus

There is no clear focus as to the teaching of online searching, how it should be taught, where, and how extensive that training should be. There is no clear definition of how online searching fits into the whole of library education. What the introduction of online searching has done is to create the awareness that it is creating a realignment in the field and that as the librarian in the field integrates online into their library, those of us in education need to maintain an awareness of its effect so that it can be included in the education of the students.

ONLINE SEARCHING IN THE CURRICULUM

The single course alternative is the least costly in that only a single instructor is required and that this method is the least costly and the most easily managed method. Scheduling can be done with the least amount of disruption. However, while easy to introduce and govern, this method may mislead the student by not indicating how and where online searching should be evaluated within the structure of their educational experience and the field as a whole.

Combining online with a single other course in the information science segment of the program may indicate some degree of relationship within the field, but provides too little time to fully cover either topic well.

Integrating portions of online into the several areas where it may logically be dealt with, such as among the various reference, information science, and administrative courses may give an indication of the various places online may belong, may well lead to duplication of some basic information and skills, and fragment the experience so that the essential elements are overlooked. This alternative would also mean that most faculty members are equally able, and interested, in teaching online and in keeping up with the frequent changes in the field.

The library school program is one that, with the exception of a few schools, can be completed in one full year. This has been true for many years. Finding time in an already crowded curriculum is yet another problem. If online is added, what is to be removed?

The information needs of the larger community that is served by the library and information center has been growing as we have been told we are moving into "THE INFORMATION AGE." Information professionals are working with people in more ways that in the past as our graduates are finding roles for themselves outside of the traditional ones in public, academic, school and special libraries. The information industry has developed as a new area of employment possibilities and many library school graduates are becoming entrepreneurs and forming their own businesses.

Despite the enlargement of opportunity, the program remains generally a one-year program. As long as schools compete with one another for students, and the students have a choice as to the library school they will attend, individual schools will (and have) found it difficult on a unilateral basis to lengthen their programs.

THE "END USER"

Librarians have acted as intermediaries in locating information for the ultimate consumer of that information, the person we now refer to as the "end user." Librarians have always instructed their clients in the basics of locating information, whether that information is found in the card catalog or in one of the A&I services or elsewhere. Increasingly, we are seeing that the "end user" wanting to perform the online search.[14-15] The novice user may have difficulties because of a lack of knowledge about, and access to, manuals and thesauri. They may have difficulties in formulating efficient search strategies and lack the ability to make a search precise, but the same can be said of their use of the hard copy indexes and services.

There is a literature building on "end user" searching of online databases.[16]

The use of abstracting and indexing services within the library has meant that the end user came to the library for information. The development of databases, accessible by phone, and the training of individuals who are not librarians in accessing those databases, suggests that the role of the library may well be changing.

If many of our clients do not come to the library but can locate their information online, what is the role of the library?

NOTES

1. Charles P. Bourne & Jo Robinson. "Education and Training for Computer-Based Reference Services: Review of Training Efforts to Date." *Journal of the American Society for Information Science* 31 (January 1980):25-35.

2. Sylvia Faibisoff & John L. Bennett. "On-line Reference Retrieval Training for Effective Use: Report." *Bulletin of the American Society for Information Science* 3 (August 1977):35.

3. Faibisoff and Bennett, p. 35.

4. Trudi Bellardo, Gail Kennedy & Gretchen Tremoulet. "On-Line Bibliographic System Instruction." *Journal of Education for Librarianship* 19(Summer 1978):21-31.

5. Bourne & Robinson.

6. R. F. Guy & J. A. Large. "Online Bibliographic Searching In The Library School Curriculum." *Library Review* 30 (Summer 1981): 27-33.

7. Stephen P. Harter & Carol H. Fenichel. "Online Searching in Library Education." *Journal of Education for Librarianship* 23(Summer 1982):3-22.

8. *Directory of Online Databases* 7(January 1986):v.

9. Harter & Fenichel.

10. Ronald R. Powell & Sheila D. Creth. "Knowledge Bases and Library." *College & Research Libraries* 47(January 1986):16-27.

11. Harter & Fenichel, p. 5.

12. Guy & Large, p. 28.

13. Harter & Fenichel, pp. 5-6.

14. Leslie W. Wykoff. "Teaching Patrons to Search." *Medical Reference Services Quarterly* 4(Summer 1985):57-61.

15. Linda Friend. "Independence at the Terminal: Training Student End Users to Do Online Literature Searching." *Journal of Academic Librarianship* 11 (July 1985):136-141.

16. Sally Lyon. "End-User Searching of Online Databases: A Selective Annotated Bibliography." *Library HiTech* 2(2) (July 1984):47-50.

APPENDIX

Library/Information School at:	Date of Bulletin
University of ALABAMA	1984/85
State University of New York at ALBANY	1982/84
University of ALBERTA	n.d.
University of ARIZONA	1983/85
The ATLANTA University	1984/85
BALL State University	1983/85
BRIGHAM YOUNG University	n.d.
University of BRITISH COLUMBIA	n.d.
University of CALIFORNIA, Berkeley	1984/85
University of CALIFORNIA at Los Angeles	1985/86
CATHOLIC University of America	1984/85
The University of CHICAGO	1982/84
CLARION University of Pennsylvania	1984/86
COLUMBIA University	1985/86
DALHOUSIE University	1985/86
DREXEL University	1984/85
EMORY University	1985/86
EMPORIA State University	1984/85
The FLORIDA State University	1984/86
University of HAWAII at Manoa	1983/84
University of ILLINOIS at Ubrana-Champaign	1984/85
INDIANA University	1984/86
University of IOWA	1984/86
KENT State University	1985/86
University of KENTUCKY	1984/85
LONG ISLAND University, C W. Post	1982/84
LOUISIANA State University	1984/85
University of MARYLAND, College Park	1985
McGILL University	1984/85
University of MICHIGAN	1983/85
University of MINNESOTA	1980/82
University of MISSOURI--Columbia	1984/85
NORTH CAROLINA CENTRAL University	1983/85
University of NORTH CAROLINA at Chapel Hill	1984/85
University of NORTH CAROLINA at Greensbobo	1984/85
NORTH TEXAS State University	1985/86
NORTHERN ILLINOIS University	1985/86
University of OKLAHOMA	1984/85
PEABODY College of Vanderbilt University	n.d.
PRATT Graduate School	1983/84

APPENDIX (continued)

QUEENS College	1982/84
University of RHODE ISLAND	1985/86
ROSARY College	1984/85
RUTGERS: THE State University of New Jersey	1984/86
ST. JOHNS University	1984/85
SAN JOSE State University	1984/85
SIMMONS College	1984/86
University of SOUTH CAROLINA	1984/85
University of SOUTH FLORIDA	1983/84
SOUTHERN CONNECTICUT State University	1982/84
University of SOUTHERN MISSISSIPPI	1983/85
SYRACUSE University	1985/86
University of TENNESSEE/Knoxville	1985/86
University of TEXAS at Austin	1985/87
TEXAS WOMEN'S University	1984/86
University of TORONTO	1984/85
University of WASHINGTON	1986/88
WAYNE State University	1985/86
University of WESTERN ONTARIO	1984/85
University of WISCONSIN--Madison	1983/85
University of WISCONSIN--Milwaukee	1985/87

Development of a Bibliographic Database on a Videotex Type System

Emil H. Levine

Videotex is a generic term for commercial two way communications with a computer using telephone lines, a video display tube (VDT) and some type of keyboard. A modem is used to interface the telephone with the VDT, and in some systems special electronic devices are required to process the incoming and outgoing signals. The videotex industry now has several standards, derived from nationally sponsored developments. Typical of these is NALPS, the North American Presentation-Level Protocal Syntax. Outside the United States, several "standards" are in use, such as the French Antiope, the British PRESTEL, West German Bildschirmtext, Japanese Captain and the Canadian Telidon. The technical details of these various systems are well documented in the literature, perhaps the best presentation being in the July 1933 issue of BYTE magazine, devoted to "videotex."

For the purpose of this research, only two distinctions are made between the videotex systems. "Broadcast teletext" continually transmits (broadcasts) pages of data, repeating all the pages every few seconds. The user selects the desired page based on a menu presentation. "Interactive videotex" also uses the menu format, but allows a much greater variety in the queries. The user is not "snatching" a continuously broadcasted page, but is truly interacting with the computer to retrieve random information.

While the industry still argues over standards and terminology, videotex is evolving to mean a service that includes graphics and alphanumeric data. Thus, the U.S. interactive services, the Source

Mr. Levine is with the Office of Information Systems, Drug Enforcement Administration, 1405 I St., NW, Washington, DC 20537.

and CompuServe, which presently do not include graphics, are generally referred to as "videotex type" services. They are often excluded from discussions of videotex in the literature.

Similarly, the Source and CompuServe are not considered "on-line" services in the context of Lockheed Dialog, SDC Orbit or BRS. This is primarily due to the nature of their databases (mainly non-bibliographic), and most significantly, their query language, which is largely menu driven or uses a single key term. The major distinction, however, is the lack of a Boolean retrieval capability in these services.

This paper will discuss the feasibility of using a "videotex type" service (more precisely, CompuServe) as a medium for developing a specific bibliographic database derived from ERIC, "Uses of Computers in Education." The findings, however, are considered applicable for all videotex systems, regardless of standards or format, broadcast or interactive, graphics or text, for any specialized subject.

CompuServe, within the last year, has offered several bibliographic databases. Typical examples are "Computer Periodical Guide" and "U.S. Government Publications." They are typified as shallow with minimal indexing and their utility is questionable. Updating is aperiodic and subject placement often questionable.

The British Library, Research and Development Department, has conducted a study on the presentation of bibliographic information on Prestel, the British Post Office (now British Telecom) videotex service. This service reaches 800,000 television sets[1] and has more than 250,000 pages of information.[2] The findings are relevant to the examples in Appendix I, although Prestel uses graphics and color.

An abstract of the research noted:

> Due to the limited character set and small number of characters available on Prestel frames, the scope for typographic and spatial coding of information is limited. The possibility of using colour coding, characteristics of the Prestel display, and the basic principles of presentation of bibliographic information established in other media were noted. Alternative designs were presented for book lists and topical subjects. Designs for author, title, data and classified listings were discussed. It was recommended that the layout should be kept as simple as possible and the numbers of colours used should be restricted to two. Indentations should be used to facilitate

scanning of alphabetical entry headings, while colour should be used to emphasize certain entry elements if necessary. Emphasis was placed on designing the information according to the way in which it would be used.[3]

A second British report discusses the use of Prestel in libraries.[4] While no specific discussion was made of bibliographic databases in the report, Prestel was used to support research and reference questions. Significant observations were made by reference users which impact on the design of a bibliographic database. Major findings in the study were:

A. Its overall performance was marred by poor indexing.
B. Viewdata (Prestel) delivers information in blocks of approximately 100 words; reading more than a few of these blocks from a television screen can be particularly tiring. Thus Viewdata may well be suited for the presentation of summaries, rather than in-depth information.
C. Libraries and their clients were unanimous in expressing their dissatisfaction with Prestel's indexes. In fact, Prestel has gained some notoriety for poor indexing practices at both the system operator and information provider levels.
D. The ability of the system to provide a large range of subject matter in one place met with wide approval.
E. In reference inquiries, Prestel supplied satisfactory answers to almost half the inquiries directed to it.

Thus, the study, while not specific to bibliographic databases, provided another valuable insight to user likes and dislikes with videotex in the reference role.

In a more specific discussion of videotex applications for bibliographic databases, Nash, a Canadian author, also notes that "the size of the usual videotext page, 20 lines of 40 characters each, at most, requires information to be written in a very concise style." However, she continues to note that "On the other hand, bibliographic online databases, because they are text-oriented, can be very expansive, even full text, if the application demands it."[5]

Nash notes five developments that are significant for videotex within the context of bibliographic databases: (1) Vast amounts of bibliographic data in machine readable form; (2) Reliable and cheap data storage; (3) Creation of easy to use retrieval packages; (4) Pres-

ence of world wide telecommunication systems; (5) The microelectronics industry production of cheap terminals, microcomputers and modems.
In comparing videotex and online, Nash states:

> Making inexpensive hardcopy prints of the output is cheap in comparison to current videotex print capabilities. User modification of output in videotex is practically nonexistent and retrieval methods are still limited to menu selection or simple keyword access. The future panacea is thought to be keyword access; whether this will be so remains to be seen . . . perhaps a solution will be to offer both methods of access, menu and keyword, geared to the level of expertise of the user of the system.
>
> As a consequence of access methods, information packages being developed for the videotex mode should probably be limited in size to the number of pages that can be viewed in half hour sessions.

The similarity in the British analysis and that of Nash are striking. The "coming together" of "online" and videotex services has been informally predicted for some time. In fact, Nash concludes with a comment that videotex and online bibliographic databases are coming together in the iNet trial in Canada, but fails to comment further on that experiment.

MENU VERSUS KEY TERM RETRIEVAL

Recent Bell Laboratories research on user preferences for menu or keyword (attribute) retrieval is also considered highly relevant to successful use of bibliographies in videotex.

Murray Hill library users were given the choice of "a menu-oriented system, in which books were hierarchically organized by their Dewey Decimal numbers, and a keyword system . . . most users chose the keyword system. . . . Twice as many keyword users reported successful searches as menu users."[6]

The preferred system used a single key term and did not have a Boolean capability.

In a follow-on study, Bell Labs found that:

. . . we have compared keyword and menu access in two textual databases. We suggest that keyword access is preferable when the database is complex and predictable and that the menu access is preferable when the database is simple and unpredictable. A simple and predictable database is probably boring and a complex and unpredictable database is probably unmanageable.[7]

This experiment consisted of observing preference in searching of news stories (simple and unpredictable) using either keywords or menus. While users, based on the first study of the Dewey Decimal system (complex and predictable), preferred key terms, they preferred the menu in searching news stories.

Correlation of the findings in these studies leads to a number of factors that should impact on the design of a bibliographic database on videotex. These are:

A. Screen size
B. Screen format limitations
C. Lack of Boolean
D. Key Term/Menu retrieval options
E. Large amount of data that can be searched
G. Fatigue rate of user
H. Degree of indexing

These factors provide a guide to the design of a user acceptable videotex bibliographic database.

A number of conclusions can be drawn from these limited studies concerning user requirements and the capability of videotex to meet the requirements.

A. Indexing is critical. The nature of video viewing requires that the user quickly find his citations. (This, however, is counter to the profit motive associated with all existing videotex systems, i.e., the practice of charging for connect time.)
B. The size of the screen constrains the format.
C. The user probably should have a choice of menu driven or keyword search strategies.
D. The lack of a Boolean "or" capability requires the development of a controlled vocabulary and the method of displaying valid search terms, integrated within the menu scenario.

Given the constraints of videotex, four design models are apparent: (1) Card Catalog; (2) Key Term; (3) KWIC/KWOC; (4) Menu.

CARD CATALOG-SUBJECT INDEXING MODEL

A videotex bibliographic file could be modeled exactly like a conventional card catalog. This has several advantages. Most users would have some experience with a card catalog. True videotex systems could even present the data using graphics resembling the physical card catalog cabinet and row of cards with subject tabs. Standardized subject headings would be available. A subject heading list would be maintained online, perhaps in a form similar to the Sears Subject Listing. An alphabetical menu could segregate the file in the same manner as a drawer in the card catalog. The menu screen could equate to Author, Title and Subject card cabinets. The contents of a "drawer" could be displayed alphabetically in the menu in the same manner as the physical subject heading cards in the card catalog. At that point, the user could "browse" through the citations. One "page" on the screen could equate to 2-3 cards.

This model might require physically storing the same data records in several locations, in the same manner as the library card.

KEY TERM MODEL

Citations could be stored in one massive file with logical delimiters and a search conducted by a single key term. The CompuServe Online Glorier Encyclopedia is an example of this type of searching. This systems allows both exact and limited (final truncation) matching. The search is relatively fast. Limited feedback is provided to assist the searcher. The videotex bibliographic file could be broken into logical, exclusive categories and the key term software used to search these categories. As a further aid, an alphabetical list of valid search terms, using an "explode" format, could be integrated with the search scenario.

KWIC/KWOC MODEL

A highly unconventional videotex display model is a modified KWIC/KWOC format. This model is unconventional in that KWIC/

KWOC is normally associated with hard copy output and that KWIC is usually presented in a single line, which would be restrictive in the 40 character format. However, there is no reason that the KWOC or modified KWIC format could not be generated for a 40 × 24 screen. The scroll feature associated with videotex would further enhance the browsing capability normally associated with bibliographic retrieval. While unusual, the literature has reflected some interest in both interactive and modified formats.[8]

MENU MODEL

The last design follows the more conventional videotex approach, that of menus which lead to more menus and finally reduce the choice to a subset small enough for meaningful browsing. Within the context of a bibliographic database on "Uses of Computers in Education," these choices can logically be broken into school class groups such as K, 1-6, K 6, 7-9, and 7-12. Further, the menu could be categorized by year of publication (i.e., 1981, 1982, 1983, 1981-1983, 1979-1980, etc.). The database could be categorized by topic, English, Literature, Math, Foreign Languages, Science, etc., which could be further classified.

Selection of specific menu heading up to this point are straight forward and obvious from the classification criteria in education. The specific classifications at the lowest levels, however, challenge the information provider to overcome problems in indexing for videotex, as reflected in the previously cited literature. These problems may not exist in the key term model; however, they may in the Subject Heading model, depending on the specificity of the subject headings.

DETERMINING INDEXING REQUIREMENTS

Based on the previously referenced research, it would appear that the users might desire either menu or key term options. Regardless, the constraints of the screen size and the comments concerning the importance of indexing show a requirement for precisely determining the information requirements of the user and then presenting the citations in a format to optimize their viewing. Within the design constraints of this model (a database on the "Uses of Computers in

Education''), two sets of knowledge support such a design problem. The first is the availability of that data within ERIC, and the second is the preference of obvious users of such a database in some sort of rank order. A correlation of rank order of user preferences with the rank order of such references in ERIC, should assist the information provider in optimizing the system within the design constraints.

Rank Order of User Requirements

It is obvious that the menu must reflect the requirements of the user. These requirements can be ascertained through use of a rank order test in which a group of knowledgeable educational professionals would rank order classes of information and a consensus would be derived for a overall rank order. This research involved 12 professional educators, all holding advanced degrees in education and involved in daily activity associated with the uses of computers in education. All subjects were enrolled in a graduate level seminar in the use of computers in education at the time of the research. The choice of terms (subject headings) were derived from the ERIC Thesaurus. This selection of 20 terms was based on discussion in the seminar and a reflection of postings of these terms in the ERIC thesaurus. After the list of 20 terms were determined, a basic program was written to provide a rank order test. This paired-comparison test was given to each member of the class. The program generated 380 (n × n-l) pairs. Each member of the seminar was asked to circle the item of choice in each pair. (The initial confusion associated with this methodology was overcome by asking ''If you were offered books on the two subjects, which one would you read first?'') Eight subjects responded. (Past experience in this methodology and the literature show that subjects taking a paired comparison test in excess of 100 choices will often tire and not mark consistent choices. This was reflected in two tests, which were discarded.) The results were tabulated and a rank order of interest obtained. This provided a statistical basis for a rank order of professional interests.

Rank Order of the Literature

A Lockheed DIALOG query was made on each of the 20 subject areas in ERIC. In ambiguous cases (i.e., computers [and] programming for ''computer programming''), the Boolean capability of DI-

ALOG was used. This resulted in a rank order of postings of the same 20 concepts used in the paired comparison test.

User Preferences/ERIC Citations Rank Order Comparisons

The paired comparison test provides a rank order of user preference. Within the context of the ERIC-videotex bibliographic scenario, it was considered useful to compare this rank order to the rank order of postings of the same concepts in ERIC, as derived in the DIALOG queries. The appropriate statistical test for such a rank order comparison is the Spearman Rho test (10), the null hypothesis being that the two rank orders are independent. Table 1 provides the matrix for the Spearman Rho. Table 2 shows the compilations and results, that there is not a meaningful correlation between the rank

Table 1 - Rank Order of User Preferences
and Rank Order of Same Data in
ERIC.

	USER PREFERENCE (A)	ERIC RANK POSTINGS (B)	RANK DIFFERENCE (A-B)	= D^2
1	Uses in Education	16	-15	225
2	Computer Literacy	9	-7	49
3	Animation	11	-8	64
4	Specific Programs (i.e. Math)	8	-4	16
5	Computer Simulation	15	-10	100
6	Teleconferencing	12	-6	36
7	Software Selection	10	-3	9
8	Computer Aided Instruction	1	7	49
9	Programming	5	4	16
10	Computer Networks	4	6	36
11	Computer Oriented Programs	2	9	81
12	Computer Managed Instruction	6	6	36
13	Science Education	3	10	100
14	Peripheral Equipment	14	0	0
15	Computer Models	18	-3	9
16	Computer Centers	20	-4	16
17	Computer Aided Testing	7	10	100
18	Computer Engineering	19	-1	1
19	Computer Games	17	2	4
20	Hardware Selection	13	7	49

Σ D=0[1] ΣD^2=996

[1]As a check, this column should equal zero.

order of user preference and the rank order of information in the candidate database.

The rank order of user preferences assists in identifying the most significant educational concepts. This, in itself, is a reason for conducting such a test, especially given the space/screen constraints of videotex. Column D2 of Table 1 also provides some insights to the success or failure of the system. The larger the number, the less the correlation of rank order. In such a scenario, it would allow the information provider to determine if the information in the database would match the requirements of the user. In Table 1, it would appear that many preferences of the users would not be met by the candidate database. A close examination of the number of postings might result in elimination of certain concepts, or perhaps combining them with similar concepts.

The previously cited research and the rank order comparisons provide a basis for designing the videotex bibliographic database within the ERIC/"Uses of computers in Education" scenario.

INITIAL MENUS

The initial menus will classify the database by grade structure. This will offer the option on specific grades, classes of grades or all grades:

1. K	5. 7-9
2. K-3	6. 10-12
3. 1-3	7. 7-12
4. 4-6	8. ALL

The next menu will offer a range search of dates of documents in the bibliography.

1. 1980	5. 1980-1981
2. 1981	6. 1982-1983
3. 1982	7. ALL
4. 1983	

A subject oriented menu will collapse the twenty headings into logically combined groups, using the user preferences as a guide.

TABLE 2 - Calculation of the Rank Order
Correlation Between User
Preference and Data in ERIC.

$$(Rho) = 1 - \frac{6\ (D^2)}{N\ (N^2-1)} \qquad N=20$$

$$(Rho) = 1 - \frac{5976}{20\ (400-1)}$$

$$(Rho) = 1 - \frac{5976}{7980}$$

$$(Rho) = 1 - .749$$

$$(Rho) = .251$$

Values of Rho at 5% and 1%
Levels of Significance

N	.050	.001	
18	.475	.625	Rho is not significant at either
20	.450	.591	the 5% or 1% level. Therefore,
22	.428	.562	the null hypothesis cannot be
			disproved.

1. Uses in Education
2. Computer Literacy
3. Simulation/Models
4. Telecomms/Networks
5. Hardware/Software Selection

6. CAI
7. Programming
8. CMI
9. Specific Programs
10. Computer Aided Testing

Following the specific category selection, the user will have the option of browsing through a list of valid key terms or entering the search directly. This is a feature not presently available on the few existing videotex bibliographies.

1. List Key Terms
2. Enter Key Term

The search would be conducted if "2" were chosen after a Key Term was entered. If "1" was chosen, the user would view a list of valid Key Terms, revert back to this menu, select "2" and enter the valid Key Term.

This unique feature would overcome the previously cited complaints of poor indexing. The system would also offer to the knowledgeable user the option of going directly to the last menu page for entry of the Key Term. This would offer users the option of either the menu approach or Key Term retrieval.

The actual display would list titles of each item in ERIC, ten to a page (perhaps in a modified KWIC/KWOC format). Each title would contain a number. The user would enter the number to view the entire abstract.

The cited research, rank order correlations and suggested approach will eventually be tested within a live environment, CompuServe. While it is anticipated that several changes will be made, based on a better understanding of that operating system, the key factors essential for a successful bibliography on videotex, isolated by previous research, will be included in the test. These include utilizing the limited screen size and format in manner that will allow users to rapidly browse with minimum fatigue. The lack of Boolean will be aided by the unique provision of all valid Key Terms; this will also overcome previous criticism of "poor indexing." The user will have the options of a menu, Key Term search, or both. Despite previous failures of bibliographic presentations on videotex, it is anticipated that this approach, drawing on evaluations and suggestions in the literature, will be successful.

NOTES

1. Miller, D. "Videotex: Science Fiction or Reality?" *BYTE* Vol. 8, No. 7, July 1983, 42-56.

2. Hudson, G. "Prestel: The Basis of an Evolving Videotex System." *BYTE* Vol. 8, No. 7, July 1983, 61-78.

3. Reynolds, L. "The Presentation of Bibliographic Information on Prestel." BLRD Report 5536, Royal College of Art, Graphic Information Research Unit, London, 1981.

4. Pollard, R. "Videotex in Libraries: An Assessment of the British Experience and Directions for the Future." *The Online Age – Assessment/Directions*. Collected Papers Presented at the 12th Mid-Year Meeting of the American Society for Information Science. May 22-25, 1983, p. 52.

5. Nash, M. "Videotex Versus Online Bibliographic Databases: A Canadian Prospective." *Online Review*, Vol. 6, No. 4, August 1982, 291-96. (Plus personal interview with Nash at ASIS annual meeting, October 1-4, 1983, Washington, DC.)

6. Geller, V. J. & Lesk, M. E. "How Users Search: A Comparison of Menu and Attribute Retrieval Systems on a Library Catalog." Bell Laboratories Internal Memorandum, Murray Hill, NJ, 1981.

7. Geller, V. J. & Lesk, M. E. "User Interfaces to Information Systems: Choices vs. Commands." Proceedings of Research in Information Retrieval, Sixth Annual International ACM SIGIR Conference, Bethesda, MD; 6-8 June 1983, pp. 130-135.

8. Lesser, M. L. "Information Retrieval — Quick and Dirty." *Microcomputing*, May 1982, 64-68.

9. Stalcup, W. Proceedings of the ASIS Annual Meeting. Vol 19, 1982. (Stalcup used a cleverly formatted indented KWIC index to compress titles into limited space.)

10. Isaac, S. & Michael, W. B. *Handbook in Research and Evaluation*. San Diego: EdITS Publishers, 1975, p. 130.

BIBLIOGRAPHY

Geller, V. J. & Lesk, M. E. "How Users Search: A Comparison of Menu and Attribute Retrieval Systems on a Library Catalog." Bell Laboratories Internal Memorandum, Murray Hill, NJ, 1981.

Geller, V. J. & Lesk, M. E. "User Interfaces to Information Systems: Choices vs. Commands." *Proceedings of Research in Information Retrieval*, Sixth Annual International ACM SIGIR Conference, Bethesda, MD; 6-8 June 1983.

Hudson, G. "Prestel: The Basis of an Evolving Videotex System." *BYTE* Vol. 8, No. 7, July 1983.

Isaac, S. & Michael, W. B. *Handbook in Research and Evaluation*. San Diego: EdITS Publishers.

Lesser, M. L. "Information Retrieval — Quick and Dirty." *Microcomputing*, May 1982.

Malloy, R. "Videotex Brings the World to Your Doorsteps." *BYTE* Vol. 8, No. 7, July 1983.

Miller, D. "Videotex; Science Fiction or Reality?" *BYTE* Vol. 8, No. 7, July 1983.

Nash, M. "Videotex Versus Online Bibliographic Databases: A Canadian Prospective." *Online Review* Vol. 6, No. 4, August 1982.

Pollard, R. "Videotex in Libraries: An Assessment of the British Experience and Directions for the Future." *The Online Age — Assessment/Directions*. Collected Papers Presented at the 12th Mid-Year Meeting of the American Society for Information Science. May 22-25, 1983.

Reynolds, L. "The Presentation of Bibliographic Information on Prestel." BLRD Report 5536, Royal College of Art, Graphic Information Research Unit, London, 1981.

Stalcup, W. *Proceedings of the ASIS Annual Meeting*, Vol. 19, 1982. (Stalcup used a cleverly formatted indented KWIC index to compress titles into limited space.)

Woolfe, R. *Videotex — The New Television/Telephone Information Service*. London: Heyden and Son Ltd., 1980.

Computer Aided Indexing at NASA

Ronald L. Buchan

NASA's computer aided indexing activity has peaked in recent years with the development of the NASA Lexical Dictionary, retrospective indexing and the demand index. Any use of computers in indexing and retrieval constitutes my definition of the term "computer aided indexing." The term "automatic indexing" has historically been used for KWIC and KWOC indexes that require no human intervention. The term "machine-aided indexing" will be used to describe a particular application and enhancement of the NASA Lexical Dictionary in indexing complete citations including abstracts. This paper will be divided into two parts: Part 1 NASA Thesaurus Activity and Part 2 NASA Lexical Dictionary Activity.

PART 1: NASA THESAURUS ACTIVITY

The present NASA Thesaurus is in its fifth edition, but its origins go back to two earlier works. Both were cooperative efforts by several government agencies. One was the TEST thesaurus entitled Thesaurus of Engineering and Scientific Terms and was published in 1967, the same year that the first NASA Thesaurus was published. The other was the AEC-DDC-NASA-OTS composite vocabulary, published in 1964. A description of the computerization of the of the NASA Thesaurus can be found in William Hammond's report Construction of the NASA Thesaurus: Computer Processing Support, published in 1968.

The author is a Lexicographer at the NASA Scientific and Technical Information Facility, P.O. Box 8757, BWI Airport, MD 21240. The Facility is operated by RMS Associated. (No copyright protection is asserted for this article.)

All 14,700,000 postings to the 16,835 NASA thesaurus terms were accomplished and verified through a computer aided indexing activity. This traditional use of computers in indexing has been augmented by the development of many new uses of the computer that enhance the NASA Thesaurus or make new forms of indexing available. Beside the main thesaurus terms there are nearly 4,000 cross references in the NASA Thesaurus. The Hierarchical Listing shows some 150,000 interrelationships between terms, all of which are maintained by the computer. The Access Vocabulary has over 40,000 entries.

NASA Printed Thesaurus

There are various computer programs in force for the production of the NASA Thesaurus. First of all there is a maintenance program which adds new terms, transfers terms and deletes terms. This program handles all types of terms (broader, narrower, and related) as well as use, used for, and scope notes. The program automatically provides for entering the reciprocal of a related term or used for term, as well as traditional broader and narrower term relationships. There is a complicated program which identifies "missing structure" for broader and narrower terms. The Access Vocabulary is created and maintained by other programs. The main term and cross references are "KWOCed," producing a modified KWOC index that is more readable. Two other programs support the Access Vocabulary, the capitalization file and the embedded term lists. These two lists direct changes in the Access Vocabulary so that words not in the initial position show capitalization and terms within terms are accessible. Since initial letters of inverted terms are capitalized this feature only shows the capitalization of acronyms or designators. Thus 1, HEAO shows in all caps rather than upper/lower case. Likewise the term electro-acoustics has acoustics embedded in it and is presented as Acoustics, Electro. These features of the printed NASA Thesaurus would not be available without the computer.

Hierarchical Listing		*Access Vocabulary*
GLOBAL	AIR POLLUTION	Magnetism, Aero
GS	POLLUTION	USE AEROMAGNETISM
	.ENVIRONMENT	
	POLLUTION	
	..AIR POLLUTION	Magnetism, Antiferro

	...GLOBAL AIR	
	POLLUTION	USE ANTIFERROMAGNETISM
RT	EARTH	
	ATMOSPHERE	
	ENVIRONMENTS	Magnetism, Dia
	POLLUTION	
	MONITORING	USE DIAMAGNETISM
	POLLUTION	
	TRANSPORT	

The generic structure (GS) permits a display which shows the interrelationships between broader and narrower terms. This information cannot be conveyed by simply marking terms BT and NT. The Access Vocabulary also shows the embedded terms.

NASA Online Thesaurus

The NASA online thesaurus differs from the printed NASA Thesaurus in that it does not show interrelationships between broader and narrower terms or scope notes. The online thesaurus is updated on almost a daily basis, so it has a currency that the printed thesaurus and its supplements do not have. The online thesaurus gives postings that are more up to date than those in the Combined File Posting Statistics. Parts of the thesaurus structure may be displayed at one time. You can display only the broader terms, only the narrower, only the related terms, or only the used for terms. If a term has a very extensive structure, such as "satellites" with 517 terms in its structure, it is better to use the printed thesaurus. The online and the printed thesaurus complement each other and should be used together. Using the command x ts/thesauri, you get the following display of the thesaurus structure.

	EXPAND TS/THESAURI			
REF	DESCRIPTOR	TP	OCC	TS
R01	-ST/THESAURI	N	110	8
R02	RT/INDEXES			
	(DOCUMENTATION)	N	3041	20
R03	RT/INFORMATION			
	RETRIEVAL	N	5165	24
R04	RT/KWIC INDEXES	N	47	
R05	RT/NOMENCLATURES	N	290	8
R06	RT/SPACE GLOSSARIES	N	43	6
R07	RT/TERMINOLOGY	N	460	4

R06	RT/TERMS	N	67	2
R09	RT/WORDS			
	(LANGUAGE)	N	636	24

Information retrieval is expedited with the thesaurus structure by allowing the user to simply select the R number of the term he is interested in. After making the desired sets the data can be manipulated with standard Boolean algebra.

Retrospective Indexing

Before the development of retrospective indexing, sets of new NASA Thesaurus terms only contained references that were added since the term was added. With retrospective indexing new terms are more fully indexed to all appropriate records. With this computer aided indexing technique both major and minor terms are added when needed. The way retrospective indexing works is to make a search on the title and the abstract, then print each set off-line. The search number and set number are entered the following day in a program to add major (title) and minor (abstract) terms to the record. When terms appear in both title and abstract, they are made major. A listing of such commands is automatically made by the program and is sent to a file where it can be edited if necessary. After editing the commands are moved to the transaction file and added overnight to the citation. Variant spellings and synonyms can all be handled at any time by using retrospective indexing to make them accessible. Retrospective indexing has been in effect since November, 1984.

Frequency Command

The frequency command is the most powerful NASA/RECON command. With it you can get a listing of the most frequently used terms in a set. Without the computer, the display of the frequency of thesaurus terms posted to a set would be impossible. The powerful frequency command enables one to determine the term "landscape" of a set. In searching the text and/or title, one is able to determine the composition of the term frequency for that set. Frequency works on any set where there are two or more postings to the same term. Frequency works on an author set, text set, report number set, contract number set or corporate source set. This is invaluable in developing a good search strategy using NASA Thesaurus terms. The frequency command will display terms from up to 500 citations. If the set is larger than 500, say 1,000, it will select about every other one so that a random sample of terms is achieved.

```
              1 3041 ST/INDEXES (DOCUMENTATION)
           TERM FREQUENCY DISTRIBUTION – SET 01 –
             500 CITATIONS – 00470 SUBJECT TERMS
REF             SUBJECT TERM                    FREQ
F001            INDEXES (DOCUMENTATION)         0500
F002            BIBLIOGRAPHIES                  0161
F003            INFORMATION RETRIEVAL           0136
F004            ABSTRACTS                       0085
F005            INFORMATION SYSTEMS             0068
F006            DATA BASES                      0050
F007            LIBRARIES                       0040
F008            INFORMATION DISSEMINA-
                TION                            0038
*************************************************************
MORE
```

Demand Index

In the recommendation section of her thesis entitled Online Database Search Strategies and Thesaural Relationship Models, Alice Chamis states on p. 170 that the seventh recommendation for further research is "The feasibility of creating indexes to searches from the frequency list of terms of terms should be investigated." NASA now offers this service through its Demand index. This recently developed capability offers various indexes, a computer generated abbreviated title entry, and an accession number which leads to the full entry. A subject index using NASA Thesaurus terms, an author index, a corporate source index, a contract number index and a report number index are all provided for most searches that can be done on NASA/RECON. A new series of Special Bibliographies are now available. An online stored search can be made which results in an indexed search like the demand index.

Category Listing

Using a classification scheme of NASA Thesaurus terms, a broad listing of thesaurus terms by subject term can be made offline by the Lexicographer. Each NASA Thesaurus term is assigned one or more category codes. Without this computerized category listing, a user looking for biology terms would have to look through some

17,000 terms and manually list the 2,500 terms dealing with biology. This offline capability provides easy access to such information.

STAR & IAA Annual Subject Indexes

In addition to the computerized aspects of compiling a printed index, the STAR & IAA Annual Subject Indexes lists narrower terms to terms that have their narrower terms contained in the index. The following is an example of this feature:

        AIRCRAFT NOISE
            NT   JET AIRCRAFT NOISE
            NT   SONIC BOOMS

The user of the printed index would probably miss these important term relationships. Having them spelled out for each broader term is definitely user friendly. It should be noted that only narrower terms contained in the index are listed.

It can be seen from the above description of computer aided indexing of NASA Thesaurus Activity that NASA's research in the area has paid off.

PART 2: NASA LEXICAL DICTIONARY ACTIVITY

The term NASA Lexical Dictionary activity is used to describe an umbrella of computer aided indexing activities including subject switching and machine-aided indexing. Subject switching is using the computer to translate controlled vocabulary, including translating groupings of terms to one or more NASA terms. This is accomplished by giving words and phrases logic codes along with appropriate translations. Subject switching is most cost effective when your input is in machine readable form. Subject switching is machine-aided indexing in its simplest form. For the purposes of this paper, machine aided indexing is the processing of natural language into an appropriate controlled vocabulary. Work on the NASA Lexical Dictionary was begun in January 1982.

DOD Subject Switching

The NASA Lexical dictionary is strongly rooted in the work done at the Defense Technical Information Center. NASA STI Facility has had a close working relationship with DTIC since its inception. DTIC citations have been added to STAR first manually, then with tapes. It was natural then that DTIC was the first candidate for subject switching. In order to accomplish this it was necessary to construct the NASA Lexical Dictionary file containing the complete DTIC thesaurus and appropriate translations to NASA Thesaurus Terms. Exact matches of terms were accomplished first. Next the intellectual effort was made to determine appropriate translations for terms. Sometimes two or more DTIC terms translated into a single NASA term. Sometimes more than one NASA term was needed to translate a DTIC term. Finally many terms could not be translated and were identified as such. Eventually all terms were translated to a NASA term or list of terms or zeroed out as untranslatable. The results were encouraging and showed a savings of three minutes of indexer time per document.

DOE Subject Switching

The next file of the NASA Lexical Dictionary to be built was the DOE subject switching file. The same approach was used as with DTIC. Those working on the project were much more familiar with the art of "subject switching." This file will translate over 25,000 DOE terms when complete. As with DTIC, the citations are received on tape and can be processed expeditiously.

LCSH Machine-Aided Indexing

Subject switching from one term to another is one thing, processing natural language is quite another. As a transition to full machine-aided indexing it was decided to try out the NASA Lexical Dictionary on the machine readable book records. This worked surprisingly well and was used against both Library of Congress Subject Headings and titles.

Machine-Aided Indexing

In order to handle natural language it is necessary to break sentences up into phrases and eliminate certain words such as verbs.

This is done by coding words by predetermined functions. This code is contained in the NASA Recognition Dictionary which currently has over 120,000 words and their codings. This enables the computer to break up sentences into manageable phrases which can then be translated into NASA Thesaurus terms. This system, based upon the location of words within a phrase, worked well. At present the natural language file has some 58,000 entries. The RTOP (Research and Technology Objectives and Plans) file was selected to test out machine-aided indexing. RTOPs deal with current research and contain long abstracts, thus they are ideal candidates for machine-aided indexing. The larger the size of the natural language file and the recognition dictionary, the greater the number of possibilities that can be translated. Machine-aided indexing offers not only a way to improve the consistency of indexing, it offers a way to more economically index since most of the indexing is done by machine and only requires indexer review.

BIBLIOGRAPHY

Automatic indexing: A state-of-the-art report. Washington, National Bureau of Standards, Feb. 1970, 298 p.

(Buchan, R. L.) Advanced thesaurus topics (NASA Scientific and Technical Information Facility), 1983, 10 p.

Buchan, R. L., Eckert, P. F. Aerospace bibliographic control in Aeronautics and space flight collections. *Special Collections*, 3(1/2), 1985/86, 195-229.

(Buchan, R. L.) The NASA online thesaurus (NASA Scientific and Technical Information Facility) 1985, 6 p.

(Buchan, R. L.) The printed NASA thesaurus and its products (NASA Scientific and Technical Information Facility) 1985, 13 p.

Buchan, R. L. Retrospective indexing, talk at NASA Scientific and Technical Information Facility before the ASIS ALP SIG Regional Meeting, January 18, 1985.

Chamis, A. Y. Online database search strategies and thesaural relationship models. Thesis, Case Western Reserve University, May 1984, 307 p.

DDC retrieval and indexing terminology: posting terms with hierarchy and KWOC. Alexandria, VA, Documentation Center, May 1979, 367 p.

Energy data base subject thesaurus. Oak Ridge, Tenn., Nov. 1984, United States Dept. of Energy, 983 p.

Hammond, W. Construction of the NASA thesaurus: Computer processing support. McLean, VA, Aries Corp. 1968, v.p., NAS-1629, NASA CR-95396, N68-28811.

Hammond, W. & Rosenborg, S. Indexing terms of announcement publications for government scientific & technical research reports. Spine title: AEC-DCC-NASA-OTS composite vocabulary, vol. 1, alphabetic listing, vol. 2, structured listing. Silver Spring, MD, Datatrol Corp., 1964, vol. 1, 447 p., vol. 2, 466 p.

International aerospace abstracts. Annual index 1985.

Kirshbaum, J. & Williamson, R. E. NASA automatic subject analysis technique for extracting retrievable multi-terms (NASA term) system. Linthicum Heights, MD, Informatics Information Systems Co., 1978, 27 p., NASA-CR-157398, N78-30992.

Klingbiel, P. H. Machine-aided indexing, talk at NASA Scientific and Technical Information Facility before the ASIS ALP SIG Regional Meeting, January 18, 1985.

Klingbiel, P. H. Phrase structure rewrite systems in information retrieval. *Information Processing and Management*, 21(2), 1985, p. 113-126. A85-44770.

Lexical dictionary developed at STI facility. *NASA STI-RECON Bulletin & Tech Info News*, Feb. 1984, p. 2.

Milstead, J. L. *Subject access systems: Alternatives in design.* New York: Academic Press, 1984, 212 p.

NASA combined file posting statistics, based on the NASA thesaurus, January 1968 January 1986. NASA STI Facility, 337 p.

NASA lexical dictionary publication to press. NASA STI-RECON Bulletin & Tech Info News, Aug./Sept./Oct. 1984, p. 2.

NASA STI facility operations manual. Nov. 1985. NASA Thesaurus section 530.2.

NASA thesaurus, volume 1, hierarchical listing, 1985 edition. NASA Scientific and Technical Information Branch, NASA SP-7053, 1985, 852 p.

NASA thesaurus, volume 2, access vocabulary, 1985 edition. NASA Scientific and Technical Information Branch, NASA SP-7053, 1985, 402 p.

NASA thesaurus, volume III, Appendixes, preliminary edition, December 1967. Office of Technology Utilization, Scientific and Technical Information Division, 1967, v.p.

NASA thesaurus—online. NASA RECON user's bulletin, 81/12, Dec. 1981, p. 1-5.

Retrospective indexing for new terms. *NASA STI-RECON Bulletin & Tech Info News*, Nov./Dec. 1984, p.2.

NASA/RECON, user's reference manual. NASA Scientific & Technical Information Branch, looseleaf, n.d.

Scientific and technical aerospace reports, annual index, 1985.

Silvester, J. P. Lexical dictionary, talk at NASA Scientific and Technical Information Facility before the ASIS ALP SIG Regional Meeting, January 18, 1985.

Silvester, J. P., Newton, R., Klingbiel, P. H. An operational system for subject switching between controlled vocabularies: a computational linguistics approach. NASA Scientific and Technical Information Branch, 1984. 96 p. NASA CR-3838.

Special bibliographies available. *NASA STI-RECON Bulletin & Tech Info News*, Feb. 1986, p. 3.

Thesaurus of engineering and scientific terms prepared for United States Department of Defense by Office of Naval Research Project Lex in joint operation with Engineers Joint Council, 1967, 696 p.

Trial period for indexed searches. *NASA STI-RECON Bulletin & Tech Info News*, Oct. 1983, p. 1.

Managing Database Information: An Index to Online Databases

Steven D. Atkinson
Michael Knee

Small computers assist librarians in providing reference services in academic, special, public, and school libraries in several ways: (a) information management, (b) instruction, and (c) accessing, storing, and re-formatting information. Budgeting, monthly annual reports, and the compilation and analysis of statistics are examples of applications for purposes of information management. Other such applications include the development of database price guides, indexes to locally searchable databases, and public relations materials. Small computers have also become useful in traditional library instruction and the teaching of online search skills for intermediaries as well as end users. Microcomputers are now being used as "dumb terminals" for accessing databases and downloading information for reformatting or further searching. Recently database vendors and producers have begun to provide their databases and software on CD-ROMs and laser disks for microcomputer searching.

Figure 1 provides an outline of these various computer functions and applications. The key to the development and implementation of each of these functions is selection of an appropriate microcomputer with peripherals and software. The purpose of this article is to describe one application for information management; that is, to show how a microcomputer can be utilized to generate an index to online databases available through an academic library reference department.

Mr. Atkinson is Assistant Coordinator of Computer Search Service at the State University of New York at Albany Library, 1400 Washington Ave., Albany, NY 12222. Mr. Knee is Physical and Mathematical Sciences Bibliographer and Reference Librarian in the same library.

****

FUNCTIONS	APPLICATIONS
Information management	Budgeting, monthly/annual reports, statistics, database price guides, database indexes, database listings, public relations materials
Instruction	Computer assisted library instruction and teaching online search skills
Accessing, storing, re-formatting information	Online searching, downloading, searching databases mounted on CD-ROMs or laser disks

FIGURE 1
MICROCOMPUTER FUNCTIONS AND APPLICATIONS IN REFERENCE SERVICE

****

INTRODUCTION.

The State University of New York at Albany (SUNYA) University Libraries Computer Search Service currently provides access to BRS, DIALOG, WESTLAW, CAS Online, WILSONLINE, and BRS/AFTER DARK online systems. Members of the computer search, collection development, and reference service staffs select vendor services and new databases for their support of undergraduate, graduate, and research programs on the SUNYA campus. As of February 1986, the Computer Search Service provides access to over 250 databases.

The computer search process begins at the reference desk, where the library patron asks for a computer search or the reference librarian, recognizing the complexity of a manual search, proposes the online search option. In either case, the reference librarian must suggest one or more databases to be searched by a search analyst or by the patron with the SELF SEARCH service. To make such referrals, a reference librarian must know what the relevant databases are in various subject areas. At SUNYA reference librarians rely on the following aids for suggesting databases:

a. knowledge of print indexes/abstracts or reference tools online
b. use of an alphabetical listing of databases currently available
c. use of printed database directories
d. use of online database directories
e. suggestions from other reference librarians or search analysts
f. knowledge from previous search referrals

Often options (a), (b), (e), and (f) are the only avenues pursued. Although options (c) and (d) would yield more and, perhaps, more appropriate databases, these directories would also lead to vendors and databases not available through the University Libraries. In order to facilitate the use of vendor services and databases and to improve reference service, a customized index was proposed in the fall of 1984. This index would provide subject access to all databases available through the Computer Search Service and would also facilitate ready reference use of databases for verification by reference librarians. As new databases are added to the service, the staff is informed of their availability and print counterparts on a monthly basis. The new files are also added to the database subject index, which is updated annually.

BACKGROUND

The Computer Search Service had previously implemented a project to create documentation to assist reference librarians, search analysts, and library patrons.[1] The documentation from the project includes:

a. *Database Fact Sheets* — comprehensive compilations of information about each database. They are intended primarily for the use of search analysts and contain such information as search cost estimates, vendor availability, thesaurus availability, connect hour and printing rates, and names of searchers.
b. *Databases, Searchers and Prices* — a briefer report that compiles in one list an alphabetical display of available databases, brief subject descriptions, search labels or file numbers, a list of assigned searchers, and price estimates.
c. *Search Service Brochure* — a listing of databases arranged by broad subjects, with added text, it is produced annually to advertise the service.

The aim of the current project is to enhance, not to replace, this documentation.

HARDWARE/SOFTWARE/PRINTER

The hardware employed for storing and producing this information is based on the Osborne Executive I microcomputer with 128K of internal memory and two 200K single sided, double-density disk drives. A five megabyte Trantor hard disk drive driven through the Osborne's IEEE 488 port augments the system's storage capacity and speeds up input/output operations. Reports are printed on a Daisywriter letter quality printer, which provides sufficient clarity. The Executive 1 is CP/M based and is supplied with WordStar, SuperCalc, two versions of BASIC, the UCSD-P operating system, and Personal Pearl, a database management system. The Personal Pearl and Wordstar software are the basis for the projects described in this article.

At the time the index project was proposed, three major projects utilized the Osborne configuration.[2] This situation not only came close to exhausting the five megabyte hard disk memory but also caused the one work-station to be tied up for long periods of time by each project. It was evident that a second microcomputer was needed. Grant funds from the SUNYA Office of Research allowed for the purchase of a second microcomputer and printer. A newspaper indexing project was transferred to the new computer, which freed up memory and time on the Osborne and allowed this project to proceed.

PERSONAL PEARL

Personal Pearl database management system employs four utilities to collect and organize information: design forms, design reports, enter data, and produce reports.

Design Forms

It is necessary to design a data entry form in order to collect data; that is, for this project, to capture the subject headings and vendor availability information for each database. The data entry form design is a three step process:

  a. Designing the form on the Osborne screen by specifying each item to be included in the form and the amount of space it will occupy;
  b. Defining the data input areas as either alpha or numeric, input required or not required, and calculations required or not required; and

c. Installing the newly-designed form into the computer memory ready for use.

Figure 2 illustrates the data entry form for this indexing project.

Design Reports

It is necessary to design a report so that the data input appears in a logical, readable format when it is printed out. There are four steps in designing a report:

a. Designing the layout of the report on the Osborne screen,
b. Defining the data output areas in the report using the names specified in the Data Entry Form,
c. Establishing the priority in which the data is to be sorted, and
d. Installing the report into the computer system.

Enter Data

Once the data entry and report forms are created, indexing can begin. To enter data, the blanks on the data entry form (see Figure 2) are filled in with the database name, subject heading, and vendor availability. When the blanks are completed, the information on the screen is saved to a file by entering the "control U" command. As subsequent headings are entered for a single database, the "control N" command is utilized. It repeats the database name and vendor

```
*************************************************************************
*                                                                     *
*    ENTER DATABASE NAME:_____     *
*                                                                     *
*    ENTER DATABASE SUBJECT HEADING:_____     *
*                                                                     *
*    ENTER VENDOR AVAILABILITY:_____                        *
*                                                                     *
*                                                                     *
*                                                                     *
*                                                                     *
*    _____ ENTER DATA __ CONTROL KEY COMMANDS _____          *
*         U -- Save/replace record        B -- Switch ADD/EDIT        *
*         N -- Duplicate last item        Z -- Get next record        *
*         P -- Print current record       W -- Get previous record    *
*         I -- Tab forward                O -- Delete current record   *
*         Q -- Help                       ESC  EXIT                    *
*                                                                     *
*                  FIGURE 2 - DATA ENTRY FORM                          *
*                                                                     *
*************************************************************************
```

availability information from the previous stored record; only the new subject heading needs to be entered, thus reducing the amount of rekeying and possible errors. This operation is repeated for all subject headings assigned for every database to which Computer Search Service provides access.

Produce Reports

This feature sorts the data and either produces a printed copy of the index or sends it to the word processor for further editing and reformatting. An example from a page of the final report is shown in Figure 3.

Once the design forms and design reports are set up, there is no need to redesign these forms when new databases or subject headings are added. Updating the index is done by entering new data into the data entry form and then producing a new report from the original report form. The final report, again, can be sent to the printer or to the word processing file for additional editing or formatting.

Selecting and Assigning Subject Headings/Keywords

The database keywords or subject headings were generated from four sources:

a. the database documentation created by the database vendors,
b. the database thesaurus or database user manual created by the database producers,
c. BRS' database FILE headings from the SU (subject) paragraph, and
d. the Knowledge Industry Publications database KIPI subject headings on BRS.

The headings from the FILE database were retrieved by selecting all databases and printing the database name, search label, and SU (subject) paragraph. The headings from the KIPI database were retrieved by searching the names of vendors to which SUNYA subscribes. These headings were sorted offline by vendor name and the database name, search label/number, and subject headings were printed. The heading from these sources were augmented with additional keywords based on the compilers' personal knowledge attained by searching certain databases. The number of headings as-

```
DATABASE  KEYWORD                    DATABASE NAME                                    DATABASE AVAILABILITY

LIBRARY SCIENCE                      ERIC                                             A,B
LIBRARY SCIENCE                      INFORMATION SCIENCE ABSTRACTS                    D
LIBRARY SCIENCE                      LISA/LIBRARY AND INFORMATION SCIENCE ABSTRACTS   D
LIBRARY SCIENCE                      SOCIAL SCISEARCH                                 A,B
LIBRARY SCIENCE BIOGRAPHIES          MARQUIS ONLINE PRO-FILE                          D
LIFE SCIENCES                        BIOSIS PREVIEWS                                  A,B
LIFE SCIENCES                        LIFE SCIENCES COLLECTION                         D
LIFE SCIENCES                        WILEY CATALOG/ONLINE                             D
LIFE SCIENCES                        ZOOLOGICAL RECORD                                D
LIFE SCIENCES COLLECTION             LIFE SCIENCES COLLECTION                         D
LIGHT TECHNOLOGY                     COMPENDEX                                        B
LIGHT TECHNOLOGY                     INSPEC                                           A,B
LINGUISTICS                          ARTS AND HUMANITIES SEARCH                       A,B
LINGUISTICS                          BILINGUAL EDUCATION BIBLIOGRAPHIC ABSTRACTS      A,B
LINGUISTICS                          ERIC                                             A,B
LINGUISTICS                          LANGUAGE AND LANGUAGE BEHAVIOR ABSTRACTS         B
LINGUISTICS                          MLA BIBLIOGRAPHY                                 D
LINGUISTICS                          PSYCINFO                                         A,B
LINGUISTICS                          SOCIAL SCISEARCH                                 A,B
LITERACY                             EDUCATION INDEX                                  W
LITERARY BIOGRAPHY                   BIOGRAPHY MASTER INDEX                           D
LITERARY CRITICISM                   ARTS AND HUMANITIES SEARCH                       A,B
LITERARY CRITICISM                   HUMANITIES INDEX                                 W
LITERARY CRITICISM                   MLA BIBLIOGRAPHY                                 D
LITERATURE                           ARTS AND HUMANITIES SEARCH                       A,B
LITERATURE                           ATLA RELIGION DATABASE                           A,B
LITERATURE                           CANADIAN BUSINESS AND CURRENT AFFIARS            D
LITERATURE                           HUMANITIES INDEX                                 W
LITERATURE                           MAGAZINE INDEX                                   B
LITERATURE                           MAGAZINE INDEX ASAP                              D
LITERATURE                           MIDDLE EAST:  ABSTRACTS AND INDEX                D
LITERATURE                           MIDEAST FILE                                     D
LITERATURE                           MLA BIBLIOGRAPHY                                 D
LITERATURE                           NATIONAL NEWSPAPER INDEX                         B
LITERATURE AND RELIGION              ATLA RELIGION DATABASE                           A,B
LOANS                                FINANCIAL INDUSTRY INFORMATION SERVICE           D
LOCAL AGENCY RESEARCH REPORTS        NTIS BIBLIOGRAPHIC DATABASE                      A,B
LOCAL HISTORY                        AMERICA:  HISTORY AND LIFE                       D
LOCOMOTION                           ZOOLOGICAL RECORD                                D
LOGIC                                MATHFILE                                         A,B
LOGIC                                PHILOSOPHERS INDEX                               D
LOS ANGELES TIMES                    NATIONAL NEWSPAPER INDEX                         B
LOW STOCK PRICES                     MEDIA GENERAL                                    D
MACHINE INTELLIGENCE                 INSPEC                                           A,B
MACHINE INTELLIGENCE                 ROBOTICS INFORMATION                             A,B
MACHINE READABLE CATALOGING          OCLC                                            B
MACROMOLECULAR CHEMISTRY             AMERICAN CHEMICAL SOCIETY PRIMARY JOURNAL DATA   A,B
MACROMOLECULAR CHEMISTRY             CA SEARCH                                        D
MACROMOLECULAR CHEMISTRY             CA SEARCH AND CA CONDENSATES                     A,B

        A=AFTER DARK    B=BRS    D=DIALOG    WL=WESTLAW    W=WILSONLINE

                    FIGURE 3 - SAMPLE PAGE OF INDEX
```

signed to each database ranges from four to twenty five, and the total number of headings for the 250+ databases is approximately 2,500.

Composition of the Index

The main section of the database index is obviously the listing of subject headings/keywords with assigned databases and vendor availability. Other sections were included to help reference librarians make database suggestions and referrals. For example, a list of subject headings assigned to each database is included to assist in discovering other headings/keywords for locating additional databases and to verify the subject content of a single database.

In addition, there is a listing of databases with their search labels/numbers to help reference librarians with the sign-on process using the files for ready reference purposes. The names and call numbers of print database directories owned by the University Libraries are also provided. Finally, an introduction is included to explain the purpose, background, and scope of the index.

Database Directories and Databases of Databases

The number of databases and vendors has grown considerably over the past ten years. Likewise, there has also been an increase in the number of directories of databases and database vendors. These directories are available in both print and online searchable formats. A few are even available in floppy disk format to be accessed using a microcomputer. The following list was compiled from articles appearing in *Database Reference Services Review*, and *Library Journal*.[3,4,5,6,7]

Databases of Data-bases — Online	Producer	System Availability
BRS FILE	BRS, Inc.	BRS
Computer Readable Databases	Martha E. Williams	DIALOG
Database Finding Aid	Alert Consultants	APPLE II, IIe as DIF, ASCII TEXT or DBMASTER or IBM PC
Directory of Online Databases	Cuadra Associates	WESTLAW, DATASTAR, TELESYSTEMS QUESTEL, Floppy Disks
EUSIDIC Database Guide	Learned Information	European Space Agency
Hi-tech Data Base Buyers' Guide	Information USA	dBASE or LOTUS 1,2,3 formats
Industry Data Sources	Information Access Corporation	BRS DIALOG

Knowledge Industry	Knowledge	BRS
Publications	Industry	
Database	Publications	
	and American	
	Society for	
	Information	
	Science	

Database Directories — Print

Abstracting and Indexing Services Directory. Detroit, MI: Gale Research Co., 1982-.

Answers Online: Your Guide to Informational Databases. Berkeley, CA: Osborne McGraw-Hill, 1985.

Business Information: Applications and Sources. Randor, PA: Chilton Book Co., 1983.

COIN: A Directory of Computerized Information in Canada. Edmonton, Alberta, Canada: Alberta Research Council, 1983.

Computer Data and Database Sourcebook. New York: New American Library, 1985.

Computer-Readable Databases: A Directory and Data Sourcebook. Knowledge Industry Publications for American Society for Information Science. White Plains, NY: Knowledge Industry, 1985.

Computer-Readable Databases: A Directory and Data Sourcebook. Chicago: American Library Association, 1985.

Data Base Alert. White Plains, NY: Knowledge Industry Publications, 1984-.

Data Base Directory. White Plains, NY: Knowledge Industry Publications in cooperation with American Society for Information Science, 1984-.

Data Base User Service. White Plains, NY: Knowledge Industry Publications, 1984-.

Database Finding Aid. Byron Center, MI: Alert Consultants, 1984.

Databases and Clearinghouses: Information Clearinghouses for Education. Columbus, OH: Ohio State University, National Center for Research on Vocational Education, 1979-.

Databases for Business: Profiles and Applications. Randor, PA: Chilton Book Co., 1982.

Databases in Europe. Luxembourg: Commission of the European Communities, 1982.

Datapro Complete Guide to Dial-up Databases. Delran, NJ: Datapro Research, 1984.

Datapro Directory of On-Line Services. Delran, NJ: Datapro Research, 1985-.

Directory of Agricultural Databases, 1985. Urbana, IL: Coordinated Science Laboratory, 1985.

Directory of Online Databases. Santa Monica, CA: Cuadra Associates, 1979-.

Directory of Online Information Resources. Rockville, MD: Capital System Group, 1978-.

Directory of Periodicals Online: Indexed, Abstracted, and Fulltext. Washington, DC: Federal Document Retrieval, 1985-.

Directory of United Nations Information Systems. Geneva, Switzerland: Interorganization Board for Information Systems, 1979-.

Encyclopedia of Information Systems and Services 1985-1986. Detroit, MI: Gale Research Co., 1971-.

Encyclopedia of Medical Organizations and Agencies: A Subject Guide to Medical Societies, Professional and Voluntary Associations, Foundations, Research Institutions, Federal and State Agencies, Medical and Allied Health Schools, Information Centers, Database Services, and Related Health Care Organizations. Detroit, MI: Gale Research Co., 1983.

Espial Database Directory: Current Canadian Information Contained in Selected Databases and Databanks. Toronto, Ontario, Canada: Espial Productions, 1982.

EUSIDIC Database Guide. Oxford, United Kingdom: Learned Information, 1983.

Federal Database Finder: A Directory of Free and Fee-based Databases and Files Available From the Federal Government. Potomac, MD: Information USA, 1984-.

Geoscience Numeric and Bibliographic Data. Glenside, Australia: Mineral Foundation, 1981.

GTE Telenet Directory of Computer-based Services. Viena, VA: GTE Telenet Communications Corp., 1984.

Guide to Information from Government Sources. Randor, PA: Chilton Book Co., 1983.

Guide to Online Databases. Boca Raton, FL: Newsletter Management Corporation, 1983.

HARFAX Directory of Industry Data Sources: The United States and Canada. Cambridge, MA: Ballinger, 1982.

HARFAX Directory of Industry Data Sources: Western Europe. Cambridge, MA: Ballinger, 1983.

Hi-tech Data Base Buyer's Guide. Chevy Chase, MD: Information USA, 1985.

Inc. Magazine's Databasics: Your Guide to Online Business Information. New York: Garland Publishing, 1984.

Information Industry Marketplace: An International Directory of Information Products and Services. New York: Bowker, 1980-.

Information Sourcebook for Marketers and Strategic Planners. Randor, PA: Chilton Book Co., 1983.

Information Sources: The Annual Directory of the Information Industry Association. Washington, DC: Information Industry Association, 1982-

International Directory of Databases Relating to Companies. New York: Unipub, 1979.

Libraries, Information Centers and Databases in Science and Technology: A World Guide. New York: K. G. Saur, 1984.

North American Online Directory 1985: A Directory of Information Products and Services with Names and Numbers. New York: Bowker, 1985.

Omni Online Database Directory 1985. New York: Collier Macmillan, 1984.

Online: A Guide to America's Leading Information Services. Bellevue, WA: Microsoft Press, 1985.

Online Bibliographic Databases: Directory and Sourcebook. London: Aslib, 1981-.

Political Terrorism: A Research Guide to Concepts, Theories, Databases, and Literature. New Brunswick, NJ: Transaction Books, 1984.

R & D Database Handbook: A Worldwide Guide to Key Scientific and Technical Databases. Ft. Lee, NJ: Technical Insights, 1984.

Reston Directory of Online Databases: Your Computer's Phone Book. Reston, VA: Reston Publishing Co., 1984.

Which Database? Headland, Hartlepool, Cleeland, United Kingdom. Headland Press, 1981.

CONCLUSION

These reference tools are invaluable sources of information on database availability from vendors on a national or worldwide basis. Libraries should make these tools readily available. Reference librarians and library users, however, also need to know more specifically what is available inhouse. Since databases are rarely cataloged, guides and indexes to databases need to be developed.

This locally developed subject index was made available at SUNYA in January 1986. It is now being used and evaluated by reference librarians. This feedback will be used to make changes in its format and content.

NOTES

1. Atkinson, Steven D. & Watkins, Steven G. "Managing Database Information: A Microcomputer Application in a Computer Search Service." *Online* 9 (1) January 1985: 52-66.

2. Watkins, Steven G., Knee, Michael & Atkinson, Steven D., "The Osborne Executive for Indexing, Accounting, and Information Management." *Small Computers in Libraries* 5 (10) November 1985: 24-27.

3. Ingebretsen, Dorothy L., Borgman, Christine L. & Case, Donald. "Database Guides: An Annotated Bibliography." *Database* 8 (3) August 1985: 89-100.

4. Feldman, Beverly. "Database Directories: Review and Recent Developments." *Reference Services Review* 13 (2) Summer 1985: 17-19.

5. Janke, Richard V. "Three New Online Directories: How They Measure Up." *Database* 8 (4) December 1985: 6-9.

6. Tenopir, Carol. "Database Directories: The Rest." *Library Journal* 110 (15) September 15, 1985: 56-57.

7. Tenopir, Carol. "Database Directories: In Print & Now Online." *Library Journal* 110 (13) August 1985: 64-65.

WESTLAW:
Online Legal Reference Searching in a Social Science Library

Richard Irving
Henry Mendelsohn

This article will describe the use of WESTLAW, a full text automated legal database, in a special library whose collections and resources are devoted to applied social science and public policy research. The rationale for acquiring WESTLAW and its usefulness for supporting research and education in the applied social sciences are described.

The Graduate Library for Public Affairs and Policy supports undergraduate and graduate education in criminal justice, social welfare, library science, public affairs, public policy and public administration in particular and the educational and research mission of the State University of New York at Albany in general. Towards these ends the Graduate Library maintains a core collection of legal materials. The law collection is specifically tailored to meet the needs of graduate education in Criminal Justice (MA and PhD) but also serves to support legal research in other social science disciplines such as social welfare, public administration, sociology, political science, education, business, and so forth.

The law collections consists of both primary and secondary sources and is built around but not limited to the publications of the West Publishing Company. Thus, it was a logical decision to acquire WESTLAW, West's online database, when the opportunity presented itself.

The two authors are librarians at the Graduate Library for Public Affairs and Policy, State University of New York at Albany, 135 Western Ave., Albany, NY 12222.

ACQUIRING WESTLAW

The decision to acquire WESTLAW was preceded by several circumstances. Part of the law collections had previously been moved from the Main Library of SUNYA to its present location in a branch library on the East Campus located a few miles from the Main Campus. The printed law collections were then streamlined by cancelling subscriptions for most state digests and other duplicative or esoteric materials. More than several thousands of dollars (and a lot of shelf space) were saved by cutting the little used and in some cases duplicate legal materials.

However, the elimination of these legal sets did cause a few patrons some inconvenience. Also many important but ephemeral materials were never owned and thus not available and were available for purchase only at considerable costs. There was also the problem of the materials being split between the two libraries. Patrons would go to one library with citations to series housed in the other library. It would take a considerable amount of time to track down alternative citations. Initially there was also a great deal of confusion as to which materials were in which library. Patrons were understandably annoyed about having to travel back and forth between libraries.

Compounding the confusion was (and still is) the fact that most of the clientele of the Graduate Library are not legally trained and thus not familiar with legal terminology or the contents of primary legal documents and the methods of accessing them.

The majority of students and faculty that use the Graduate Library have backgrounds in the social sciences. When attempting legal research they generally encounter at least one of the three following problems: (1) a lack of familiarity with the primary sources of legal materials and of the means of accessing those materials; (2) a lack of familiarity with legal vocabulary and concepts; (3) a need to consult legal sources not so much for legal argument or principle but rather to understand the social or public policy consequences or likely consequences of legal actions.

While the acquisition of WESTLAW would not solve all of these problems it seemed that it would help alleviate them. The opportunity presented itself when the state of New York sought to acquire access to WESTLAW for its state agencies' libraries. SUNYA successfully petitioned the N.Y.S. Division of Budget to be included in the contract being drawn up. It was pointed out that it would be cheaper to subscribe to WESTLAW than purchase expensive legal sets. It was noted that WESTLAW also contains some materials online for which there are no printed equivalents. For example, WESTLAW Case Highlights and WESTLAW Tax Highlights summarize cases of significant and current developments in federal tax laws respectively. Another feature called "Insta-Cite," provides the complete line of history, both prior and subsequent for a case. (More about "Insta-Cite" later.)

Thus, SUNYA was able to join other New York State agencies in accessing WESTLAW. A group rate proved to be less expensive than if SUNYA had subscribed individually.

POLICY AND PROCEDURE

Once the contractual matters were settled, a WESTLAW terminal was acquired. The WESTLAW Custom Terminal, referred to as WALT, consists of a keyboard and a video display screen. A printer may be attached. In addition to the alphabet keys are the command function keys. These keys perform functions merely by striking them. For example, there is a Shepardize key which, when struck, automatically Shepardizes whichever case is on the video display screen. The WALT terminal is also programmable and when programmed to do so, will automatically dial into WESTLAW and many other database systems such as Dialog and BRS.

The next step was to develop policies concerning use and price structures. It was decided that WESTLAW policies and procedures would parallel as closely as possible policies and procedures already in effect for other computerized databases. It was determined that GLPP would provide access to WESTLAW in support of graduate and undergraduate programs and the research needs of faculty and staff of SUNYA. Such service includes retrospective, current awareness and quick reference search requests within the subject coverage and time periods available in WESTLAW.

It was decided that suitable search requests to be referred to WESTLAW searchers for indepth searching would include complex multi-term searches, subjects not easily searched in the printed legal materials, complex Shepardizing of cases, searches on sections of WESTLAW for which there are no corresponding print sources, comprehensive searches such as research for a review article, book, dissertation, thesis, or indepth term paper, or other requests that cannot be satisfied by using printed legal materials. Patrons must bear part of the cost for indepth searches while SUNYA picks up the rest of the costs.

A distinction was made between indepth searches for which the requester would pay partial costs and quick reference search requests for which patrons would not be charged. Categories of quick reference search requests are identification of incomplete, incorrect, or garbled citations and case names, identification of appropriate reporters for manual searching, Shepardizing of cases, directory type information and any other searches deemed suitable for WESTLAW quick reference by trained WESTLAW searchers. As in other quick reference searches of Dialog and BRS Databases, WESTLAW quick reference searches are provided free of charge.

ADVANTAGES OF WESTLAW

Brownmiller et al. (1985) cite three situations in which an online search is advantageous. For our discussion of WESTLAW we have rearranged the three situations into four and identified them as follows:

1. Enhanced Access Flexibility—"when an available print index is inadequate because the access points in the published indexes are insufficient to extract the required information";
2. Timeliness—"when an available print index is inadequate because of inevitable delays in the printing and distribution of the index";
3. Search Time Efficiency—"when it is clear that a quick online search would obtain the same or better results than a lengthy manual search";
4. Collection Enhancement—"when an online search is the only option in a reference context because no printed source is available, either because the library doesn't subscribe to it or because there is no print equivalent of the online file."

Brownmiller et al. identify the types of reference queries which are particularly well suited for online searching (and which our policies closely parallel):

1. Bibliographic verification of incomplete or garbled references;
2. Current information—information too recent to appear in a printed index;
3. Obscure topic—terminology of a subject is such that it is unclear which subject heading, if any, in a printed index would be most appropriate;
4. Coordinated subject—question can only be answered by coordinating two or more subject headings or concepts;
5. No printed source—either no print equivalent exists for the online file or the library doesn't subscribe to the printed index.

WESTLAW has proven to be extremely useful in answering all of these types of reference questions. Three factors contribute to the value of WESTLAW in a social science setting. First, as noted above, our users are generally unfamiliar with legal cites and are therefore likely to bring garbled references to the reference desk. Second, our users are more familiar with social science terminology and are therefore likely to find the terminology in legal reference works foreign or inapplicable to their research. Third, since SUNYA does not support a law school or legal practice the printed law collection is limited in scope and WESTLAW enhances the scope of our collection by providing access to additional legal materials.

CASE LAW DATABASES

For purposes of brevity we will restrict our discussion to WESTLAW's retrieval capabilities regarding its case law databases, although many of WESTLAW's search advantages apply to its other databases as well. The case law databases on WESTLAW correspond to West's printed case reporter series. The Graduate Library has the following printed sets of West reporters; *Supreme Court Reporter, Federal Reporter, Federal Supplement, Federal Rules and Decisions*, the seven *Regional Reporter Series, New York Supplement*, and the *California Reporter*.

Ultimately, to locate a case in a reporter series one needs the citation to the case including the name of the reporting series, volume number within the series, and the page within the volume. There are many different reference sources a person may consult to obtain the citation. To a large extent the choice of reference source is dependent upon the information the researcher starts with. However, digests are the reference sources specifically designed to provide access to case reporters. A digest is "An Index to reported cases, providing brief statements of court holdings or facts of cases, which is arranged by subject and subdivided by jurisdiction and courts" (Blacks Law Dictionary, 5th ed., p. 410). Most digests are also broken down into series which cover the cases of a designated time period. Thus, knowing the date of a decision is very useful information in locating a case through the digests. There are three access points to each digest series. First, if the user knows the appropriate topic name he/she can go directly to the volume(s) containing that topic. Second, if the title of the case is known access can be through "Table of Cases" Indexes which accompany each series. Third, if the researcher is searching by subject he/she can consult the "Descriptive Word Index" which accompany each series. Entries in the "Descriptive Word Index" refer the user to appropriate topic(s) for any given subject. The Graduate Library houses three digest systems published by West which provide us with access to the West series of case reporters mentioned above. They are the *American Digest Series*, the *Federal Digest Series*, and the *New York Digest Series*.

We shall be focusing on the advantages WESTLAW provides in comparison to the digests in responding to reference queries. The four situations identified above as appropriate for online searching are used as a guide to our discussion.

ENHANCED ACCESS FLEXIBILITY

Most of the enhanced flexibility provided by WESTLAW is due to the fact that it allows for free text searching of both the full text of the case plus the editorial information added by West. Each case on WESTLAW is broken down into ten fields. Chart One identifies the fields, describes the information contained in each field, and gives examples of the factual information which can be searched in each field. All of the fields can be searched independently except for the date field which can only be used to limit a search to a particular date or range of dates. Also, it should be noted that the digest field simply combines the headnote, topic, and citation fields. The digest field is particularly useful for performing searches combining subjects (topics) with free text terminology.

CHART ONE

FIELD	DESCRIPTION OF CONTENTS	ACCESS OPTIONS
Date	Date of Decision	Specific Date, e.g., May 14, 1984 Range of Dates, e.g., 1979-1984 Date Before, e.g., before 1984 Date After, e.g., after 1984
Title	Full Name of the Case	Any party or parties listed in the decision Full names of any party or parties Order of plaintiffs and defendants doesn't have to be correct
Citation	Citation - Volume number, abbreviation for reporter series, page number	Volume number and page number in that order
Court	Abbreviation for the Court the Court which decided the case and the date of the decision	All cases decided within a state or group of states Only cases decided by the highest appellate court of a state or states Only cases decided by intermediate or lesser state courts Decisions of a particular circuit of the United States Court of Appeals Decisions of a particular United States District Court Decisions of a particular state in the United States Court of Appeals Decisions of a special court, e.g., United States Court of Military Review
Judge	Name of judge authoring the majority opinion	Last name of judge authoring the majority opinion
Opinion	Name of the court; docket number; full text of the decision	Court Docket number Names of the attorneys arguing the case Names of expert witnesses Names of organizations filing amicus curiae briefs Free text search for unique words and/or phrases

CHART ONE cont'd.

FIELD	DESCRIPTION OF CONTENTS	ACCESS OPTIONS
Synopsis	Summary of the history and facts of the case; judgement of the court; resolution of the issue	Lower Court Decision Cite Lower Court Judge Name Judgement of the court, i.e. affirmed, reversed, etc. Names of judges concurring or dissenting with majority opinion Free text search for unique words and/or phrases
Topic	West digest topic number, topic name, key number, text of key line	West digest topic number West key number Topic name Free text search for words and/or phrases in the text of the key line
Headnote	Text of the headnote as well as information in the topic field	Free text search unique facts, words, phrases. Particularly useful for locating cites to statutes, rules, or dollar amounts
Digest	Combination of the citation, topic, and headnote fields	Any of the search options available in the topic, citation, or headnote fields or any combination thereof Particularly useful for combination of a topic (subject) search with a free text search when two or more concepts are combined

Source: Westlaw Reference Manual, pp. 9/1-9/27, St. Paul, Minnesota: West Publishing Co. 1985.

A couple of examples of reference questions which we used WESTLAW to answer may serve to demonstrate its usefulness. The first example illustrates WESTLAW's capability in retrieving cases given garbled or incomplete citation.

Example One

A patron was looking for a cite to a South Carolina case, decided after 1976, reviewing the death penalty sentence of Terry Roach. We first searched the "Table of Cases" volumes in the appropriate digest series without success. We next tried the descriptive word approach again without success. At this point we turned to WEST-LAW. We entered the South Carolina case database (SC-CS). The following search query was used:

Date(after 1976 & Title(Terry + 2 Roach) & synopsis(death)

The following case was retrieved:

State v. Joseph Carl Shaw and James Terry Roach, 255 S.E.2d 799 (1979)

The reason the case had not been retrieved through the "Tables of Cases" was that it was listed under the co-defendant's name "Shaw." Since we were able to search the full title of the case on WESTLAW it greatly facilitated the search.

WESTLAW has also been useful in locating cases decided by particular judges, argued by particular lawyers, or in which an organization has filed an amicus curiae (friend of the court) brief, or in which unique phrases are found.

Example Two

A patron was looking for a federal abortion case in which "Lawyers for Life" filed an amicus curiae brief. A manual search would require that the patron search the Federal Digests for cites to all cases dealing with abortion and then read enough of each case to determine if "Lawyers for Life" had filed a brief. We decided to use WESTLAW. We entered the ALLFEDS database which contains all U.S. Supreme Court, U.S. Court of Appeals, and U.S. District Court cases reported since 1946. The following query was entered:

Opinion(Lawyers + 2 Life /s amic!) & synopsis(abortion)

Two cases were retrieved:

Reproductive Health Services v. Freeman, 614 F.2d 585 (1980)
Mahoning Women's Center v. Hunter, 610 F.2d 456 (1979)

There are two other ways WESTLAW facilitates reference service by increasing the variety of access points. First, it provides more unique jurisdiction databases than its print counterparts; e.g., the ALLFEDS database used in the example cited above. Chart Two lists some of these special jurisdiction databases which in most instances are not available in printed format. Second, WESTLAW has special subject databases for federal and state court decisions. Searchers should be wary of using the subject databases in searching for cites to recent cases. Many cases appear on WESTLAW before headnotes are written for them. Cases are apparently assigned to subject databases according to headnote topic.

Thus, relevant recent cases may be available on WESTLAW but not yet entered into the specialized subject databases. In addition to providing a wider variety of access options, the subject and jurisdiction databases permit more time efficient reference searching. The subject databases are listed on Chart Three.

TIMELINESS

WESTLAW has two advantages over the printed format in this regard. First, the cases themselves appear on WESTLAW before they are available in the printed format. Frequently, cases are found with a message "Not Yet Published" indicating the print version is not available. Patrons can get a copy of these cases for the print cost. This is of particular value to researchers, many of whom need quick access to current cases. Second, even if the case has been printed it will be difficult to locate manually until the printed in-

CHART TWO

Database	Contents
ALLFEDS	U.S. Supreme Court U.S. Court of Appeals U.S. District Court
CTA 1	U.S. Court of Appeals - First Circuit
CTA 2	U.S. Court of Appeals - Second Circuit
CTA 3	U.S. Court of Appeals - Third Circuit
CTA 4	U.S. Court of Appeals - Fourth Circuit
CTA 5	U.S. Court of Appeals - Fifth Circuit
CTA 6	U.S. Court of Appeals - Sixth Circuit
CTA 7	U.S. Court of Appeals - Seventh Circuit
CTA 8	U.S. Court of Appeals - Eighth Circuit
CTA 9	U.S. Court of Appeals - Ninth Circuit
CTA10	U.S. Court of Appeals - Tenth Circuit
CTA11	U.S. Court of Appeals - Eleventh Circuit
CTADC	U.S. Court of Appeals - District of Columbia Circuit
ALLSTATES	Consolidation of court decisions from all 50 states and the District of Columbia
50 Individual States and D.C.	Cases from any particular state's courts as reported in a West reporter series
e.g.	
Alabama Cases, AL-CS	All Alabama State Court decisions reported in West's <u>Southern Reporter</u>

dexes are published which may be considerably after the case appears. WESTLAW eliminates this problem.

WESTLAW can also be used to update a manual "Shepards" search. There is a time lag between when a decision is reported and when it is picked up in the printed Shepards' volumes. The manual search can be updated by free text searching the cite of the case you are "Shepardizing" within the most recent cases of any of WESTLAW's databases.

CHART THREE

SUBJECT	COVERAGE
FEDERAL	All the federal subject databases include U.S. Supreme Court, U.S. Court of Appeals, and U.S. District Court reported decisions. Additions to this basic coverage will be noted in this field.
Antitrust and Business Regulations	Basic
Federal Admiralty	Basic
Federal Bankruptcy	Basic plus U.S. Bankruptcy Court decisions
Federal Communications	Basic
Federal First Amendment	Basic
Federal Copyright	Basic
Federal Energy	Basic
Federal Financial Services	Basic
Federal Government Contracts	Basic plus U.S. Court of Claims decisions
Federal Labor	Basic
Federal Patents	Basic
Federal Securities	Basic
Federal Tax	Basic plus U.S. Court of Claims
STATE	
Education	Education cases for all states or any individual state
Family Law	Family law cases for all states or any individual state
Insurance	Insurance cases for all the states or any individual state
Securities	Securities cases for all the states or any individual state

TIME EFFICIENCY

As noted above the many additional access points provided by WESTLAW makes it much more efficient in retrieving cases than the printed indexes. The fact that it can perform coordinated searching of more than one concept or fact also increases its efficiency in comparison to the digests which require sequential searching.

A typical search in the digests starts by narrowing the search to a series which covers the date of the case. Then the user consults either the "Table of Cases," or the "Descriptive Word Index" to locate the appropriate topic. Then the topic is searched by jurisdiction and date within jurisdiction. The less information the user starts with the more time he/she can expect to spend finding the searched for case. Lacking the date or approximate date of the decision can be particularly time consuming. Searching for cases containing two concepts may require two independent searches.

WESTLAW provides three advantages regarding time efficiency. First, WESTLAW allows a variety of starting points, only a few of which must be known to retrieve the case. Not knowing the date or approximate date of decision is not a particular burden on WEST-LAW. Neither is not knowing the jurisdiction or the appropriate legal topic. Efficient WESTLAW reference searches can be performed without knowing any of these bits of information, which are nearly essential for performing a manual search. Second, WEST-LAW allows one to retrieve cases by combining facts none of which could retrieve the sought case by themselves, e.g., a search combining the exact date of decision and court issuing the decision will quickly retrieve the desired case. Third, WESTLAW permits the coordinated searching of two or more concepts. This can be two or more legal topics (subject descriptors), two or more free text terms, or any combination of topics and free text terms.

Example Three

A patron was looking for a recent New York State case deciding the issue of whether a professional licence acquired during marriage is subject to equal distribution, as marital property, during divorce proceedings. We decided to use WESTLAW for two reasons. First, because it was a recent decision which might not be reported yet in the printed reporters and if it was reported might not be covered by the digests. Second, because it required the combination of several concepts, divorce, equitable distribution, and professional licenses. We entered the New York cases database (NY-CS) and entered the following query:

Date(after 1984) & synopsis("equitable distribution" & licence!) & divorce

We retrieved the following case:

O'Brien v. O'Brien, 106 APP.Div.2nd 223, 485 NYS2d 548 (February 11, 1985)

The patron indicated familiarity with this case but thought that there had been a more recent decision regarding the case. To find the later decision we entered an "Insta-Cite" command on WEST-LAW. "Insta-Cite" reports the case history of a case complete with parallel citations. In this instance "Insta-Cite" yielded both an earlier and a later decision regarding the same case. The cite to the later case:

O'Brien v. O'Brien, 66 NY2d 576, 54 USLW 2348 (December 26, 1985)

For recent cases the searcher should not use a topic search but should instead use free text searching in the synopsis field. This is because many cases appear on WESTLAW before they are assigned subjects (topics) and headnotes by the West editors. If a topic search is used these cases will not be retrieved.

COLLECTION ENHANCEMENT

As mentioned above, the Graduate Library's law collection is intended to support the curricula and social science research needs of the schools of criminal justice, social welfare and public administration. Thus, our law collection is limited and tailored toward the subject interests of our faculty and students. WESTLAW provides access to many resources which have not been purchased in printed format because the cost of acquiring and storing them cannot be justified based on the occasional use they might receive.

WESTLAW has extensive holdings of administrative and specialized case reporters which are of occasional interest to the Graduate Library's users, e.g., Decisions of the Merit System Protection Board, U.S. Comptroller General Opinions, Decisions of the Federal Communications Commission, and Attorney General Opinions for most of the states and the federal government.

For the last few years WESTLAW has been adding on a selective basis the full text articles from law reviews and journals. Such databases can be used to verify bibliographic information and to print an article from a journal not owned by the Graduate Library.

ADDED FEATURES

WESTLAW has several specialized features which have proven to be especially useful in answering reference queries. One of these special features is "Insta-Cite." As noted previously, "Insta-Cite" allows the searcher to obtain the complete case history, with parallel citations, for any retrieved case, by just striking the "Insta-Cite" key. "Insta-Cite" also provides the docket numbers, complete date, jurisdiction, and record of action for each decision. For persons who are not trained in legal research techniques this has proved to be a particularly useful way to check on the status of a case.

The Shepards' database on WESTLAW is also useful. A searcher can "Shepardize" a retrieved case by striking the Shepardize key on the terminal. Once in the Shepards' database, the WESTLAW software allows the searcher to quickly narrow the search to cites to a particular headnote, those with a particular treatment, from a particular jurisdiction, or any combination of the three. This can save the user considerable manual search time and the reference staff considerable time in explaining how to use the printed Shepards' volumes.

CONCLUSION

WESTLAW has proven to be an important addition to a social science library. It offers enhanced access flexibility, timeliness, time efficiency and collection enhancement to a library not entirely devoted to legal research. Its costs are more than offset by these four factors.

REFERENCES

Brownmiller, Sara et al. "Online-Ready-Reference Searching in an Academic Library." *RQ*, Spring 1985, 320-326.
Nolan, Joseph R. & Michael J. Connolly, Eds. *Black's Law Dictionary* 5th ed. St. Paul: West Publishing Co., 1979.
Westlaw Reference Manual. St. Paul: West Publishing Co., 1985.